Everyday Desistance

CRITICAL ISSUES IN CRIME AND SOCIETY

Raymond J. Michalowski, Series Editor

Critical Issues in Crime and Society is oriented toward critical analysis of contemporary problems in crime and justice. The series is open to a broad range of topics including specific types of crime, wrongful behavior by economically or politically powerful actors, controversies over justice system practices, and issues related to the intersection of identity, crime, and justice. It is committed to offering thoughtful works that will be accessible to scholars and professional criminologists, general readers, and students.

For a list of titles in the series, see the last page of the book.

Everyday Desistance

THE TRANSITION TO ADULTHOOD AMONG FORMERLY INCARCERATED YOUTH

LAURA S. ABRAMS
DIANE J. TERRY

RUTGERS UNIVERSITY PRESS

New Brunswick, Camden, and Newark, New Jersey, and London

978-0-8135-7347-2
978-0-8135-7446-2
978-0-8135-7447-9
978-0-8135-7448-6
978-0-8135-7449-3
978-0-8135-9088-2

Cataloguing-in-Publication data is available from the Library of Congress.

A British Cataloguing-in-Publication record for this book is available from the British Library.

∞ The paper used in this publication meets the requirements of the American National Standard for Information Sciences—Permanence of Paper for Printed Library Materials, ANSI Z39.48–1992.

www.rutgersuniversitypress.org

Manufactured in the United States of America

This book is dedicated to the young men and women who graciously offered their time and insights to make this project a reality.

Contents

FOREWORD

MY FIRST REAL EXPOSURE to the idea of juvenile delinquency and the lives of teenagers growing up in difficult circumstances occurred when I read S. E. Hinton's *The Outsiders* as a child. Immersing myself in the experiences of Ponyboy, Soda, Johnny, and the other Greasers gave me an idea of how my life might have been very different if I had been born into a dysfunctional family or a turbulent neighborhood. In short, the fictional boys in *The Outsiders* offered me an early experience in learning both sociology and empathy.

I have now spent most of my adult life studying troubled teens who have committed serious crimes and spent significant time in juvenile correctional facilities and/or adult prisons. The world does, indeed, look different from their perspective, and it's a view we must take seriously if we are to have any hope of improving the lives of troubled young people in the United States.

Laura Abrams and Diane Terry have done just that in *Everyday Desistance: The Transition to Adulthood among Formerly Incarcerated Youth*. This is an important book and should be considered vital reading for anyone who cares about young people who are struggling to come of age amidst crime, violence, and the complicated web of youth justice in the United States. While grounding the book in the context of the extreme inequality in the Los Angeles area, Abrams and Terry meet their goal of giving a "nuanced picture of desistance," change, and the difficult road to adulthood some must travel. They show us exactly what it is like to be "living in the heart of trouble," as one of the young men they follow so aptly phrases it.

The young people in these pages have had difficult lives, and their incarceration has in many ways "piled on" to the obstacles they already faced growing up in harsh environments and circumstances. It can undoubtedly be confusing and frustrating for less privileged youth growing up in the relatively rich environment of Los Angeles. Despite the wealth in the city, there were no real safety nets in place for young people striving to overcome their daily struggles and trouble with the law. Abrams and Terry clearly illustrate the power of resilience in these disadvantaged young adults before and after going through the "juvenile justice maze." They highlight the importance of social welfare agencies, mentors, and good fortune for young people trying to build new lives in the community.

Abrams and Terry smartly prioritize the voices of the system-involved young adults, letting them tell their own stories in their own ways. The result is a powerful indictment of our current youth justice system and its many failings. The authors complement the raw and thoughtful voices of their subjects by offering astute analyses that highlight larger issues and provide context for the young adults' experiences.

These alumni or survivors of the maze of juvenile justice frequently view the system as setting kids up for failure. Many cycled through several placements, including foster homes, sentences in youth camps and correctional facilities, and parole violations before returning to the community for what they hoped would be the last time. Because their lives were often characterized by instability before their stints in juvenile justice facilities, these young adults face extra challenges in returning to the community and learning how to negotiate housing and jobs and to meet their basic needs. In their efforts to become fully realized adults, they struggle in dealing with social service agencies, family and romantic relationships, and the daily challenges of parenting and caring for others.

Abrams and Terry guide the reader through the stories of these emerging adults, and they identify patterns and strategies the young people used for reintegrating into the community. They note three typologies of desistance: "On the Road," "Running in Circles," and "Still in the Game," suggesting that those who want to turn away from crime often face a difficult and zigzagging road. They return to their communities and must once again face all of the temptations and trials of the street and crime-involved lifestyles.

In my own research with incarcerated youth I distinctly remember hearing both staff members and African American and Latino youth talking about the real dangers these young men would face upon their release. The fears for their physical safety were tangible. The youth spoke about having to hide from enemies on the outside who had held simmering grudges for months and years and were patiently awaiting their chance for revenge. They planned to take jobs out of the public eye so that they would not be visible targets for those looking to do them harm. I felt a sad recognition in reading the accounts in *Everyday Desistance* of youth facing the same fears and obstacles nearly a generation later. Abrams and Terry perfectly capture the confusing new realities young adults face in returning to a community where friends have become enemies and the perceived danger they live and breathe takes a toll on their relationships, their psyches, and their quality of life.

Many of the youth profiled in this book attempt to create new identities when they return to the community, changing their appearance, altering their speech, and finding new peer groups. Abrams and Terry highlight the particular challenges for "crossover youth"—youth who have aged out of the foster care system and have troubled, if any, relationships with their biological families. A cherished yet elusive goal for these young people is the idea of finding a home, although the meaning of "home" varies among the participants.

Everyday Desistance is powerful for including both young men and young women in this study, a welcome change from previous research and reporting that has generally focused on one or the other gender. By following both women and men through the process of reentry, readers are allowed a glimpse into the different values and challenges faced by each. As one example, caretaking was an important component of life on the outside for the young women, particularly as they often emerged from juvenile justice agencies and immediately took on the responsibility for their children, their boyfriends, and their extended families. The men did not face these challenges in the same way.

Abrams and Terry conclude their book with a number of recommendations and policy suggestions specifically derived from their data. Readers can take this information a step further by figuring out how they can apply these hard-earned lessons to their own communities. Young people in every community need a vision for a hopeful future, and social welfare and justice agencies must help to light the path to show them how to achieve it. Mentors can help them to first imagine better futures and then help them to cultivate the tools that will make such futures a reality.

In the novel *Ordinary People*, the middle-class father of a suicidal son remarks to himself: "Growing up is a serious business. He, Cal, would not be young again, not for anything. And not without sponsors: a mother and father, good fortune, God" (p. 13). The young adults struggling through *Everyday Desistance* are almost entirely without such sponsors. We, as community members, should learn from the powerful analysis that Abrams and Terry have offered us and find ways to honor the experiences of these young adults. If we take their voices and their views seriously, we can help young people in similar situations find their way to a better life.

Michelle Inderbitzin, PhD

REFERENCES

Guest, Judith. 1976. *Ordinary People*. New York: Penguin Books.
Hinton, S. E. 1967. *The Outsiders*. New York: Penguin Books.

Everyday Desistance

CHAPTER 1

Introduction

THE LAST TEN YEARS have witnessed significant shifts in American juvenile justice policy. As public sentiment has moved away from a primarily punitive discourse regarding young people in trouble with the law, states have increasingly adopted community-based alternatives to incarceration with a focus on rehabilitation. A number of factors have contributed to these changes, including a dramatic decline in juvenile crime rates, a persuasive body of research on adolescent brain development, major philanthropic investments in juvenile justice reform, and widespread documentation of the high costs and poor outcomes associated with juvenile incarceration (Mendel, 2011; Perruti, Schindler, & Zeidenberg, 2014). Underlying this newer discourse is the notion that teenagers do not cognitively or emotionally mature as rapidly as previously believed, making their criminal culpability more akin to children than to adults. Moreover, views from inside the system, documented in works such as Richard Ross's photo exposé *Juvenile-in-Justice* (2012) and journalist Nell Bernstein's (2014) critical book *Burning Down the House: The End of Juvenile Prison* have fueled public perception that juvenile confinement is unnecessarily harsh, ineffective, and indeed not a suitable place to house children (Mendel, 2011).

As the disturbing economic, social, and psychological consequences of youth incarceration are increasingly publicized, rates of juvenile detention and incarceration have simultaneously plummeted. In 1997, the Office of Juvenile Justice and Delinquency Prevention's (OJJDP) census of residential placement documented 105,000 youth in US juvenile justice placements on a given day, compared to just over 61,000 in 2011 (Sickmund, Sladky, Kang, & Puzzanchera, 2013). This represents a 40 percent decrease in the confined juvenile population in less than 15 years. Notwithstanding these dramatic changes, a group of young people continues to interface with the juvenile justice system with significant consequences for their future well-being. Members of this group are highly likely to be male youth of color—particularly African American—and to have a history of involvement in public systems, such as child welfare, mental health, and special education (Hager, 2015). They also tend to live in lower-income neighborhoods where they are subject to intensive policing, racial profiling, and monitoring.

For the young people who continue to traverse through the revolving door of probation, detention, and corrections, the juvenile justice system is where they experience a large part of their adolescent development. They often live apart from their families, disconnected from mainstream schools, and exposed to the considerably negative trappings of institutionalization. Several scholars have recently sought to document and unravel the complexities of the experience of juvenile incarceration (Abrams & Anderson-Nathe, 2013; Bernstein, 2014; Fader, 2013). These works have examined the subjective experience of living in a correctional setting, how these institutions shape youth identities, and why correctional programs—even those with a therapeutic leaning—often fail. In this book, we pose a different set of questions: What does everyday life look like for young people who age out of the juvenile justice system? How do young people navigate the transition to adulthood while attempting to stay out of the hands of the law? This book is about everyday desistance: how young adults construct their lives after growing up in the juvenile justice system, neither giving up on their goals nor experiencing a simple or straightforward pathway to success. While the media tends to portray formerly incarcerated youth as either doomed to fail or miraculously able to succeed against all odds, we rarely hear about those whose experiences lie in between these extremes. Our intention is to illustrate how young men and women who were incarcerated during much of their adolescence navigate the challenges and opportunities associated with desistance from crime alongside becoming an adult.

EMERGING ADULTHOOD AND FORMERLY INCARCERATED YOUTH

The young people whose stories comprise this book are considered to be "emerging adults," referring to the developmental period between traditional understandings of adolescence and adulthood (Arnett, 2000).

The concept of emerging adulthood itself reflects some of the major demographic shifts of the past fifty years, such as the tendency for young people to delay childbearing and marriage and to live longer under the care of family members (Federal Interagency Forum, 2014; Furstenberg, 2010). Scholarship and popular literature alike have characterized emerging adulthood as a time of rapid change, exploration, and extended opportunity to consider life pathways (Arnett, 2000; Henig & Henig, 2012; Jay, 2012). For economically and racially privileged young adults, this exploratory period often takes place in a college setting, an arena that offers some sense of protection from real-world responsibilities (here we invite you to envision college parties, summer internships, and spring break trips to Florida). However, unlike their more privileged peers, a substantial number of emerging adults are not afforded a protected or nurtured passage to adulthood. By contrast, upon reaching the age of legal maturity, young people with histories of foster care, homelessness, school disruption, and early age of parenthood must fend for themselves, and often their own children and families, to meet even their most basic needs. This group of more marginalized young adults is replete with those who have had contact with the juvenile justice system. For, although juvenile incarceration rates have steadily declined over the past 20 years, the US juvenile justice system still interfaces with more than 1.2 million youth annually, of whom more than 250,000 are detained and roughly 100,000 are placed in out-of-home care annually (Sickmund, Sladky, & Kang, 2015).

As a whole, formerly incarcerated youth enter adulthood with significantly fewer economic and social capital resources than other young people their age, even compared to those from similar socioeconomic backgrounds (Uggen & Wakefield, 2005). This is partially because of time spent in institutional settings that are far removed from real-world circumstances and developmental opportunities. For example, institutionalized young people have far less control over their daily routines and fewer opportunities to learn from their mistakes or to take natural risks than those who remain at home (Chung, Little, & Steinberg, 2005). Yet paradoxically, formerly incarcerated young adults also find themselves navigating major responsibilities at younger ages, as they are more likely to live on their own, work full-time, and become parents than their same-aged peers (Foster & Gifford, 2005). In this sense, the transition to adulthood for formerly incarcerated youth can be viewed as expedited in a context in which many middle-class young people are actually delaying the adoption of adult roles and responsibilities.

To date, researchers have focused on the poor outcomes associated with juvenile incarceration. For example, studies have shown that at least half, and even up to 85 percent, of formerly incarcerated youth will return to the criminal justice system within two to five years of their release from confinement (Trulson, Marquart, Mullings, & Caeti, 2005), and fewer than 20 percent will complete high school (Osgood, Foster, & Courtney, 2010). Even if these young people circumvent the high likelihood of criminal recidivism, they often face the larger realities of resource-poor neighborhoods, a dearth of well-paying jobs, and the dangers of community and police violence (Mears & Travis, 2004). Moreover, many face risks of police profiling in simply going about their daily lives. For formerly incarcerated young people, particularly men, these dangers are amplified and persistent due to the mark of a criminal record (Abrams & Terry, 2014). This research evidence has provided ammunition for advocates to demand action to fix this broken and ineffective system.

With this background, our book takes a different approach to this increasingly familiar script. Although we fully acknowledge that the juvenile justice system continues to create a group of youth who are disadvantaged as they enter adulthood, we contend that these young men and women are a great deal more than just their bleak odds. As such, this book intends to provide a richer, nuanced view of the transition to adulthood among young men and women with histories of juvenile incarceration. Specifically, we focus on the ordinary experiences, decisions, and challenges that these young people encounter as they enter early adulthood and make important decisions concerning crime, friends, partners, work, and school. We find that while these young people's concerns are partially constructed by the past, they also have high hopes and dreams for their futures. We believe that the crossroads of adulthood is a pivotal juncture, and we hope that our book will contribute to a better understanding of what these young people need in order to thrive.

RESEARCH ON DESISTANCE FROM CRIME

Criminal desistance, which can be defined as the movement toward the complete termination of offending behavior, is a key concept informing this book. Criminal desistance is a process that involves a multitude of factors, including personal motivation to change, social support, and access to mainstream institutions such as employment and schooling (Maruna, 2001; Mulvey et al., 2004). An extensive body of literature has theorized criminal desistance among adolescent offenders. Most experts have acknowledged that a large percentage of those who were involved in crime as minors end up reducing or ceasing their criminal activity altogether in young adulthood (Laub & Sampson, 2003; Moffitt, 1993). Criminologists also generally concur that desistance for young adults hinges on a blend of internal motivation and external opportunities for change (Mulvey et al., 2004). Despite this agreement, there are still some key debates about how and why previously delinquent youth terminate offending in young adulthood.

One of these points of conversation concerns the degree to which maturation and age play a role in launching a process of desistance for adolescents. From a developmental view, research has found that certain characteristics associated with chronological age appear to reduce young people's involvement in criminal activity over time. These include biological factors (i.e., impulse control, suppression of aggression) as well as behavioral traits associated with maturity (i.e., increased hopefulness, empathy, and reasoning) (Monahan, Steinberg, Cauffman, & Mulvey, 2009). An emerging body of neuroscience has supported these ideas, finding evidence that the younger brain is more prone to judgment errors, impulse, and peer pressure than the more mature brain (Maroney, 2011). Implicit in this reasoning is the notion that becoming an adult involves becoming more focused and mature, and therefore less drawn to a criminal lifestyle. Thus, desistance in young adulthood can be viewed as a normative process of cognitive and emotional maturity. This science may explain why most adolescents will age out of crime around the transition to adulthood period.

Taking a slightly different view on the age-crime curve, life course theory suggests that it is not age or maturity per se, but rather critical life turning points that can shift the criminal trajectories of adolescent offenders. These turning points may include events such as marriage, parenthood, and employment; events that often occur in the young adulthood period (Sampson & Laub, 1993). These roles and responsibilities operate as social bonds that formerly incarcerated individuals can latch onto to enact desistance. According to the life course perspective, these social bonds work independently of childhood experiences, in that even those young people with risks for persistent offending may terminate criminal activity when they experience these turning points (Laub & Sampson, 2003).

Departing from both maturation and life course theories, criminologists have also attributed desistance to a set of complementary internal and external shifts that facilitate a gradual process of change. For example, Peggy Giordano theorized a set of cognitive transformations that must occur for desistance to take place. These include such shifts as openness to change as well as willingness to latch onto available opportunities, or "hooks," for change (Giordano, Cernkovich, & Rudolph, 2002). These hooks can include marriage or childbearing, but may also include school, peer groups, or other opportunities to change one's course. Building on Giordano's ideas, Shadd Maruna's (2001) study of criminal persisters and desisters in the United Kingdom found that successful desisters disassociated themselves from their offender identities and actively took on new identities as law-abiding individuals. On the contrary, persisters did not disentangle themselves from criminal identifications and associations in a similar way. Accordingly, he asserted that although young adulthood may be a prime age to terminate offending due to a process of maturity, internal cognitive and identity related shifts must occur in order to set these events in motion.

Scholars have also suggested that environmental and neighborhood context ought to be more fully integrated into theories of criminal desistance (Abrams & Snyder, 2010; Laub & Boonstoppel, 2012). Social and ecological contexts certainly have great influence over criminal patterns, in that young people's social networks, familial influences, ties with local institutions, and larger disparities in economic opportunity play a significant role in rates of offending and recidivism (Sampson, Raudenbush, & Earls, 1997). The relevance of neighborhood context to desistance is also supported by research finding that communities with high densities of crime, violence, and poverty can contribute to criminally persistent behaviors, even compared to lower-income areas without such intensive risk factors (Grunwald, Lockwood, Harris, & Mennis, 2010; Kubrin & Stewart, 2006; Mennis & Harris, 2011).

For our purposes, this rich set of ideas contributes to an understanding of desistance from crime among formerly incarcerated young men and women who are transitioning to adulthood. From these theories, we understand that factors such as age, maturity, social bonds, internal motivation, external hooks for change, and neighborhood conditions may all converge to facilitate a process of desistance for young adults. Part of the richness of the narrative approach of this book is that we can look at how all of these elements play out in a young person's life, examining how desistance among these young adults unfolds within their particular life histories and as situated within their relevant social contexts. In this sense, we hope that our book contributes to this important body of theory on mechanisms of desistance in young adulthood.

GENDER AND DESISTANCE

Within the literature, there are also various perspectives concerning gender differences in the desistance process. Arguably the bulk of desistance research, and particularly large longitudinal studies, have focused mostly on men (Glueck & Glueck, 1950; Sampson & Laub, 1993). Yet although young women have been increasingly represented in all stages of the juvenile justice system over the past two decades, they are still more likely to terminate offending in adulthood than young men (Piquero, Schubert, & Brame, 2014). A significant question thus remains unanswered: How does gender influence desistance mechanisms during this particular life stage?

One perspective attributes gender differences in desistance to young women's tendency to seek out and make use of supportive social bonds. In this view, women's desistance is more likely to be facilitated by close relationships than the more formal bonds that often frame men's desistance experiences, such as employment (Benda, 2005). Yet paradoxically, while the social bond of marriage is important for men's desistance, it is less clear that marriage operates similarly for young women (Bersani & Doherty, 2013). This may be at least partially attributed to young women's choice of romantic partners that inadvertently perpetuate their own criminal associations (Leverentz, 2006). Moreover, as the age of marriage continues to rise, this formal social bond may become less critical for young women in regard to triggering desistance.

Other scholars have found desistance to be a largely gender-neutral process, in that life events such as work, marriage, and childbearing operate very similarly for both males and females (Uggen & Krushnitt, 1998). In Giordano's view, once cognitive transformation has occurred, both men and women may seek out pro-social relationships that are conducive to fully disengaging from crime. Given this understanding, the core elements of desistance, including "readiness to change" and "hooks for change," operate largely similarly for both men and women (Giordano et al., 2002).

With this background, we understand that far less is known about young women's desistance compared to the relatively more robust studies on young men. Our intention in this book is to contribute to this important discussion by exploring the mechanisms that play a role in desistance for young men and women within the same developmental period and similar social context of urban Los Angeles.

GOALS AND STRUCTURE OF THE BOOK

This book brings to light the words and stories of young men and women who are carving out their pathways to adulthood after spending significant time within the trappings of the juvenile justice system. The young people whose stories comprise the core of this book are marginally employed, sporadically enrolled in school, and often insecurely housed. Some are still involved in crime and spending time in and out of jail and prison, while others, despite major adversities, have changed their lives in significantly positive ways. Although there is a substantial body of knowledge about the failure of formerly incarcerated youth to achieve "normative" (i.e., middle-class) adult milestones, current literature and theory lack a rich description of the everyday challenges that these young people face, the ways they navigate these barriers, and the personal victories they achieve along the way. By bringing these stories into sharper focus, we aim to expose our readers not only to the magnitude of the strength and grit often required to overcome these barriers, but also to the need for social and institutional supports that can help to guide these young people into the futures that they desire.

This book is based on nearly three years of field research, including 70 in-depth interviews with seventeen formerly incarcerated young men and eight young women between the ages of 18 and 25. Situated in Los Angeles County, we began our fieldwork in the winter of 2010, spending an initial period of time gathering the stories of 15 young men who had spent time in a local correctional facility. To gather additional insights, particularly from young women, we then recruited ten additional participants (eight young women and two young men) from community-based programs serving formerly incarcerated youth in Los Angeles County. This second wave had been placed in multiple types of facilities, ranging from detention to the state youth prison. All of the participants took part in two in-depth qualitative interviews and ten participated in three or more interviews over the course of two years. More detail about our methodological approach is provided in the appendix.

This work is organized into several thematic chapters. In chapter 2, The Road to Juvie, we situate the reader in the context of Los Angeles County and introduce the 25 participants who took part in this study. We delve into some of the major race and class disparities in Los Angeles County, such as poverty, child maltreatment, and the education system, while at the same time weaving in the individual stories of these young men and women in order to bring this broader information to life. Related to the overall context of Los Angeles, we describe the young people's various pathways into delinquency as recounted from their own memories and perspectives. By placing the individual stories in their context, we set the groundwork for the situated life history perspective that undergirds the book as a whole.

In chapter 3, Locked Up and Back Again, we describe the participants' journeys through the juvenile justice system, from their first forays into the system to their eventual release into adulthood. Most of these young people became trapped in a system that cared little for their safety or personhood, and they were repeatedly incarcerated for probation violations or petty offenses. Others had crossed over from foster care into the juvenile justice system when they fled abusive or unstable homes. In spite of an overriding sense of being a "throwaway," some of these young men and women also found moments of hope and transformation within the system: through volunteer mentors, a caring probation officer, or a family member or friend who inspired them to take a different outlook on their future. This chapter sets the stage to understand how these formative experiences laid a foundation for their transition to adulthood.

In chapter 4, And Now I'm an Adult, we illustrate how these young people situated themselves as young adults after spending much of their adolescent years in and out of the juvenile justice system. We highlight two major themes: "making ends meet" and "on the margins" that capture the essence of their quest to earn a living, find a place to call home, and put food on the table for themselves and their partners, family members, and/or children. For those who were able to support themselves financially, their search for stable work entailed a great deal of determination, self-sacrifice, and often, foregoing higher education. By contrast, those who were living on the margins faced an array of logistical and personal barriers that precluded them from entering the mainstream workforce altogether. As this chapter illustrates, even the most prepared and dedicated young adults were quite vulnerable to poverty and falling through the cracks of mainstream opportunities.

In the next two chapters, we focus on young men and their processes of criminal desistance. Chapter 5, Dangers and Decisions: Navigating Desistance as a Young Man, lays out three patterns of young men's desistance, including those who were "on the road" to desistance, those who were "running in circles," and those who were still "in the game." We describe differences in these groups with regard to their decision-making around issues such as changing their appearance and contending with the pressures of old friends and influences. Chapter 6, You Can Run but You Can't Hide, then examines the core experience of "being marked," meaning being targeted by old friends, enemies, and the police. This experience posed challenges to desistance for all of the young men in the study who found themselves grappling with the internal and external reminders of their pasts. We also suggest that members of the three groups adopted different strategies for dealing with being marked, each of which had consequences for their own desistance journeys, sense of safety, and overall well-being.

Chapter 7, Finding a Net to Fall Back On: The Young Women's Journeys, examines the criminal desistance experiences of the young women. Overall, we found that the young women did not undergo the same struggles with criminal desistance as the young men. In particular, it was easier for them to leave their old associations and criminal ties behind. However, they most certainly faced their own set of challenges in young adulthood. Through the young women's stories, we illustrate how they tried to build lives free from criminal activity while also facing some potentially grave risks to their economic survival and personal safety. We also look closely at the ways that the young women forged their relational lives, which both facilitated and hindered the process of desistance in noticeably gendered ways.

We conclude the book with two chapters: one on desistance theory and one on policy and practice recommendations. In chapter 8, Everyday Desistance: Theory Meets Reality, we return to our initial questions about young adult desistance and gender differences, and summarize our major conclusions. We comment on how our work extends and refines current theory and pose some questions for further research. In chapter 9, Policy and Practice Reforms: Supporting the Pathway to Adulthood, we propose some answers to looming questions about how young adults can safely navigate the difficult pathways involved in criminal desistance. We use the young people's stories and our analysis of them to propose what social institutions and policymakers can do to better prepare formerly incarcerated youth to become functional and productive members of our communities.

Last, in the appendix, we describe the methods that we used to collect the data for the book and note the strengths and limitations of our approach. We hope that this detailed methodological explanation will be useful and instructional for other students and scholars who are seeking to engage in similar work.

CHAPTER 2

The Road to Juvie

THE TRANSITION TO ADULTHOOD among the 25 young men and women in this study took place in the diverse landscape of Los Angeles County. Los Angeles is the most populated county in the United States and is home to more than a quarter of all residents in the entire state of California. In 2010, the 4,084 square miles that comprise the county housed over 10.4 million people (US Census Bureau, 2012). Put into perspective, Los Angeles County is more heavily populated than 42 US states and is the first in the nation to reach ten million residents.

Los Angeles is culturally, ethnically, and linguistically diverse and is home to a large population of immigrants, particularly from Mexico. As of 2014, 48 percent of county residents identified as Hispanic and 35 percent identified as foreign-born (US Census Bureau, 2014). The racial and ethnic composition of the county has changed significantly over the past several decades. From 2000 to 2010, the number of Hispanic residents increased by 10 percent while the African American population decreased by 7.8 percent (US Census Bureau, 2014). Due to these changing demographics, historically African American neighborhoods in the southern part of the county such as Compton and Watts (see figure 2.1) are now comprised of a majority Hispanic population. These demographic shifts have contributed to changes in the social, cultural, and political landscape of the region as a whole.

Known for being the gang capital of America as well as an epicenter of Hollywood glitz and glamour, Los Angeles is riddled with paradox. One such irony is extreme wealth disparity, as Los Angeles has the second-highest rate of millionaire growth as well as the second-highest number of millionaires in the United States (Fisher, 2011). The millionaire lifestyle is proliferated throughout popular media with images of sprawling mansions, designer clothing, lavish parties, and other "rich and famous" eccentricities. Yet even with the enormous wealth ushered

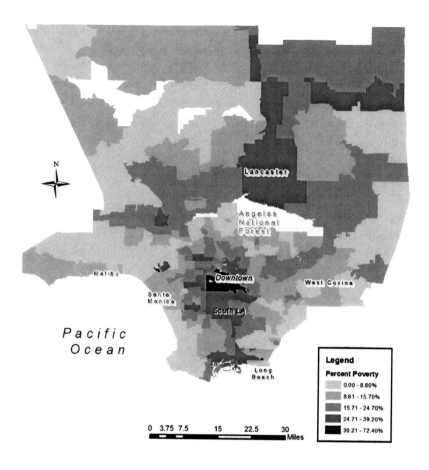

FIGURE 2.1. Los Angeles County Poverty Rates. Map created by Christina Tam.
Data Source: US Census, American Community Survey, 2013

in by the largest entertainment industry in the world, a strikingly high percentage of Los Angeles residents experience economic hardship. The US Census finds that in 2011, the poverty rate for Los Angeles County was 18.2 percent. Yet when factoring in the cost of living, public benefit levels, and housing prices, Stanford University economists estimate the real poverty rate in Los Angeles to be 26.9 percent, which is the highest poverty rate in all of California. Moreover, at least one in four children in Los Angeles County grow up poor (Willen, Mattingly, Levin, Danielson, & Bohn, 2013).

Poverty in Los Angeles is geographically clustered in particular neighborhoods and regions, most often in areas with high concentrations of immigrant families and people of color. According to urban economists, the region defied national economic trends in the latter part of the twentieth century due to an increase (rather than a decrease) in areas of concentrated poverty, defined as census tracts in which 40 percent of households or more fall below the federal poverty level (Matsunaga, 2008). These areas of concentrated poverty are located in the inland and southern parts of the county, which are geographically distanced from the wealthy Westside beach communities of Santa Monica and Malibu. Figure 2.1 displays areas of Los Angeles County with the highest levels of economic need corresponding to the darker grey hues. One can see from this map how areas with the highest need are clustered together in particular regions—east of downtown, South Los Angeles, and in the more remote northern part of the county (i.e. Lancaster and its surroundings).

In sum, growing up in Los Angeles, young people are subject to a society of extremes. On the one hand, they experience the media version of Los Angeles: mansions, millionaires, fancy cars, and Hollywood glitz and glamour. Yet at least one in four children grow up in poverty alongside a set of harsh social conditions that are ripe for media hype (i.e., the gangster lifestyle, violence, and hip-hop music), yet in reality restrict access to the resources and privileges enjoyed by their more advantaged counterparts.

It is in the crux of these paradoxes that the young people in this study forged their own pathways into the juvenile justice system. Several of these individuals were raised in stable homes with parents who worked, encouraged their children to pursue education, and made efforts to provide their children with a supportive home environment; while others struggled with absent or incarcerated parents, foster care, and material deprivation. Despite these differences, all of their childhood and adolescent experiences played out alongside the backdrop of under-resourced neighborhoods and schools that provided several pathways to crime and scant opportunities for educational or other successes.

PATHWAYS TO DELINQUENCY

The 25 young adults who took part in this study shared some common life experiences. They were all between the ages of 18 and 25 when we met them, had lived at least part of their lives in Los Angeles County, and had spent at least six months incarcerated during their adolescent years. Despite these similarities, their pathways to delinquency and the juvenile justice system were quite diverse. Extant research and theory on the causes of delinquency provided us with some guidance on the interpretation of their life histories and in particular, their forays into the system.

Juvenile delinquency stems from a number of interrelated factors such as family instability, child abuse/neglect, neighborhood conditions, school failure, substance use, and association with anti-social peers (Thornberry, Huizinga, & Loeber, 2004). More recently, researchers have found that toxic stress, meaning the stress caused by repeated exposure to violence and material deprivation, is linked to the development of violent and other anti-social behaviors (Duke, Pettingell, McMorris, & Borowsky, 2010). These factors often interact with one another. For example, drug use and school failure are both strongly associated with delinquency, yet these issues also correlate with both child maltreatment and poverty. Likewise, a young person may be drawn to an anti-social peer group or a gang, but family stress and poverty may limit a parent's ability to protect a child from these associations. As such, it is often difficult to disentangle the root causes of a young person's involvement in delinquent or criminal activities.

There are also known gender variations in the causes and correlates of delinquency. For example, young women in the juvenile justice system have significantly higher rates of diagnosable mental health conditions than their male counterparts, including depression, anxiety, behavioral disorders, and suicidal ideation (Abram, Teplin, McClelland, & Dulcan, 2003; Cauffman, 2008; Trupin, Stewart, Beach, & Boesky, 2002). Sexual abuse, family problems, and low self-esteem are also more common among detained females compared to males (Bloom, Owen, Deschenes, & Rosenbaum, 2002; Trupin et al., 2002). Overall, family, physical, and emotional traumas tend to be precursors for young women's delinquency. This may be true for young men as well, but these factors are more widely documented among young women.

Given what is known about multiple and co-occurring precursors to delinquency, we examined the participants' life histories to better understand their various pathways into the juvenile justice system. In this process, we

TABLE 2.1.

Pathways to Delinquency and Demographic Information

Pseudonym	Gender	Race	Age at First Interview	Age at First Incarceration	Gang History
Pathway 1: Early Delinquent Activity					
SCHOOL TROUBLES					
Evan	M	African American	21	14	Yes
Jerry	M	Latino	23	14	Yes
Keira	F	African American	18	16	Associated*
Mario	M	Latino	23	13	Yes
Oscar	M	Latino	19	13	Yes
NEIGHBORHOOD ORIGINS					
Amber	F	African American	18	12	No
Carlos	M	Latino	20	15	Yes
Chris	M	African American	24	15	No
Eduardo	M	Latino	19	14	Yes
John	M	Latino	19	15	Yes
Peter	M	Pilipino	23	14	Yes
Pathway 2: Later Start Delinquency					
Anthony	M	African American	20	17	Associated*
Cesar	M	Latino	23	17	Yes
Shawn	M	African American	22	16	No
Steven	M	Latino	24	17	No
Pathway 3: Family Difficulties					
POVERTY AND SURVIVAL					
Gabriel	M	Latino	24	16	Yes
Greg	M	White	23	17	No
Maria	F	Latina	19	16	Yes
Mike	M	African American	24	10	No

Pseudonym	Gender	Race	Age at First Interview	Age at First Incarceration	Gang History
CROSSOVER YOUTH					
Carina	F	Latina	20	12	No
Desiree	F	African American	20	14	No
Irene	F	Latina	20	15	Yes
Lupe	F	Latina	19	13	No
Sara	F	Latina	18	13	Associated*
Tyrone	M	African American	20	14	No

* May have associated with a gang, but did not join a gang per se.

found a great deal of overlap, with family problems, peer groups, and school problems serving as the primary origins of anti-social behaviors. For some, these behaviors were rooted more firmly in peer and neighborhood factors, while for others, they were more readily linked to family problems. Moreover, akin to what is known about gender differences, the young women largely attributed the origins of their juvenile justice involvement to family problems and related traumas.

Table 2.1 introduces the reader to the 25 participants, displaying basic demographic information along with what we identified as each individual's primary pathway toward delinquency. These pathways include early delinquent activity (school and neighborhood origins); later start/peer influenced; and family difficulties (poverty and survival, and crossover youth). Following this table, we further define each pathway through the lens of the participants' narrated life histories.

Pathway One: Early Delinquent Activity

A quest for thrill-seeking, often combined with a desire for respect from peers, led several of these young men and women into delinquent activities in the late elementary or early middle school years (roughly ages nine through twelve). The young people in this pathway were united by their getting into trouble with the law at an earlier age and by having a strong attraction to the excitement of a fast-paced life. Within this pathway, we culled out two subgroups: (1) those who began getting into trouble in a school setting for reasons such as fighting or defying authority; and (2) those who formed informal crews with their neighborhood friends and whose primary source of trouble was rooted in these associations. For all of the young people in Pathway One, thrill-seeking and defiant behavior eventually escalated into more serious troubles such as gang membership, heavy drug and alcohol use, school dropout, and increasingly more dangerous crimes and criminal associations.

SCHOOL TROUBLES. In order to understand how a child goes from engaging in elementary school mishaps to sleeping in a locked cell, it is important to provide some context on the complexity of the Los Angeles educational system. The school system is a microcosm of the larger county in that the extreme wealth and racial disparities that characterize the region as a whole also shape children's educational opportunities and experiences. With 85 school districts and vast differences in resources, public schools range from those with Olympic-size pools and Ivy League–bound students to struggling schools with tattered texts and abysmal graduation rates. State-level funding cuts and outdated funding formulas have contributed in part to these vast disparities. Historically, school districts received "revenue-limited" funding from the state that resulted in inequitable funding allocations between wealthier and poorer neighborhood schools. This distribution did not take into account the fact that the latter districts typically served a disproportionate number of students with significant learning, emotional, and social needs, and thus had a greater need for state resources. California only recently passed legislation to rectify this imbalance and fund school districts in a way that better reflects the diverse needs of their student population (EdSource, 2016).

Black and Latino students in Los Angeles County are more likely to attend schools in under-resourced and racially segregated academic environments. According to the UCLA Civil Rights Project (2011), approximately 40 percent of Latino youth and black youth in the region attend schools where 90–100 percent of the students come from racially under-represented groups. By comparison, most white students attend schools where they comprise 50 percent or more of student enrollment. The schools where youth of color make up the majority of the student body face significant challenges that inhibit learning, including overcrowding, high suspension rates, limited access to college preparatory courses, and restricted funding for electives, aides, tutoring, and other amenities relative to their wealthier counterparts (Orfield, Siegel-Hawley, & Kucsera, 2011).

Disparities in educational opportunity affect students as early as elementary school, making it hard for disadvantaged students to catch up to their more advantaged peers. In third grade, only 31 percent of economically disadvantaged children in Los Angeles County test as reading-proficient, compared to 64 percent of economically advantaged students (California Department of Education, 2013a). These early achievement disparities eventually translate to differences in high school graduation rates. Overall, 75 percent of youth in the county earn a high school diploma or GED. Yet, while 81.8 percent of white youth earned a diploma or GED in 2010, only 65.5 percent of Hispanic and 59.4 percent of African American youth achieved the same marker (California Department of Education, 2013b).

Under-resourced and racially segregated school settings typified the educational experiences of the young people in our study, and for those in Pathway One, laid the foundation for their eventual foray into the juvenile justice system. For example, when we met Oscar, he impressed us as a friendly and introspective 19-year-old Latino young man who was focused on earning a college degree and becoming a social justice advocate. In telling us his story, however, Oscar painted a completely different image of his childhood self. Oscar's troubles may have started at home, but they became cemented in the school setting. He grew up with his parents, older brother and sister, and two younger siblings in a mixed black and Latino neighborhood in South Los Angeles. While he clearly loved his family, he described his relationship to his parents as "complicated" as he often felt singled out as the "bad seed" compared to his siblings.

Oscar began getting into trouble in school at a young age, and in some ways the stressors of the two environments—home and school—seemed to feed off of each other. His first recollection of school trouble was when he was suspended from kindergarten. He explained that his teacher promised him a treat and then changed his mind; in response, Oscar started picking up all the chairs from the desks and throwing them onto the floor. He continued to get in trouble for similar behaviors throughout his elementary and middle school years, with the severity of his problems escalating with each passing year. He explained: "It would go from little fights over snacks to like, it wouldn't just be fist fights. All of a sudden middle school came and there were knives and weapons and stuff. I started adapting to that and I've always had a personality of wanting to be the toughest. And I remember in the sixth grade the teacher asking me 'what sign are you?' And I said 'Leo.' And he said, 'Oh Leo. No wonder.' And so then in my head I was like, okay, this is how I'm supposed to be. So then I took that and ran with it."

Living up to the "bad seed" image projected onto him by adults and authority figures was an ongoing challenge for Oscar. He described how among his group of school and neighborhood friends "it was always a battle for the top to see who was the baddest in anything." On a more introspective note, he described how "a lot of the troubles I got myself into were because I was always defending other people who couldn't defend themselves." He went on to explain that because he had developed a reputation as a good fighter, his friends always came to him when they needed help: "And I would always run up to somebody, fighting them, defending them. Whoever it was. And even on random occasions, I remember walking down the streets, and if I saw someone getting hassled, then I would go up to whoever was hassling that person and fight them off or do whatever I had to do. So I always got in trouble for being a defender."

By seventh grade, Oscar was expelled from his local middle school as a result of his involvement in a school riot. Unfortunately, being in such serious trouble at the tender age of 12 did not dissuade him from going down an even more hardened path. Instead, after a cycle of fighting, school suspensions, expulsions, and transfers to six different middle schools, he felt satisfied that he had officially earned his reputation as a serious troublemaker. With this reputation in tow, Oscar never found a school where he could succeed. His behavior became increasingly reckless as he got older and tried harder to live up to his image; by age 13 he and his friends joined a neighborhood gang. That same year he was arrested after a minor encounter with the police turned into an altercation that resulted in his first of many trips to court and juvenile hall.

Another member of the school troubles group is Keira, an 18-year-old African American young woman. Wearing a brightly colored leopard print shirt and with multiple facial piercings, Keira was an animated talker with a quick wit. Her home life was not without troubles. As an infant, she was removed from the custody of her mother due to substance abuse, and was subsequently raised by her paternal grandmother and father in a low-income housing project, along with three of her fourteen siblings. Despite a mostly stable home situation, Keira recalls always longing to be closer to her mother and feeling jealous of the siblings who had the chance to live with her. Due to her mother's ongoing addiction struggles, Keira was permitted only weekend visits and eventually was legally adopted by her grandmother.

Keira recalls enjoying elementary school, but that feeling changed when she transitioned to middle school. She explained that her troubles began when a group of girls threatened her due to jealousy and she started to fight back. The school responded with harsh disciplinary practices: starting with suspension, then home schooling, and eventually expulsion. While on a home study program, Keira recalled that the work was minimal, describing the learning as "a joke." She explained: "It wasn't like a real homeschool because they don't do homeschool, so like one of the teachers just gave me a packet. And the packet—I had to do it on the computer but when I was at home on the computer I was on like MySpace and stuff."

Following her home schooling experience, Keira was moved to an "opportunity high school" (we discuss these alternative, opportunity schools further in chapter 3) even without successfully completing middle school. At this school she felt she was doing better, but she was expelled in tenth grade, this time for something she considered rather minor. She explained: "I had a scarf on my hair—my hair wasn't finished, like all the way done. I had a scarf and I didn't want to take it off, so the principal told me if I didn't take it off I was going to get kicked out of the school and he kicked me out because I didn't take it off." Exasperated after this experience, Keira decided to drop out of school altogether. Then 15, her tough reputation and lack of structure led to hanging out with friends who were, in her words, "robbing people, stealing things, and getting high." After stealing cell phones and other small items, she and her friends would sell them to get money for drugs. Eventually Keira's reckless behavior led to her first arrest for being a passenger in a stolen car. While she was let off the hook for that charge, she did not return to school. Continuing to run around with the same group of friends, she was soon arrested again for a felony, and this time she spent a few months in juvenile hall.

Released on house arrest, Keira was mandated to return to school as part of the terms of her probation. By that time, she was supposed to be a junior in high school, but she had fallen far behind academically and became discouraged. Eventually she stopped going to school altogether and fell back into her patterns with her friends. Her grandmother grew tired of her recklessness, repeatedly called the police to arrest her for defiance, and eventually kicked her out of the house. Keira subsequently spent time "couch surfing" with friends and hiding from the police— finally returning to stay with her biological mother. At the time that we met her, she was still technically on the run from the law.

Oscar and Keira had vastly different upbringings, family structures, and points of entree into the juvenile justice system. However, the common thread running through their narratives was the heavy-handed response of the school system in dealing with their behavioral issues. Rather than intervening on their behalf or providing support for their struggles, both Oscar and Keira received punishments such as suspensions and expulsions that further isolated them from school and did little to deter them from future problems in school or with law enforcement.

Unfortunately, these experiences of school push-out are not atypical for students of color, who are far more likely than their white counterparts to be subject to harsh disciplinary action for similar types of infractions (Fabelo et al., 2011). This tendency is driven in part by educational policies. Following national trends, Los Angeles public schools in the 1990s implemented a series of zero-tolerance policies that permitted schools to readily suspend or expel students for a variety of reasons, ranging from serious incidents (i.e., fighting), to minor infractions (i.e., talking back to a teacher). Youth of color are disproportionately impacted by these policies, and African American students in particular receive the worst consequences. For example, in the 2009–2010 school year for the Los Angeles Unified School District (LAUSD), 23 percent of African American male students were suspended compared to 19 percent of Latino males, and just 5 percent of white males (Losen, Martinez, & Gillespie, 2012). African American males with disabilities represent the most vulnerable subgroup, with nearly 40 percent of these youth being suspended in this same time period.

Such punitive measures can have long-lasting impacts on students' educational outcomes. Experiences of suspension and expulsion result in less classroom instruction time and are linked to poor academic performance and an increased risk of dropping out of high school (Advancement Project, 2010). Further compounding the problem is that students under zero-tolerance policies are more likely to be picked up by the police and arrested for minor offenses such as truancy. Many advocates and policymakers refer to this trend as the "school-to-prison-pipeline" because the culmination of these harsh disciplinary actions results in students being literally pushed out of the school system. This ultimately weakens youths' connectedness and engagement with school and increases their likelihood of future contact with the juvenile justice system (Fabelo et al., 2011; Heitzeg, 2009). For Oscar and Keira, this pattern appeared to hold true.

NEIGHBORHOOD CREWS. The second set of youth in Pathway One also began to get into trouble at young ages, yet their confrontations with the law were rooted more firmly in their neighborhoods and less so in school. Most of these youth began committing minor crimes with peer groups, such as petty theft, curfew violations, or tagging (i.e., a form of graffiti). However, their behaviors worsened over time, especially as they began to form neighborhood crews or joined formal gangs with older and more criminally sophisticated members. And once they got involved in these more established criminal networks, they began participating in activities that landed them in the arms of the law.

Nearly all of the young men and women in our study had some degree of childhood and adolescent exposure to gangs and community violence. Los Angeles has a particularly rich history of organized gangs, gaining visibility with the Crips and the Bloods, African American gangs that originated in the South Central Los Angeles corridor. These gangs formed during the early 1950s during periods of integration to protect black residents from harassment and physical attacks from local white gangs. These groups later morphed into organized civil rights groups concerned with racial equality, community improvement, and activism. The 1965 Watts Riots were, in large part, an organized protest against racism and lack of economic opportunity for blacks in Los Angeles. Gradually, the combination of white flight, the loss of well-paying urban industrial jobs in South Los Angeles, and the influx of the crack cocaine drug trade shifted African American gangs into more criminal and violent organizations (Davis, 2006).

Along with their African American counterparts, Mexican gangs formed as early as the 1940s in the barrios of East Los Angeles. Historian James D. Vigil (1988) explains that racism, housing segregation, poverty, and poor-quality schools pushed immigrant youth out of mainstream society and into organized street gangs. Despite the emphasis on family ties and culture within Mexican families and communities, parents as workers were subject to labor exploitation and long work hours, so they were often unable to provide the supervision required to keep their children in school and out of gangs. Since the 1940s, Mexican gangs have expanded at a rapid pace that parallels the continuous flow of Mexican immigrants into Southern California. These gangs are both neighborhood- and family-oriented such that multiple generations of family members have belonged to the same organizations (Vigil, 2008).

Beginning in the 1970s, unstable political conditions in Central America forced another wave of migration to Southern California, mainly from El Salvador, Guatemala, and Nicaragua. Central American immigrants and refugees have at times intermingled peacefully with their Mexican American neighbors, yet they have also formed their own transnational gangs such as the notoriously violent MS-13. Transnational gangs are different from domestic gangs with regard to sophistication, organization, and control. They are also heavily involved with the international drug trade (Monteith, 2010). As such, the barrios that once served as a safe haven for Mexican newcomers are now more dangerous, with frequent occurrences of violence between Mexican and Central American gangs (Vigil, 2008).

The Los Angeles Police Department estimates that 450 gangs are currently active in the city of Los Angeles, meaning many more would be counted in the county as a whole (LAPD, 2014). Latino/as comprise more than half of these gangs (Los Angeles Almanac, 2014). In 2007, the mayor's office took steps to fight gang violence by implementing a comprehensive plan that blended prevention, intervention, and suppression strategies. Since the inception of this initiative, gang crime fell 15 percent in areas of the city that received targeted intervention and prevention services, and witnessed a 35 percent decrease in gang-related homicides overall (Advancement Project, 2011). Despite these efforts, gang-related violence remains a serious problem, especially for the south and east areas of the county where most of our study participants were raised and/or still reside. Moreover, the LAPD indicates that gang membership actually increased from 2009 to 2014 (LAPD, 2014). Thus, although the FBI reported that violent crime rates in California reached a 46-year low in 2013 (Public Policy Institute of California, 2014), children living in the poorest Los Angeles neighborhoods at that time were still subject to a high likelihood of exposure to gang violence. The Advancement Project (2006), a Los Angeles–based research and advocacy organization, explains why gang violence often defies overall crime patterns: "[G]*ang* crime does not follow general crime trends. In spite of recent declines in citywide crime rates, *gang* crime and violence in Los Angeles are up. It is a problem because it destroys the lives of thousands of children and the quality of life in hundreds of neighborhoods. It is also wasteful; Los Angeles gang crime costs taxpayers and crime victims over $2 billion every year" (p. 9).

As many of our participants' life stories illustrate, gangs were quite pervasive in the neighborhoods where they were raised. For some, joining a gang served as a rite of passage as they transitioned to middle school or sought protection from a neighborhood clique. Others were not directly involved in gangs, but were still affected by the culture through gang-affiliated family members, or by simply living in communities controlled by gang violence and the drug trade. To contextualize the pervasiveness of gangs and neighborhood violence and their influence on young people living in its midst, we offer a few of our participants' life stories.

When we met Eduardo, he was 19 years old and had been out of juvenile probation camp for almost two years. He appeared to be relaxed and content; he spoke in the leisurely manner of a young man who had a somewhat carefree perspective on life. Yet in other respects, he was much more guarded about his past life than the other young men we had met. He was born and raised in the city of Pasadena, a more middle-class enclave of the county, where he lived with his mother, two younger siblings, and grandparents. He described having a close relationship with his mother while he was growing up, and that she, along with his grandparents, consistently served as positive role models for him. He also recounted a fairly stable childhood where he often played outside with his family and neighborhood friends. As Eduardo recalled, middle school was "when all the trouble started," when he and his friends started doing the "crazy stuff" that he attributed to the influence of hanging out with older teens. He explained: "I mean, you get there and I knew a lot of the eighth graders cause we're all from the same area so we all know each other. So we get there and you're already with the older kids, and you see what they're doing. And you're in the sixth grade, and you're hanging with them. It's like, you're gonna step it up. You gotta grow up a little bit." Around this same time, he and his crew of friends were jumped into their neighborhood gang. Eduardo explained that they didn't feel pressured to join the gang but rather, he and his friends were "already doing the things that gang members do," such as stealing, fighting, and selling illegal goods, so they figured "why the hell not?"

When he entered high school, Eduardo was arrested for stealing bikes. He was charged with robbery, sent to juvenile hall for one week, and then released on probation and house arrest. His involvement with the juvenile justice system peaked at that point; between the ages of 14 to 17 he rotated in and out of detention and other placements for probation violations, fighting, and more robberies. He attributes much of this pattern ris's story represents a different type of youth on the same path; one who was not in a formal gang per se, but who forged an informal partnership with neighborhood friends and family members centered around delinquent, and later more serious, criminal activities. Chris was born and raised in a northern, remote, and less urban part of Los Angeles County that is known for methamphetamine labs, drug dealing, and high crime rates. His parents divorced when he was three years old, and from then on his mother raised Chris and his three siblings on her own. According to Chris, his mother worked very hard to provide a stable home and resources. Chris shared fond memories of his childhood growing up with his mother, sister and brothers, grandmother, and a host of cousins in the neighborhood. He remembered going to school, playing with his brothers, and having all of his basic living needs met.

For many years, Chris had gotten into trouble in fits and starts. In early elementary school he had minor fights with other kids at school. However, he began getting into more severe trouble around age 10 when he and a group of his close neighborhood friends started stealing. At first, they stole gum and candy from the grocery store, as he remembered, "for fun." However, this more benign form of delinquency escalated once they realized they could sell the items they stole for profit. Aside from the fact that his activities made him some money, Chris admitted that his behavior was partially influenced by having his older brother and cousins as role models, as they had spent large chunks of their own adolescence and adulthood entangled with the criminal justice system.

By middle school, his behavior became more severe as his informal crew got involved in burglary, fighting, and selling drugs. Chris summed up his group's escalating behavior as follows: "stealing got worser. Intimidation got worser. The lack of judgment got worser." He and his crew had also started to carry guns, which carried a series of consequences, as he explained:

LAURA: Why, at 15, were you carrying a gun?
CHRIS: Beating up on people.
LAURA: Intimidating?
CHRIS: Yeah, but I mean like, as far as retaliation.
LAURA: For someone getting shot?
CHRIS: No, for beating up on people at parties and things like that. Or people getting shot too. A lot of people get shot out here, you feel me? So people might confuse you with somebody else and shoot at you, or something like that. And then we actually was beating up on people and getting into it. So you never know who they might confuse us for. So that was necessary.

Chris ended up going to juvenile hall for the first time for a gun charge when he was just 15; this became a pattern of being locked up that would continue throughout his teen and young adult years.

Chris and Eduardo are similar in that both were engaging in minor delinquent activities, such as stealing from a store, from a fairly young age. However, it was clear that their affiliations with peers, family members, and/or older guys from their neighborhoods accelerated their entree into more serious crime and, eventually, into the juvenile justice system. Both acknowledged that they consciously chose this path, despite the fact that they each grew up with supportive parental figures in their homes. As we will see in later chapters, the influence of environmental context on individual decisions around crime remained a consistent theme in the lives of many of these young adults.

Pathway Two: Late Starters

The young men in Pathway Two had a relatively later start in delinquency or trouble with law enforcement compared to those in Pathway One. Contrary to the popular depiction of incarcerated youth as coming from broken homes and disorganized communities, these youth had mostly intact and supportive families and did reasonably well in school, at least until high school. Though none of the participants in this group experienced the advantages of being highly economically privileged, they had certain protective factors at work in their lives that deterred them from getting into serious trouble at younger ages, such as living in neighborhoods with relatively low levels of crime and having parents who encouraged them to succeed in school. However, these young men committed crimes during high school largely due to their peer group associations, or what they attributed to a series of bad choices. In this way, their narratives illustrate how at times, even with a number of protections in place, one bad decision or life change can bring about a series of long-lasting repercussions.

Anthony, for example, was a soft-spoken and polite African American young man who was very popular at the continuation school where we met him. He was raised in a rural area in central California with his mother, brother, two half-siblings, and several extended family members. He had few memories of the biological father that he and his younger brother shared, but that did not seem to trouble him too much. Growing up in a rural community, Anthony recalls being very close with his brother, maternal grandparents, and great-grandparents. He described his childhood as quiet and peaceful and shared memories from his elementary years: "I really just helped my granny, my grandpa with they garden. Yeah, with like chickens and stuff in the backyard and all that. Dinners on Sunday and all that. We're really family-oriented." Further disrupting stereotypes of system-involved youth, Anthony performed well in school, played on the school football team, and was a generally happy person.

Anthony's troubles began around age 15 when he moved from his rural community to urban South Los Angeles. By then his mother was busy raising his two younger siblings from a second marriage and wanted to move to Los Angeles because of what Anthony identified as "her own personal issues." They rented an apartment near their cousins, whom Anthony recalls as being heavily involved with gangs and drugs. Reflecting on the major turning points in his life, he pinpointed what he remembered as the cause of his delinquency:

LAURA: Why do you think you went from doing good to doing all this other stuff?

ANTHONY: The environment I was in. It's a whole different thing, like, you gotta adapt to your environment.

Soon after he moved, his beloved grandmother and grandfather both succumbed to illnesses and passed away, which caused him to feel despondent. He recalled, "I stopped caring. My granny and grandpa died, I didn't care no more." At the same time that he lost two of his most treasured and supportive relationships, he was forced to navigate a whole new urban landscape with social cues and experiences that he felt unprepared to handle.

At his large urban high school, Anthony was frequently threatened with weapons and feared for his safety. He recounts the first time he was pressured to join a gang: "Well the first time, they wanted to try to put me on 5–8 [the name of a gang], I told them no, whatever. And after school they tried to jump me." His mother and cousins frequently intervened to protect him, but the pressure did not stop until he finally aligned himself with a gang, although he never became a full-fledged member. Once that happened, he also started to steal, cut school, and sell marijuana. He continued: "I started ditching to be with the girls. Hanging out with all the popular kids. Every school I went to, I was always popular. So I started ditching with the girls or whatever. Started selling drugs and stuff. There ain't no reason for me to be at school if I'm trying to make money."

As a late starter, Anthony didn't have formal contact with the police until he was 17. By then he had dropped out of high school and was still involved in stealing and selling drugs. Upon his first major arrest, he faced trial as an adult. He took a plea deal and spent only eight weeks incarcerated, but then was placed on two years of adult probation. During that time, Anthony became a young father to an infant with complicated health needs, tried to return to school, and moved out of his mother's house and in with his criminally active cousins. When we met him at age 20, he was still trying to finish high school and had positive intentions to be a great father. Nevertheless, when we tried to contact him a week later for his second interview, he was back in jail facing a felony assault charge.

Steven was another member of the late starter pathway. He grew up in the eastern edges of Los Angeles County with his two younger sisters, mother, and father, who he described as a disciplinarian who stressed hard work and education. His dad was raised in the city of Compton and had experienced his own share of hardships while navigating adolescence, which made him determined to raise Steven in a nurturing environment that would support his future success. With his father's guidance, Steven grew up focused intensively on school and sports. He did get into trouble from time to time, mostly when he got caught sneaking out to play with his friends when his dad wanted him at home. It was not until his teenage years when he changed high schools that his behavior began to shift. Part of this change was the allure of drugs; he started smoking weed regularly during his sophomore year and soon he was dabbling in heavier drugs such as pills and methamphetamines.

During his senior year, Steven and a group of friends decided to rob a liquor store to get beer and cigarettes for a party. They got out of the store without getting caught, but when the police started to investigate in the following weeks, they pulled Steven aside for questioning and he panicked. Having never been in any serious trouble before, he ended up confessing to the crime and was arrested. To make matters worse, the police found him in possession of a knife on the day of his arrest. With the weapons charge, combined with his friends blaming him for the robbery, Steven faced the possibility of being tried and sentenced as an adult (a process we will further explain in chapter 3).

Steven and his lawyer fought his case and he ended up serving only three months in juvenile hall before being released on probation. However, he returned home with a negative attitude and a penchant for fighting, a skill he had picked up while detained. He explained, "when I came out everybody was doing the same, and I was like, my mind was on a different trip. I came out of juvie like, 'I am the shit.'" This attitude led to Steven getting into multiple physical altercations at parties while under the influence of alcohol or drugs. He also started using crystal meth on a more consistent basis. Over the next three years, Steven rotated in and out of jail for probation violations and minor offenses, all related to his drug use.

There are a number of common threads running through these two narratives. Both young men were raised in families that provided love, structure, and support. However, changing school environments and friendships exposed them to peer pressures and scenarios they weren't fully prepared to handle. These stories illustrate the power of environmental changes during such critical years. While Anthony and Steven were clearly cognizant and responsible for the choices they made, their stories left us wondering how their lives may have been different had they not experienced these abrupt life changes, or had they received greater supports through these transitions.

Pathway Three: Family Difficulties

The third pathway includes the remaining young men and the majority of young women who faced extreme poverty and other very difficult family issues such as child maltreatment, foster care, parental incarceration, homelessness, and parental substance abuse. While several young people in Pathways One and Two also experienced family troubles, these struggles were more extreme in the lives of the Pathway Three youth and appeared to contribute more directly to their delinquency. We also divided these young adults into two subgroups: (a) "poverty and survival," meaning those whose foray into crime can be attributed mostly to material need; and (b) "crossover youth," referring to those who got caught up in crime largely because of home instability and placement in foster care.

All of the young people in Pathway Three were raised in troubled and under-resourced neighborhoods. As explained earlier, Los Angeles is a region of economic extremes. Poverty is particularly hard hitting for children growing up in Los Angeles County, as more than 25 percent of children live below the federal poverty line, compared to 20 percent across the United States (US Census Bureau, 2014). African American and Hispanic youth are more apt to live in impoverished conditions in Los Angeles than are children from other racial groups (Willen et al., 2013), further cementing a feeling of marginalization from the material culture portrayed in the media.

POVERTY AND SURVIVAL. Poverty can lead directly to criminal activity when young people feel compelled to provide basic material goods for their families. Mike, an African American young man, is one example of how the basic need to survive turned into delinquency and trouble with the law. He arrived at our first interview wearing dark jeans, a starched t-shirt, and a red baseball cap. Given the neighborhood we were in and the histories of many of the young people we had interviewed up to that point, we thought the color of his cap was a sign of possible gang affiliation. As it turned out, he was not a gang member and his involvement in crime had very different origins.

Mike grew up in a very poor part of South Los Angeles with his parents and two sisters. His parents divorced when he was five years old, which brought a great deal of upheaval to his life, including his mother's subsequent addiction to crack cocaine and inability to provide a stable home life. As a result of his mother's addiction, Mike grew up living with his father at one point, and then with his grandmother, but with very scant resources. He was acutely aware of the financial problems in his various homes and he relayed vivid memories of lacking basic living needs and struggling with evictions and homelessness. One of the earliest childhood memories he shared with us was when he received a bicycle for Christmas. This moment stood out to him because it was the last Christmas that his mother was able to buy him a present. It was also the last Christmas that his parents were together. He described life after their divorce:

DIANE: What are your memories of your dad before your parents split up?

MIKE: He was good. Like when they was together, he took care of me you know? Like he took care of the house and all that. But when he left, everything just went downhill.

DIANE: How so? How did it go downhill?

MIKE: Like my mom, she had problems with paying her rent, having a place for me to stay, you know, like every since then I ain't had no Christmas. Like every since then. Until I got older you know.

Mike also struggled in school while growing up, mostly related to his financial hardships. He was embarrassed to be around other kids who had more money than he did, so he often ditched school and instead did small jobs around the neighborhood to earn money for food and clothing. When he couldn't find work, he would steal. His first arrest was at the very young age of ten for stealing food from a local store; he was hungry and there was no food in his house. For this crime, he was sent to juvenile hall for one week, but he admitted that he "continued to do bad stuff" after returning home. Although his family tried to help him, he felt mostly on his own because his immediate family members were dealing with their own stresses, and his extended family members distanced themselves from him because they viewed him as a criminal. For all of these reasons, Mike grew up feeling that he had to fend for himself in life, which often meant stealing to meet his basic living needs—a survival pattern that continued throughout his adolescence and into early adulthood. By age 14 he was sentenced to serve time in a probation camp, and he then moved in and out of various juvenile justice institutions until he turned 18.

Gabriel, a Latino young man, provides another example of how poverty can lead to delinquency and crime. When we met Gabriel, he was 24 years old, happily married, and he had a well-paying job at a manufacturing company. He was large in stature, wore glasses, and within the first 15 minutes of the interview, he captivated our attention with his detailed, insightful narrative of his journey deeply in and then totally out of crime. Gabriel grew up in Watts with his parents, three younger brothers, and two older sisters. He shared that his family of eight was very poor, despite the fact that both of his immigrant Mexican American parents worked full-time jobs. He recalled, "it was real difficult for us to live. We went through a time where we had poverty real hard. We used to look for pennies, nickels, quarters and dimes between our furniture to go ahead and buy a pound of beans so we could at least eat. So it was difficult. My mother, my father, used to both work about 14 hours a day." As the oldest son, Gabriel felt the weight of his family's financial struggles. During the day, he was a straight-A student who had dreams of being a psychiatrist. Outside of school, however, he worked hard to help fill the gap left by his parents when they were away at work; he picked up his siblings from school, made sure they had dinner, and got them ready for bed.

By the time he was 14, Gabriel began to seek out opportunities to contribute to the household income. He started hanging around some of the older guys from his neighborhood, who eventually convinced him to start selling marijuana. Full-fledged gang activity soon followed. He described how this one decision soon led him headfirst into the drug trade: "And I just thought of the easiest way out. And I'm like 'well, if I'm making $400 selling marijuana part-time after school, what would happen if I started selling other stuff?' So I started making crack and selling crack. Then they introduced me to crystal meth and speed and ecstasy. And once I knew it, I was already wrapped up in something that I just couldn't get out of, you see? It's easy to get in. It's so easy. You just fall right in."

At age 16, Gabriel caught his first set of charges for possession of a firearm, possession of narcotics, and grand theft auto. Because it was his first arrest, he served only a relatively short sentence of six months in juvenile hall. When he was released on house arrest and probation, he quickly returned to selling drugs. At a certain point, he was earning a significant amount of money, so he decided to relocate with a few friends to a different state. Over the next year and a half, he got deeper into selling drugs, was rearrested twice, and found himself trapped in a cycle from which he saw no easy way out.

Mike was different from Gabriel in the sense that his crimes seemed to be fueled by meeting his day-to-day needs, while Gabriel admitted that at a certain point, he was driven by ambition and the desire to acquire more and more material possessions. Both of their initial forays into crime, however, reflect a larger reality of children and adolescents growing up in poor neighborhoods: feeling trapped by the confines of poverty and viewing crime as a viable alternative to being hungry and poor. Yet what neither young man realized was that the lure of quick money would soon lead them into a juvenile justice system that then became a revolving door of its own.

CROSSOVER YOUTH. Economic hardship is often related to risk for child welfare intervention. However, of the numerous children who are exposed to violence, abuse, or neglect, only a small number wind up in the hands of the Los Angeles County Department of Children and Family Services (DCFS). This troubled county agency is one of the largest child protective organizations in the nation, investigating more than 131,000 reports of child maltreatment in 2010 with more than 30,000 substantiated cases. As a point of reference, these figures accounted for 34 percent of substantiated abuse and neglect cases in the entire state of California (Needell et al., 2014). While child maltreatment is not unique to poor youth, DCFS services in Los Angeles are typically rendered to youth of color in areas of concentrated poverty. Families of color, particularly those who are African American and Latino, have disproportionate contact with child welfare agencies at each stage of the system, including higher rates of reports to the authorities for suspected abuse and neglect, and longer length of stay in out-of-home placements (Harris & Hackett, 2008).

DCFS, like the Los Angeles County Probation Department (which will be elaborated on in chapter 3), is a highly political and fractured organization. The department has witnessed numerous major leadership changes in the past 15 years, due in part to disorganization, alleged neglect of the youth in its care, and high-profile child beatings and murders among families that DCFS had previously investigated. In 2013, following the torture and murder of then 8-year-old Gabriel Fernandez at the hands of his previously investigated caregivers, the Los Angeles County Board of Supervisors appointed an expert Blue Ribbon Commission to investigate the internal problems with the organization. The results of this investigation found dire conditions in need of comprehensive reform: "The Commission believes that there is a State of Emergency that demands a fundamental transformation of the current child protection system. Nothing short of a comprehensive approach to reform will lead to the seamless and comprehensive child welfare system that the County has needed for decades" (Blue Ribbon Commission on Child Protection, 2014, p. 10). Among other major problems, the commission charged DCFS with neglecting youth in its care, failing to provide adequate emergency response to reported incidences of abuse and neglect, and lacking sufficient suitable placements for foster youth.

Foster youth and youth under child welfare supervision who are cycled into the juvenile justice system are often referred to as "crossover youth" or "dual status youth." Researchers have estimated that anywhere from 9 to 29 percent of probation youth are from the foster care system; if youth with any child welfare history are included, this overall figure rises substantially (Herz et al., 2012). In Los Angeles County, depending on the charges and disposition of a juvenile court case, some DCFS youth retain their child welfare status and benefits, whereas others are terminated from DCFS and turned over entirely to probation. Many consider crossover youth to be the most vulnerable of all those within the probation system. A large study conducted in Los Angeles County using multiple linked data sources found that crossover youth are more likely to have mental health concerns, recidivate to adult prison, and have weaker employment and educational outcomes than youth from just one of these two systems (Culhane et al., 2011).

Desiree, a 19-year-old stylish and vibrant African American young mother, had spent the majority of her childhood in the child welfare system before crossing over into the juvenile justice system. She was the third child born to a teenage mother (who was also raised in foster care) who was already under the supervision of child welfare authorities due to a history of child neglect and endangerment of Desiree's siblings. By the time Desiree was born, two of her older siblings were already in foster care. At age four, Desiree remembers being "taken away in a police car" because of burns she had sustained in the home and then placed in an emergency foster home by social workers. At that time her father was in jail facing a murder charge and no family members were willing or able to care for her.

Desiree recalls her experience in foster care as abusive, which furthered her insecurity around safety and attachment. She described her array of foster parents as follows:

They're perverts, they're abusers, they're like . . . I had a few foster parents who I think were pretty good. I don't remember what they looked like or anything—I wasn't there long enough—but it was very few; maybe two or three. I think in those homes they couldn't cope with my behavior problems. . . . When I first got in the system—my mom used to tell me 'stop acting up or I won't be able to come see you' and I said 'ok, I don't understand. I'm not acting up, I just want my mom,' you know. And I don't understand to this day what I was doing but obviously I was doing something because I even . . . the places where I got comfortable, I would be gone. It's like a blink and I was gone.

Desiree started experiencing anxiety and behavioral issues that she attributed to ongoing abuse in foster care and a longing to be with her mother. DCFS subsequently labeled her as "hard to place" and transferred her to a group home for mentally ill youth where she was heavily medicated and became numb.

Desiree openly relayed many painful experiences that she suffered within the institution. She expressed her resentment toward the system while telling us humorous stories about how she would manipulate staff and play pranks on other residents. For example, she said: "I think they just thought I misbehaved because I was a little defiant. I was very defiant, honestly. And like they would tell me 'go to your room' and I used to be like—have you guys seen Dr. Doolittle? . . . And Dr. Doolittle was like 'do a little dance, make a little love'—I used to do that in the doorway and they used to get so mad at me. They used to get so mad and then they'd strap me down to the bed . . . I hated that place. . . . But it was crazy like, I don't know I was there for a long time—I thought it was home."

When a distant relative found her locked away on heavy doses of psychotropic medications, her paternal grandmother arranged to take custody of her as a kinship care provider. It was at that point that she finally met some of her other siblings who were also being raised by her grandmother. In her grandmother's care, Desiree remembers about 20 people living in a cramped house, all supported by foster care benefits for six children. She also recalled that despite being under DCFS supervision, she was even homeless for periods of time. She described: "We were living like orphans. She [grandmother] had her nails done, hair done—everything. So I'm like, now, she used to keep herself and I thought about it and it's because we're all grown now and we're not getting checks no more. And I was just saying like that's crazy how she really lived off of us. She really lived off of us and didn't take care of us like she was supposed to." Things became difficult and violent at her grandmother's home and Desiree began to act out her anger. Eventually she voluntarily returned to live with her mother while hiding her whereabouts from DCFS. However, this environment proved to be unstable as well, as Desiree recounts, her mother was still "partying and clubbing at night."

When Desiree was 12, she ran away from her mother's home after a fight and was arrested and sent to juvenile hall. Once she crossed over into the juvenile justice system, she was then frequently arrested and placed in probation group home facilities for running away, fighting, and eventually possessing weapons. In between her placements she would try to return to her mother's home, yet the stability never lasted long as she continued to run away and get picked up by the police. Eventually Desiree did two stints at a girls' probation camp, where she met a caring probation officer and other adult mentors who encouraged her to fight for her future and finish high school. Desiree returned to her mother's house, hoping to complete her high school diploma. However, when she became pregnant at the age of 17, her mother finally kicked her out of the house permanently. She gave birth to her daughter Kianna while residing in a group home for pregnant foster youth, which finally ended her cycle of running and arrests.

Lupe, another crossover youth, came to her first interview wearing baggy jeans and a backward hat, and had multiple visible tattoos. Her gender presentation was on the more masculine side of the spectrum, a posture that she had learned to embrace as she came out as lesbian in her adolescent years. Like Desiree, Lupe was "basically raised in the system" as she experienced living in multiple households, including with relatives, parents, foster homes, and, later, at juvenile camps. Yet her crossover story is also quite unique.

Born to Mexican immigrant parents who had spent time in and out of prison, Lupe was fully abandoned by her mother and physically and sexually abused by her father. At age five, her father was ordered to serve prison time for child abuse. At that point her paternal grandmother took in Lupe and two siblings as foster children, and two of her other siblings were sent to a different foster home. She recalled: "I was living with my dad and my four brothers and my mom was locked up. And then I guess she came out and my dad ended up getting locked up. So after, I don't know—I guess, a hard time, for us. And then at one point they were both locked up. I lived with my grandma, which was just hard."

Lupe stayed with her grandmother for several years but never felt quite settled at home. When she was 12, her mother fought to regain custody of her children and completed drug rehabilitation. Yet after six months together, her mother suddenly left the United States to return to Mexico, knowing that she would not be able to return to Los Angeles easily due to her undocumented status. Lupe looked back on that experience of abandonment as a significant turning point when she began to use drugs to numb her feelings, starting with inhalants and eventually moving to harder drugs.

Drug use and truancy ultimately led to stealing, fighting, and contact with law enforcement. Her grandmother, with the help of the court, placed her in a group home at age 12 to "fix" her bad behavior. Her behavior actually got worse there, as she explained: "Like, at the time I didn't really care. I just wanted to do my time and get out, you know? So I got picked up and it turned even worse. I started smoking weed, starting ditching school more often. I was really bad." After a few months of placement, Lupe ran away, and was then shuffled between various facilities including juvenile hall and locked mental health wards. She recalls just getting deeper and deeper into trouble as her behavior became more rebellious.

After several years of being in flux and on the run, she finally completed a group home placement and went to live with her aunt and uncle. There, however, her family consistently rejected her based on her masculine gender presentation. She felt that her caregivers were more concerned about her gender presentation than her sexuality. She explained:

> Actually, when I got released to them, I was dressing like a guy, you know? And I remember them telling me we're going to accept you either way, however you are. I'm like "alright." I get there like a month later and they're like "you need to change the way you dress." I'm like "what, I thought you would accept me?" She's like "yeah, I

know but I don't like my daughters to get . . . going the same way you're going" I'm like "damn that's fucked up." So I'm like "alright." They put all my boy's clothes on a yard sale. So I had good clothes, you know, nice clothes. So all that clothes went quick and they took me shopping and bought me girl's clothes. I'm like "I don't know what to wear. I don't know what to fit." Like I didn't like it, like but I had no choice like "you either wear that or you go back inside" So I was forced to dress like a girl.

Lupe's experiences of abandonment and rejection fueled her already looming addiction struggles, and she moved toward harder drugs such as ecstasy and cocaine. This destructive cycle of drug use, running away, and lockup continued until she was emancipated from the system at age 18.

The experience of being abandoned by family members and the child welfare system was a thread that united the crossover youth in our study. Their initial encounters with the juvenile justice system were different from youth in other pathways, in that their crimes were often related to the stress, discomfort, and abuse they experienced as they were shuffled between placements and homes. And, as we will see in chapter 3, being placed in juvenile halls and camps only further contributed to trauma and the development of self-destructive coping mechanisms.

CONCLUSION

Within the context of low-quality segregated schools, economic and racial segregation, restricted access to resources, family poverty and challenges, and systemic barriers to achievement, these 25 young adults came of age. While it is impossible to isolate any one factor that contributed to a pathway of delinquency, it seems evident for each individual that a blend of family problems, neighborhood conditions, school climate, and gang presence formed an environmental context that limited the youths' opportunities, and facilitated their contact with law enforcement.

This is not to deny that these young people did not exercise agency in their choice of friends and illegal activities. Rather, their stories showcased many of the systemic challenges facing children and families living in Los Angeles County, providing support for the idea that youth crime does not just happen on its own. From the youths' stories we saw how impoverished, segregated neighborhoods with limited resources to support youth structured opportunities and doled out harsh pun-ishments for nonviolent behaviors. Under-resourced schools permitted defiant behaviors to escalate without the provision of interventions that address the root causes of youths' behaviors, and inadvertently served to disconnect youth from school and stifle their motivation to succeed in academic environments. Overtaxed families, despite their intentions to support and nurture their children, were unable to prevent their chil-dren from falling further into gangs and criminal activity. Moreover, the child welfare system was unable to prevent those with histories of mal-treatment from crossing over into the juvenile justice system, and often contributed to ongoing cycles of abuse and neglect in youths' lives.

In the next chapter, we will examine these concepts further, as we explore these young people's experiences in and out of the juvenile jus-tice system as a gateway to adulthood.

CHAPTER 3

Locked Up and Back Again

IN THIS CHAPTER, WE examine the young people's pathways in and out of the juvenile justice system. We situate these stories within the vast and troubled landscape of the Los Angeles County juvenile justice system. For it was within this labyrinth of courts, halls, camps, and group homes that these young men and women spent a bulk of their formative adolescent years. As illustrated in chapter 2, many routes led these young people into the system; yet once inside, few paths led them out. The major themes of this chapter capture how these young people experienced this complex and broken set of institutions. We begin with John's story of his first arrest:

> That year [when I was 15], I had gotten stopped and picked up and taken to the station, but never officially booked or anything. They [the police] would just mess with me and take me in cause I had like a blue rag in my pocket or something. Stupid shit, just to mess with me because they had a feeling that I was gonna get into a gang . . . And they kept messing with me and shit. But the next time I really got arrested, it was right before Christmas. We used to rob people right there. And we had taken a break from robbing people. I know that sounds weird to say, but we had taken a break and we had somebody buy us some forties. And we look to our left and we see the gang unit pull up through the alley. And we just dropped our beers and started running. And next thing you know, they pull up alongside us, chasing us. And the cop hops out of the car and puts me in the back and drops me. Puts the cuffs on me. Then I got taken in that night but it was only for one night. But I finally went to the juvenile hall that time.

For John, this trip to juvenile hall was an inevitable stop on the dangerous road he was traveling. Like many of the peers he had grown up with, John considered a stint in juvenile hall a rite of passage, a minor consequence relative to the larger rewards reaped by belonging to his gang. A night in the hall was trivial in the mind of a 15-year-old boy wrapped up in the adrenaline rush of stealing, drinking forties, carrying weapons, and running with a gang. Yet in retrospect, this first night spent in the halls, even if it was inevitable, led John into a tangled maze from which he would not return unscathed.

WAITING TO GET ME: THE ROAD TO JUVIE

Several of our study participants had forged gang ties at different points in their lives, and these gang activities and associations set themselves up for eventual problems with the police. At the same time, they lived in neighborhoods where they were subject to intense police scrutiny and harassment. Due to the highly publicized murders of unarmed black men such as Michael Brown, Eric Garner, and Freddie Gray, the public has become increasingly attuned to the prevalence of police abuse and violence in communities of color. Yet in Los Angeles, advocates, activists, and concerned citizens have for many decades drawn attention to racial bias, abuse, and corruption in law enforcement organizations. The region's history over the past 25 years includes the acquittal of the four white officers who were videotaped brutally beating Rodney King, an unarmed African American man stopped for a traffic violation, and the subsequent community uprising. In the 1990s, Los Angeles was also home to the well-known "Rampart scandal" that uncovered major corruption and racial profiling in the Los Angeles City Police Department (LAPD). Over the last 25 years, these events and their detailed investigations by independent commissions have all exposed racial bias and abuse of power permeating all ranks of the LAPD (Chemerinsky, 2000; Christopher, 1991).

Based on this history and the lived realities of their family members, neighbors, and communities as a whole, the young people in our study were raised with a strong distrust of police. The young men shared numerous stories of living under police surveillance in their everyday lives. John's story, presented in the opening of this chapter, is just one of many examples of how young men operate under police surveillance until they finally succumb to formal system involvement. John grew up in a racially diverse, lower-income community that was in close proximity to some of the wealthier parts of Los Angeles. When he was an infant, his great aunt assumed guardianship of him because neither of his parents was able to adequately care for him. John described his family as tight-knit and able to meet his basic needs. However, the combination of scant supervision at home, access to drugs, and a gang-heavy presence in his neighborhood eventually lured him toward joining a gang. In middle school he began participating in many aspects of the gang lifestyle, including hanging out on the local "corner" with older gang members, holding their guns, and stealing liquor. Around the same time John started using marijuana, crystal meth, and cocaine. By age 16, he became a full-fledged gang member and dove headfirst into all that gang life entailed. Even after that first arrest, what he perceived as a setup for his own failure became further cemented in his mind. He recounted:

> I skipped out on court the first time, and I just didn't go. Then I had ended up getting my house raided. And they let me go. They didn't even take me to the station after they raided my house. . . . And they raided my house 'cause my sister was on parole, and she had given that address. And they had said "oh this is just a parole check. We're just checking for her." But the funny thing was, they let her sit on the couch, they took me out of the house in handcuffs. They had me up against the wall and shit. And they were only searching my fucking bedroom and searching the garage. And then they pulled me back inside into the restroom and they asked "oh what's your gang name?" They were harassing me. So it was for me. They were just waiting for a chance to get to me, 'cause they were really frustrated 'cause they couldn't get me. Every time they tried to stop me I would get away. So they were getting frustrated. My sister was just an excuse. So they raided my house and they had set my other court date up. And they told me "you better not miss this fucking court date. We can't get you for anything right now. But don't miss this next court date."

In retrospect, John recognized that by joining a gang he was responsible for the sequence of arrests and legal entanglements that ensued. However, he also believed that no matter what he did at that point in his life, the police were going to try to get him off the streets. At the young age of 15, he was labeled as an enemy: he was frequently arrested, set up, and treated by the authorities as someone who would inevitably wind up either locked up behind bars or dead.

Caught Up and Set Up

Following their initial arrest, the young people in our study fell into a seemingly endless cycle of placements, releases, probation violations, arrests, and incarceration. And once this cycle began, it was extremely difficult—both structurally and personally—to break free. Often the journey began at one of the three Los Angeles County juvenile detention facilities where youth await charges, proceed through their trial, or at times serve shorter sentences. In 2010, these three large juvenile halls housed approximately 1,800 youth on any given day, with an average length of stay of 21 days (Abrams, Daughtery, & Freisthler, 2011). Children even as young as eight years old are confined in these spaces, separated by gender and sometimes age. The halls also have designated units for youth with mental health conditions, special needs, and those awaiting trial as adults. These large detention facilities have elements that appear child-oriented, such as school classrooms and painted wall murals. Yet they also resemble adult jails, as the young people sleep in locked cells with concrete floors and in-cell toilets. Following an adult jail model, the youth are required to wear matching blue and grey uniforms, and the probation officers are dressed in official khaki pants and blue shirts with their last names printed on the shirt pocket. The probation officers carry handcuffs and pepper spray to handle fights between youths or attacks on staff.

Peter, one of the early starters in the study, fell into a vicious cycle of getting "caught up" in the system. Peter was born in the Philippines and moved to Los Angeles with his mother and older brother when he was seven years old. His family faced many challenges in trying to obtain their US citizenship, which meant they spent a great deal of time evading contact with law enforcement. Even as an undocumented immigrant, Peter recalled succeeding academically in elementary school. However, like many youth in this study, he started getting into trouble in middle school. He attributed much of his behavior patterns to the influence of his older brother, who was an active gang member. Peter started smoking marijuana at age 10, and by age 14 he had joined his brother's gang, was using and selling crystal meth, and was arrested for fighting.

When Peter found himself serving a one-month stint at juvenile hall for this fight, the reality of the life he had assumed hit him hard. When we asked Peter what it was like being in juvenile hall for the first time, he recalled feeling scared and lonely because he missed his mother and brother. What he remembered even more about juvenile hall, however, was the abusive and illegal behavior of the staff. He described how the probation officers would verbally and physically abuse youth in their cells, stating that the staff were "as corrupt as the kids there." Peter elaborated:

People who work there, they must have some type of power trips. They just power trip. They're crooked too, they'll do as much dirt as the kids would. They would even sell drugs to the kids like cigarettes. They would sneak you in cigarettes. Or they'll tell us like, "hey if you guys wanna, certain staff would be like what's up with a burger? You got $5?" 'Cause you know they would be sneakin' in money into the juvenile hall. So we're just giving 'em money like "here's $10. You buy me one and then I'll buy you one." So I'm like 'alright fuck it.' And then from there that feeling of, like you can kinda get away with shit, I don't know, it was just easy.

The experience in juvenile hall left a negative imprint on Peter and cemented the notion he had learned on the streets that law enforcement could not be trusted. Similar to what journalist Nell Bernstein (2014) documented about the rampant abuses in youth jails, Peter witnessed adults abusing their power with the children in their care. Thus he entered the facility as a fearful young adolescent who looked up to his brother, and he left with a feeling that the entire system was corrupt. He lost his innocence and hope at the same time.

Feeling discouraged and with no incentive to change, Peter returned to his home and neighborhood where he went back to his old friends and behaviors. To make matters worse, his brother was arrested and subsequently deported. To cope with this loss, Peter's drug use escalated to using crystal meth more habitually. Losing perspective and control with this highly addictive substance, he was soon re-arrested and convicted of assault with a deadly weapon, which landed him in a juvenile probation camp for a ten-month sentence. This charge opened a revolving door of recidivism, one that involved house arrest, probation violations, group homes and probation camps, and finally adult jail. Peter acknowledged that he was actively participating in activities that were getting him into trouble, but he also felt strongly that the justice system itself was a trap. For example, he argued that the concept of house arrest represented a major pitfall for youth, because it was unrealistic to expect a teenager to never leave the house.

Peter felt similarly set up in places such as continuation school, another component of the juvenile justice maze. Los Angeles County youth who are on probation or house arrest are all too often expelled from or barred from mainstream public schools, and in these circumstances, are sometimes sent to probation alternative schools. In theory, these alternative schools (also sometimes called community day schools) are designed to provide an educational pathway for troubled students, yet in reality they often place youth at risk for further problems with law enforcement. With dropout rates ranging from 31 percent to 51 percent (in 2012–2013), these rates are, on average, nearly double those for the Los Angeles Unified School District as a whole (California Department of Education, 2013c). Peter explained to us the social dynamics of probation schools and why they often fail: "And plus they send you to a school with a bunch of fools that's been in jail also. Like that's not cool. Everybody's just gonna fuckin' reminisce and brag about some shit. . . . I just felt like I was being set up all the time. So I didn't give a fuck about the law then. Just the whole setup. They just tryin' to get a mothafucka while he's young so they can feed the system. Get money and shit." In Peter's view, the presence of other youth with very similar attitudes and behaviors created an impossible environment for learning. Conforming to his negative picture of the juvenile justice system, he also believed that the county had an incentive to keep youth involved in the system in order to profit from their misfortunes. Probation schools were thus another cog in the wheel to set up Peter and others like him for failure.

Carlos was another young man who had a difficult time staying straight once he got caught up in the juvenile justice maze. Growing up in a close-knit Mexican American family, Carlos described himself as having a fairly average upbringing: he hung out with his friends from the neighborhood, skateboarded, and generally enjoyed going to school. However, this picture changed in middle school when he and his neighborhood friends started getting more involved with tagging. In ninth grade he joined a neighborhood crew, a seemingly small decision but one that changed his entire high school experience. He explained, "Probably that was my mistake right there. 'Cause I got into the crew." Although he participated in minor illegal activities with his crew such as tagging, Carlos did not get in trouble with the law until tenth grade when he and his sister were caught stealing food from a local school. He took a plea deal for a misdemeanor, spent a short time in juvenile hall, and was then placed on a year of probation. During that year he continuously violated his probation due to failed drug tests, which eventually landed him in a probation camp for a three-month sentence with no new actual conviction under his belt. In his own words, he started to "straighten up" about one year after leaving the probation camp. However, he started getting into fights with rival cliques, was placed on house arrest, and was eventually sentenced to another juvenile probation camp where he served a six-month sentence. There were very few new charges in Carlos's whole story, but he could never successfully complete his probation.

The probation camps where Carlos and Peter were sentenced are slated for youth who are convicted of more serious crimes in juvenile court (e.g., burglary, assault, weapons charges) or who have repeat violations. In 2011 there were 16 youth probation camps in Los Angeles County, including two designated for young women, with the capacity to house up to 1,500 youth on a given day (Abrams, Daughtery, Freisthler, 2011). The camps are located in the far reaches of the county where few families are able to regularly visit. While a typical sentence is three to nine months, they can be extended if new charges are incurred while in camp, such as for fighting—an all too frequent occurrence. Over the last 15 years, the Los Angeles County probation camps have been the subject of several lawsuits charging poor conditions for youth with disabilities, absence of quality education, failure to prevent suicide, and failure to protect youth from violence and harm from staff or other youth. The settlement of these lawsuits has led to some changes in standards of care, but certainly none far reaching enough to satisfy the youth and families whom they are supposed to serve (Newell & Leap, 2013).

While serving his probation camp sentence Carlos finally pledged himself to a gang for protection. Supporting the charge that the deeper ends of the juvenile justice system often serve to catapult youth further into crime (Bernstein, 2014; Mendel, 2011), he stated bluntly, "in camp, you have to be a part of a gang." Even as part of a gang, Carlos managed to stay out of trouble for about a year after his release. He followed the terms of his probation, landed a job, and even completed one semester at a community college. However, the police arrived at his house one day to question him about a recent crime. Surprisingly, he confessed because he "didn't want to lie to them" and he was arrested on charges of vandalism. Only this time, the stakes were higher, because he was 18 and would have to serve time as an adult if found guilty. Carlos took a plea deal for a lesser felony charge of several months in an adult jail along with three years of adult probation.

Peter and Carlos represent examples in which involvement in the juvenile justice system appeared to escalate, rather than abate, their criminal trajectory. Both young men had been in minor trouble around the time of their first arrest and may have benefitted from diversion, restorative justice, or other alternatives to incarceration that are more common in 2016 than they were just five years ago. However, they exited the juvenile halls, camps, and probation schools with mind-sets and connections that made them more prone to criminal activity. We do not mean to suggest that these young men should not have received any consequences for their crimes or that a supportive program would have necessarily changed the course of their events. Indeed, ethnographic research has shown that some youth may respond to a more punitive facility and others to a more therapeutic one, but who will respond best to a given setting is very difficult to predict (Abrams & Anderson-Nathe, 2013). Yet in hearing their stories, we could not help but wonder what roads they may have taken had they been diverted from the deeper ends of the juvenile justice system at these pivotal junctures.

FEELINGS ASSOCIATED WITH INCARCERATION

Alongside their observations about living life inside of the juvenile justice system, the men and women in our study offered deep insight into the feelings associated with the experience of youth incarceration. They articulated complex emotions about spending their adolescent years under the constraints of the system and feeling betrayed by their family members and the police. These experiences left a significant imprint on their identity development and future trajectories in mostly negative but also some positive ways.

"I Never Felt So Alone and Betrayed"

For the young women in particular, involvement with the juvenile justice system perpetuated cycles of turmoil and trauma they had already been experiencing in their home lives. Once they became entangled with the system, they continued to experience disruptions in their school, community, and home lives that negatively affected their mental health and well-being. For example, Carina grew up primarily with her father as her mother had struggled with drug addiction, and as a result, was arrested for drug possession and deported when Carina was a toddler. In her early childhood, Carina had a difficult time being cared for by an immigrant single father who spoke limited English, yet she enjoyed elementary school, friends, and her extracurricular activities. Her first contact with the justice system resulted from a home altercation with her father in which the police blamed her for the violence even though she was just 12 years old. The experience of being forcibly removed from her home and ushered into juvenile hall at such a young age was terrifying. She described: "I woke up like around ten or eleven probably. Um, when he [my father] said 'hi' all happy I was like 'hey' but um, I guess in my head I was like 'hey, what has him all happy?' I think this might be a good day. Next thing I know, like two seconds later people, police come, arrest me, put me in handcuffs and take me. And next thing you know I find out my dad put me in juvie. And at first I didn't know for what either—I was confused, I was crying, crying, crying. . . . I never felt so alone and betrayed." This sense of betrayal by her father, coupled with her young age, set a stage for some turbulent years to follow. She felt too young to handle what was happening in her life and unprepared for being labeled as violent and mentally disturbed. She explained: "Yeah, so to be betrayed like that, of course that brought out the rebellious side, like I'm not going to care anymore. But little did I know back then that all my actions only affect me, myself, and I. You know? And I guess, you know, I wasn't mentally or emotionally ready to deal with all that. I didn't even know how to deal with all that at that age."

Once she entered the system, Carina then experienced a slew of residential placements, group homes, and stints in juvenile hall lasting almost up until her eighteenth birthday. Group homes for probation youth are scattered throughout the region and house up to 1,070 youth who are dually involved in the probation/foster care system, whose families will not take them back following detention, or who have special needs such as mental health issues or disabilities (Abrams, Daughtery, & Freisthler, 2011). Carina exited the system at age 18 with only two convictions on her juvenile record, but due to ongoing problems at home and surveillance by the child welfare and probation authorities, she lived in no fewer than ten placements in a span of five years. She was also forced to take medications to calm her down that she believed made her feel more unstable. According to Carina, she didn't feel violent inside but was angry about her father's betrayal and being labeled. At times she felt suicidal.

Although Carina did not experience the same level of police monitoring as the young men, she certainly harbored strong feelings of resentment toward both DCFS and probation who were simultaneously overseeing her case. Crossover youth in Los Angeles, who are disproportionately female, often become lost in a bureaucratic shuffle. Once they enter the juvenile justice system, their DCFS caseworkers can close their case altogether (Herz et al., 2012). When this happens, a child can lose his or her foster care benefits entirely, which can include regular oversight from the social worker who is actively monitoring the youths' case and helping prepare him/her for independent living. This case closure often occurs even though a 2005 state law permitted crossover youth to be designated with a particular hybrid status wherein they maintain their relationship with both systems (Herz & Ryan, 2008). Within this shuffling game, Carina described how the cycle of probation and foster care set her up for failure, even in the absence of any new charges. In one instance: "I was on house arrest and then two or three days later I went back for messing up on my house arrest for kicking my own door down, um, 'cus why would I be kicking my own door down if I'm outside? So, I went back for four more months. Altogether I spent eight months in juvie. Um, then instead of going back home like I wanted to I was put in another placement, where I ran away." Entering the system as a terrified 12-year-old girl, she exited an almost-18-year-old young adult. With only two crimes on her record in six years, she was shuffled between homes and systems until she finally aged out of the system altogether. Throughout this journey, Carina refused to accept the institutionalized or expert version of herself as violent or crazy, because she knew deep inside that was not really her true self. In essence, she had to fight the stigma and labels that the system had imposed upon her.

For Carina, the juvenile justice system was a mostly negative experience, with some exceptions. For certain, she missed out on many of the normative rites of adolescent passage that her friends were able to enjoy. Although she had always felt shy and out of place at school, she did not get to experience school dances, a stable peer group, and many other markers of adolescent life. Yet sometimes she felt that confinement provided her time to think and heal, away from the home conflicts that led her into the system in the first place. As Carina described, her experience in the system was lonely, but also helped her to grow up just "a bit too fast."

Fighting My Fitness

A few of the young people in our study harbored a great deal of resentment about the lengthy process they endured in facing the possibility of trial in adult criminal court. It is interesting to note that the participants who faced adult charges weren't necessarily the ones who had the most serious criminal backgrounds or arrest histories. Yet due to various aspects of California's adult transfer laws, they got stuck in a long process to determine their fitness to be tried as an adult.

California statutes (as of 2015) allow for several routes for those under the legal age of criminal majority (18) to be tried in adult court, including judicial waiver (i.e., judges make the decision themselves); statutory waiver (i.e., automatic referral to adult court based on age, crime, or both); and direct file by the prosecuting attorney (i.e., prosecutorial discretion). Following the tough-on-crime policy trends of the 1990s, California voters passed the direct file option (Proposition 21) in 2000, resulting in an 88 percent increase in youth transfers to adult court between 2000 and 2009 (Lynn-Whaley & Russi, 2011). Under the statutory waiver clause of state law, a minor as young as 14 can be automatically tried in adult court for crimes such as murder, rape, and many other felonies.

Moreover, at the discretion of the judge or prosecutor, a minor may also be referred to what is known as a "fitness hearing" based on several circumstances related to criminal history and type of crime. In a fitness hearing, a youth is evaluated concerning his or her fitness to be transferred to adult court according to several criteria, including:

1. The degree of criminal sophistication exhibited by the minor
2. Whether the minor can be rehabilitated prior to the expiration of the juvenile court's jurisdiction
3. The minor's previous delinquent history
4. Success of previous attempts by the juvenile court to rehabilitate the minor
5. The circumstances and gravity of the offense alleged in the petition to have been committed by the minor (California Welfare & Institutions Code 707)

When a minor is awaiting a fitness hearing or a determination of that process, he or she is typically housed in a special unit of juvenile hall. The fitness process can take a long time—even more than a year in some cases—meaning that the young person spends a long period locked up even prior to any conviction. If the minor is found "fit" to be tried as an adult and convicted in criminal court, he or she typically remains in juvenile hall until the eighteenth birthday, at which point he or she is transferred to an adult state prison. Others may serve their sentence in the notorious California Youth Authority (CYA), now called Division of Juvenile Justice (DJJ), which consists of just three remaining state juvenile prisons that house young people up to age 25.

"There's No Way of Winning"

When we met Shawn, he was a 22-year-old African American young man, a member of the late starter pathway who got entangled in the adult transfer system. A self-proclaimed "class clown," Shawn had a reputation for joking around in school and being a "cool kid" who had a way with the girls. As an only child, he was always very close to his mother, who had worked hard to steer him away from negative influences despite raising him mostly on her own. Shawn had gotten into very minor trouble with friends during middle school and high school but overall, he described his younger self as a positive person who cared about his family and doing well in school.

Shawn had his first brush with the law during his sophomore year of high school. He and a friend were going to a neighborhood party, and his friend had brought a gun for protection. Unfortunately, the police stopped them on the way and charged them with possession of a weapon. Shawn spent a week in juvenile hall and was then placed on summary probation, a light sentence that requires youth to stay out of trouble, but is not actively supervised. About one year later, as a 17-year-old high school junior, he stole a jacket from a young man while riding a public bus. He was arrested for robbery and charged as an adult. If convicted for this one robbery, he faced spending up to 15 years in adult prison. Shawn spent the next year in juvenile hall fighting his fitness to be tried as an adult. This process is very complicated and lengthy as well as doubly difficult for a person like Shawn who had never been in serious trouble before. He explained that in many ways his good sense and values actually hindered his ability to keep his case in juvenile court, because one way to determine a minor's fitness is moral cognition: knowing right from wrong. He explained:

LAURA: Why did it take so long to fight your fitness?
SHAWN: Because when I first got in there, they gave me an evaluation or whatever. And I acted regular, like I was telling them I'm a good guy, I know right from wrong and stuff like that. And the psychologist recommended me for my fitness.

Shawn ended up having a second evaluation to assess his fitness, but this time he changed his story, explaining how he had endured a hard life, a lie that ended up working in his favor. The prosecutor eventually recommended that he win his fitness hearing and be tried in juvenile court, and he was subsequently sentenced to nine months in a juvenile probation camp. Thus for this one incident, during which no one was injured, Shawn spent a total of two years locked up fighting his fitness and then finally serving his time.

This long ordeal soured Shawn's impression of the criminal justice system. He accepted responsibility for stealing the jacket, but at the same time he remained unsettled by the fact that he could have spent 15 years in prison for a minor crime. He also had strong opinions about fitness trials as a whole; he felt that the process for determining if someone should be tried as an adult was unfair, especially for younger kids. In his view:

> That whole fitness thing it just sets you up for failure. It's like there's no way of winning it because it's criteria or whatever, and if you miss one you lose your fitness. Basically if they make you fight a fitness 'cause it's a serious crime, one of the criteria is the seriousness of the crime. You automatically gonna lose it . . . It's like, all these young kids is getting all these years and they're never gonna come home again. Like people, like they first time ever getting in trouble in their entire life, did one thing, and it's like, life. And you're never gonna come home again. That's messed up. That's just a crazy law.

Shawn's statement reflects an overriding sentiment of many of our participants that the legal system and authorities set kids up for failure. Rather than viewing juvenile halls and camps as an appropriate punishment or perhaps even a place where they might find opportunities for rehabilitation, they instead perceived the system as overly harsh and morally bankrupt.

"I Needed Time to Think"

While still feeling bitter about the structural deficits of the system, some of the young men and women also felt that their experiences behind bars provided them with space and time to reflect on their lives and formulate their hopes and dreams for the future. Irene was a 19-year-old Latina young woman who grew up in a very unstable family. She lived with both of her parents as a young child. However, her mother left her father when Irene was just three years old and took Irene with her; both of her parents were selling drugs, and Irene's mother decided to move once her daughter was old enough to become aware of what was happening around her. Irene continued to experience a great deal of upheaval with her mother. They were in a constant state of transience, moving between homes and changing elementary schools numerous times. She described having a very strained relationship with her mother that eventually turned into physical abuse. Adding to an already traumatic home life, Irene was sexually molested by a male babysitter beginning at the age of seven. By the time she reached middle school, Irene had started stealing, fighting, and using crystal meth. She also fought constantly with her mother who was using drugs as well. At age 12, Irene's mother turned her in to DCFS for her so-called incorrigible behavior.

The presence of DCFS in her life created additional chaos and instability. She was placed into a series of group homes where she would persistently go "AWOL" ("absent without official leave"). Running away, combined with breaking curfew and committing minor offenses such as stealing, resulted in her case crossing over into the juvenile justice system. Irene estimated that she was arrested about 12 times and resided in more than 10 placements during her early adolescent years. When she wasn't in placement, she was essentially homeless, often squatting in apartments, staying with friends, and fighting for her survival.

Irene managed to achieve some sense of stability around age 16. She found work and had secured an affordable studio apartment. However, she lost her job unexpectedly and desperately needed money to avoid an eviction. Consequently, she and her boyfriend decided to rob one of the "unofficial taxi drivers who worked in their neighborhood." This was only the second time she was involved with what she considered to be a serious crime. The first time her boyfriend was charged with grand theft auto, but Irene was not charged due to her minimal involvement. In the second incident, however, Irene and her boyfriend were both charged in the robbery. Because they had used a weapon, Irene was charged with two felony counts and faced serving up to 25 years in adult jail. In the end, she was tried and sentenced as an adult to a maximum of 15 years. Based on her good behavior, she ended up serving five years in the state youth prison (DJJ) and was never transferred to an adult prison.

Living in the DJJ facility proved to be a contemplative time for Irene. Established in the 1860s, state juvenile prisons in California are notoriously violent and have been subject to numerous lawsuits and facility closures. Since 2000, a declining youth offender population and shifting fiscal priorities at the state level forced the closure of more than ten of these facilities, leaving only three open units as of 2013 (California

Department of Corrections and Rehabilitation, n.d.). Housed at one of the remaining DJJ facilities, Irene used her time to regroup; she spent most days by herself, which provided her with ample time to contemplate what she wanted for her life when she returned home. Envisioning one's future is a very normative part of adolescent development. However, this process holds much more gravity for youth like Irene and Shawn who had very real and serious concerns about spending their foreseeable futures in adult prison. Rather than pondering her friendships, relationships, career options, or college, Irene's self-reflection centered around how to break free from the cycle of violence and chaos that had characterized most of her life. Part of this process involved coming to terms with the mistakes of her past and trying to figure out what aspects of her life she could change. She recalled her thought process: "I was like 'what am I doing with myself? Look, like, my boyfriend's locked up, I'm locked up, he don't care about me—like, what the heck is going on?' Nobody—even if I try to call my ex's family or my family—nobody answers. Nobody even wants to hear from me . . . and I was like 'I want to love me, because nobody else is going to love me but me.' So that's when I was like 'alright, I'm going to do my best.' So I did. Like, I kept on accomplishing . . . I wasn't acting a fool."

Like Irene, Shawn spent a large portion of his confinement grappling with troubling aspects of his past and his goals for the future. Although he had gotten into some minor trouble as a kid, he always felt that he would clean up his act once he became an adult. He never saw himself as someone who was destined for a life of crime, so he struggled with the fact that he might spend the first 15 years of his adult life in the harsh environment of state prison. Living in a probation camp further cemented his feeling that he wanted something different for his future, especially because he was surrounded by youth who were active gang members. He drew a clear distinction between himself and the other youth, especially those who said they planned to return to their gangs after they got out; he framed that manner of thinking as "stupid." Shawn recalled spending periods of time in prayer, asking God what he was supposed to learn from his situation, and seeking guidance on how to become a better person after he returned home. He also used his time to determine goals for his adulthood.

Incarceration thus represented a critical period during which Irene and Shawn decided to make better choices in their lives. Yet at the same time, their conditions also led to a sense of loneliness and isolation. Irene made only a few friends during the time she was behind bars and spent most days alone, with the exception of visits she received from church and community volunteers. She got along well enough with the staff, but she described even those relationships as part of her "hustle" in that she would be pleasant to the staff in order to obtain special privileges. In retrospect, Irene recognized that she was depressed almost the entire time she was at DJJ, which was no doubt exacerbated by the fact that she simply had nothing to do except sleep, think, write letters, and watch TV for an hour or two. In her view, the DJJ facility lacked programs to help her cope with her depression and anger, so she learned to deal with these challenges on her own. One of the major critiques of the US juvenile justice system, including in Los Angeles County, is that there is a lack of effective treatment options for the many youth who have mental health concerns (Newell & Leap, 2013). Irene's description of her time in DJJ reflects these systemic inadequacies, as they did not address her history of abuse, trauma, or depression.

Similarly, Shawn experienced a certain amount of loneliness while locked away, and he didn't form any friendships. This was due in part to his feeling that he was different from the other youth because he was not criminally sophisticated or part of a gang. Shawn also felt marginalized at the halls when he was awaiting trial. He shared stories of how staff and other youth gave him a hard time because he was not tough enough, how they constantly tried to break his spirit by testing his desire to fight, and even started rumors about him possibly being gay. While in retrospect he was able to learn important lessons about perseverance and resilience, he couldn't help but feel as though he'd been robbed of important adolescent experiences such as hanging out with his friends, playing football, going to his senior prom, and participating in high school graduation.

Despite these astute critiques of the juvenile justice maze, both Irene and Shawn were able to acknowledge that their time in confinement helped them in some respects. For example, Shawn explained that he received support to help him pass his high school exit exam, which he did not think he would have passed on his own. He also participated in various leadership opportunities at the probation camp that provided him avenues to lift some of his depression and alienation. Interestingly, Irene felt that she benefitted from the stability she received while serving her time. Prior to DJJ, Irene had experienced an adolescent period full of contrasts. On the one hand, she was a young woman who lacked the support she needed from adults in her life to help guide her through her turbulent years. Yet at the same time she was essentially living on her own, making adult decisions, and fending for herself without the tools necessary to take on such responsibilities. The combination of these circumstances influenced her decisions and choices about relationships, finances, and ultimately her decision to commit the crime that landed her in the grip of correctional authority for her foreseeable future.

While in DJJ, Irene experienced a sense of stability that she had lacked throughout her life simply because she had consistent food, shelter, clothing, and a daily routine. Like Shawn, she also credited her time behind bars with providing the opportunity to complete high school, which she doesn't think she would have accomplished otherwise. Last, she shared the opinion that her time in confinement gave her a sense of maturity and life perspective that allowed her to realize that she had been traveling down a self-destructive path. In the next section, we explore more of the unexpected ways that youth appeared to find inner strength and outside supports behind bars.

FINDING SUPPORT

As the stories in the prior section illustrate, these formerly incarcerated young people had mixed feelings about their years spent in the juvenile justice system. On the one hand they missed out on many normative adolescent life milestones and experienced the corrupt and destructive elements of institutions and systems. At the same time, for those who did not have stable homes to begin with, the system also offered them structure and routine, the possibility of meeting some caring adults, and the guarantee of three meals a day and a place to sleep. We would be remiss in telling this story if we did not articulate the types of supports that many of these young people found during their confinement.

Tyrone was one of the youth in the study who, similar to Irene and Carina, bounced between the halls, camp, foster homes, and probation group homes beginning at age 12, when his adoptive parents abruptly rescinded their guardianship. Feeling uncomfortable and alone in the numerous (more than he could even accurately count) group homes he had resided in, Tyrone began to run away, which then led to his crossover status. Although Tyrone had only one conviction on his record, numerous probation violations and running away from care contributed to three probation camp placements between the ages of 15 and 18. As he explained: "Just 'cause I was leaving my placements which you wasn't supposed to do. I would leave my placements and they'd violate me for it. And I'd be smoking weed and they'd violate me for it. And I would do six months every time I get caught." Without parents or a home to return to, the system continued to confine him, which in many ways was easier than finding him a permanent home.

While somewhat resentful of being tossed around from home to home, Tyrone also received more help and structure in some of the camps than he had ever experienced in foster care. In one camp in particular with an organized sports program, Tyrone had a very positive experience playing on a football team. He recalled: "The help that I got at that camp was that I was able to play football. I liked football but I never played but that gave me a chance to really know how to play football and know about football. . . . We had playbooks and we'd have to practice. And it was like a hands-on thing, so it wasn't like a game anymore. They gave us a chance to really see how it is. So it helped us. And they just would work with us. . . . The coaches, some of them were the staff, so it was cool like that too." The football program served as an incentive for Tyrone to do well at camp, a privilege that could be rescinded if he displayed bad behavior or got into fights. He felt that these experiences taught him leadership, teamwork, and the importance of listening to his coaches. To him, the camp was better than his foster care or group home experiences. He stated:

> I felt like I was on a team. And it was different from my experiences already of being in a group home. 'Cause I never really had a chance to have a group circle like that. And then we'd go out and put on our pads, and I felt like I was finally getting into a group, being able to communicate and relate to people more, 'cause of our skills. It was just . . . that was when I first started having visions of how I'm gonna

be successful, what can I do to be successful. Focusing on school 'cause we had to focus on class there. So I worked more. And I seen my English was always getting better, and my math was always bad. But I still would study though. We would always have to study. Not study, but we did our work and went to camp school, and tried to maintain a C average. So I started buckling down in school a little bit in camp. But then it fell back off when I got released.

Tyrone experienced positive benefits of camp life even beyond the football program. At another camp, he took part in GED classes and participated in a poetry program. But, like many of the youth, once he was released, he found himself lost and alone, and he fell back into using drugs and running away. While two of his stints in camp bolstered his spirits and hope in the short term, the child welfare and probation systems did not set him on a positive course for the long run. As is common among crossover youth, he continued to fall through the cracks without a permanent placement until he aged out of the system.

Other young men and women also benefited from support of various voluntary sector and educational programs that operated in the camps. At one of the boys' camps in Los Angeles County, a number of community-based organizations offered educational and enrichment programs that often continued upon their reentry. Cesar was one young man who took advantage of these opportunities. Cesar's mother raised him and his two siblings on her own until he was nine, when she tragically passed away in an unexpected accident. At that time, all of the children went to live with their grandmother. Cesar loved his family and never got into too much trouble growing up, but things gradually changed when he started high school and he went from tagging to forming an informal neighborhood crew. Similar to so many of our participants, soon after he joined the crew he started stealing, fighting, and selling drugs. He was incarcerated for the first time at age 17 and joined a gang after that, mostly because of the close-knit friendships he had formed with guys from the gang since childhood.

At age 18, Cesar was locked up in a probation camp, looking at his last chance to be sentenced as a juvenile, and found himself facing a bleak future without high school credits or work skills. There he linked up with a supportive program that he credited for helping him turn his life around: "I came to the realization [that my life had to change] and this program, it caught my eye because, they had yoga, poetry, acting. And I believe right now they have a watercolor class right now. But yeah they had all those classes. . . . And I did the GED, and then after that I got out, and I told 'em I really wanted to get my diploma—my high school diploma. I didn't want to get no GED. And even though it's good, I just didn't want to. And they helped me do that." Cesar continued to remain involved in this program when he returned to the community, which encouraged him to get his diploma and enroll in college. His positive experience with the voluntary sector motivated him to give back to the community and become a community activist and mentor.

At times, help and motivation appeared in unlikely ways. For Sara, her source of support came from a writing program offered inside juvenile hall. Sara grew up primarily with her father in South Los Angeles after being abandoned by her mother when she was two. At some point during elementary school, Sara's father entered a facility for drug and alcohol rehabilitation and DCFS placed Sara and her sister in a foster home. She returned home to live with her father in sixth grade, but tensions ran high and her father physically abused her. She began running away from home and was placed in foster care again around seventh grade, when her cycle of running continued. By age 14, Sara was mostly living on the streets, finding comfort and protection in gangs, drugs, and alcohol. She was never officially convicted of a crime, but was held in juvenile hall for many months nevertheless. With her history of running, her case was eventually transferred from child welfare to probation. Sara was initially very distressed about the thought of spending potentially months or years in juvenile hall. Yet once she accepted her situation, she explained: "I started getting really attached to all the staff there, I started seeing kids in there that I start having a relationship, like feeling like this is all I have now. So I started reading, I started picking up in school, like I guess that's where I made the most credits because I was actually forced to be in school and I was back on track again where getting all my grades—straight As, Bs. I guess I just started to find my way back to myself."

One of the activities that helped her to find her way back to herself was writing and poetry. She felt that the writing teachers saw her potential, which helped her to change her own view of herself:

I was participating in the writing classes . . . I would go and I'd feel really welcome every time I would come in the class, I guess they kinda like really encouraged me and helped me get through the process a lot easier because here I am thinking I'm going to be in juvenile hall for who knows how long waiting for a trial case through an adult court where other people don't really understand what's actually going on. So it came to the point where every time I'd come to class it seems like you become happier and more open and you become more freely able to write, to talk and I like, I kinda like noticed in myself, too and that's when I started realizing that I wasn't being sorta rebellious or trying to act up or be disrespectful to anybody. I was just being myself and trying to work through it.

Sara spent much of her time in the halls learning how to express herself through writing and sharing her stories. She also continued to stay in touch with the program upon her release.

Like Sara, many of the participants placed a high value on simple yet important programs such as football, poetry, writing, or gardening. While these are not the more expertly touted evidence-based programs or intensive therapies, these young people recalled the programs brought into the camps and halls by volunteers and non-profit organizations as being soothing and valuable for them at their stage of development and in the midst of crisis, fear, and betrayal. More akin to what might be offered at a summer camp than a court-mandated placement, the essence was that these programs allowed them to have fun, to see themselves in a new light, and to develop skills and confidence that helped them in the long run.

Conclusion

Los Angeles County contends with thousands of juvenile probationers each year and is one of the largest systems in the United States. For many youth, an arrest can be a blip on the screen that begins and ends with that one isolated incident. Yet for the youth in our study, this was not the case. An arrest typically led them down a pathway that reinforced patterns of self-destruction, uprooting, and trauma. Conditions of confinement made them feel angry, confused, and betrayed; probation staff and police set up these young people to fail, and for some, these experiences in themselves served to further cement their criminal propensity and gang involvement. Indeed, these young people certainly knew full well that if they did not change themselves, they would continue to face trouble with the law as adults. The stakes were only getting higher. However, they exited feeling more bitter toward the system, unwilling to comply with the rules of house arrest, and angrier about their circumstances, so the cycle of arrest and detention continued a downward spiral toward a longer term placement.

At the same time, some of these young men and women found opportunities for growth and support within the system. This occurred sometimes through the experience of confinement itself but also through connections to volunteers and sometimes staff who worked within these facilities. Thus, while the overall context of the juvenile justice maze perpetuated a sense of being caught up and set up, some of the youth were able to find pockets of hope in order to propel themselves toward a more positive future. In the next chapter we closely examine the process of moving from the juvenile justice system into adulthood.

CHAPTER 4

And Now I'm an Adult

I ain't really tried, but just based on my background and probably the way I look, it don't make no sense to just go fill out all these applications and you don't get no interviews or no none of that. They going to judge me already, so it's like why try?

—Evan

HOW DO YOUNG ADULTS juggle work, school, independence, and parenting when they have spent many of their formative years behind bars? How do they balance these responsibilities alongside the trial and error that the transition to adulthood entails? The young men and women in this study had a diverse array of challenges, opportunities, setbacks, and triumphs in working toward self-sufficiency. While some found stable jobs, housing, and friendships, others experienced a great deal of instability in all of these domains, and most fell somewhere in the middle of these extremes. Yet even with these variations, the transition to adulthood for this group of young men and women was as a whole characterized by a struggle for economic survival. This chapter presents two main themes, "making ends meet" and "on the margins," which capture the central forces shaping the transition to adulthood for these formerly incarcerated young adults.

MAKING ENDS MEET

Economic survival is critical for young adults, particularly for those who are not enrolled in college, without the backing of wealth and/ or family support, and who are vulnerable to homelessness. Statistically speaking, the odds of gainful employment for formerly incarcerated youth are quite discouraging (Uggen & Wakefield, 2005). One study of more than 500 formerly incarcerated youth in the state of Oregon found that at 12 months post release, only 28 percent were employed (Bullis & Yovanoff, 2006). In our own survey of 75 young adult men (ages 18–25) who were previously confined in a Los Angeles County youth facility, nearly 50 percent were either partially or fully employed at the time of the survey, and 75 percent had experienced undesired stretches of unemployment. Moreover, we found that the young men's unemployment was associated with a higher risk of adult incarceration (Abrams, Terry, & Franke, 2011). To further contextualize the employment landscape, it is important to note that in 2011, the overall unemployment rate in Los Angeles County was 12.3 percent, but nearly triple that number—35.1 percent—for young adults ages 16–24 (Matsanuga, 2011). This figure is much higher in areas of concentrated poverty—the parts of the county where formerly incarcerated are most likely to return (Abrams & Freisthler, 2010).

Even if one is able to overcome unemployment, it is still quite challenging to find a well- paying career in the absence of a college degree. According to the US Bureau of Labor Statistics (2013), without accounting for racial, gender, or regional disparities, the median annual income in 2012 for a person without a high school diploma was $20,122, compared to $35,170 with a high school diploma, $57,590 with an associate (two-year college) degree and $67,140 with a bachelor's degree. On the whole, formerly incarcerated youth are known to have low educational attainment. Studies have reported that less than 20 percent of formerly incarcerated youth eventually earn a high school diploma or an equivalent (Chung, Little, & Steinberg, 2005; Osgood, Foster, & Courtney, 2010; Uggen & Wakefield, 2005), compared to 92 percent of the general population (US Department of Education, 2011). Moreover, these youth typically face a complex set of barriers to educational attainment once they have aged out of high school (The Council of State Governments Justice Center, 2015).

The young men and women in our study reflected some of these bleak odds, but not all. Table 4.1 displays the various markers of young adulthood for the 25 participants (in alphabetical order), including parenting status, employment, schooling, and living situation. More than half of the participants (14 out of 25) had obtained a high school diploma or GED (high school equivalency exam), and five were enrolled at least part time in a community college or a trade school. At the time when we met, none of the young men or women had completed an associate's or bachelor's degree; however, many were working toward this goal.

In the employment domain, five of the young men and none of the young women had full-time jobs that generated enough income to facilitate independent living. The remaining 20 young adults either were working part-time or were unemployed, with a few working part-time jobs while taking courses in junior college. Among the young men who were employed, just a handful were engaged in jobs with long-term career prospects, meaning industries where they perceived growth potential, and the others were working in retail or sales-oriented positions, including some who had secured temporary or seasonal employment. As a slightly younger group, the women were mostly trying to juggle school and part-time work, and none had full time-jobs. The two mothers in the group had unique challenges with maintaining employment as they were fully responsible for the care of their young children.

Table 4.1 also indicates that there was wide variation in participants' living arrangements. Five of the young people (all were young men) earned enough money to support independent living for themselves and/or their families; five were transient or in flux during the time of our interviews; and the remainder lived with parents or other relatives. Those who were parents themselves (9 out of 25) were more likely to live in their own apartment, either through employment or public benefits. As we will see throughout this chapter, security in housing provided a stable basis from which to launch other aspects of their lives, such as career and educational pursuits.

Getting Paid: "Stand on Your Own Two Feet"

For all of these young adults, making ends meet entailed a great deal of planning, hard work, and for many, sacrificing or postponing higher education. Those who were successful in maintaining steady employment appeared to experience a confluence of positive influences: a secure housing situation, strong social support from a family member or a significant other, a mentor or someone to guide them into a job, and a personal commitment to becoming economically self-sufficient. Shawn, who we introduced in chapter 3, is one such example. His time spent in limbo between the juvenile and adult criminal justice systems left him

TABLE 4.1.

Markers of the Transition to Adulthood

Name, Age	Parent	Employment	Secondary School Status/ Post-secondary status	Living Situation
Amber, 18	Yes[a]	Unemployed, receiving public benefits	No GED/HS diploma; attending alternative school	With mother
Anthony, 20	Yes	Unemployed, sporadically looking	No GED/HS diploma; attending alternative school	With cousin
Carina, 20	No	Unemployed, looking for work	Earned HS diploma; some community college	With father
Carlos, 20	No	Unemployed, looking for work	Earned GED; some community college	With mother and siblings
Cesar, 23	No	Part-time, sporadic work	Earned HS diploma; some community college	With a friend and with family
Chris, 24	Yes	Self-employed, sporadic work	Earned GED; some community college	Temporary hotel
Desiree, 20	Yes	Unemployed, receiving public benefits	No GED/HS diploma; some community college	Transitional housing
Eduardo, 19	No	Employed with two part-time jobs	Earned GED; no current school	With mother and relatives
Evan, 20	No	Unemployed, looking for work	Earned HS diploma; no college	With mother
Gabriel, 24	No	Full-time employment	No GED/HS diploma; some trade school	With wife, on his parents' property
Gabriela, 19	No	Unemployed, looking for work	No GED/HS diploma; working toward diploma	Transitional housing
Greg, 23	No	Unemployed, not looking for work	Earned GED; no current school	With friend
Irene, 20	No	Employed part-time; sporadic work	Earned GED; some community college	Many moves, renting a room

Name, Age	Parent	Employment	Secondary School Status/ Post-secondary status	Living Situation
Jerry, 23	Yes	Employed part-time, multiple jobs	Earned HS diploma; no college	Independent and with family
John, 19	Yes[b]	Employed part-time	Earned GED; some community college[c]	With wife, child, and family
Keira, 18	No	Unemployed, not looking for work	No GED/HS diploma; attending alternative school	With mother
Maria, 19	No	Unemployed, not looking for work	No GED/HS diploma; attending alternative school	Sporadic, with relatives
Mario, 23	Yes	Employed, two part-time jobs	Earned HS diploma; attending vocational school	Renting apartment with girlfriend
Mike, 24	Yes	Unemployed, looking for work	No GED/HS diploma; no current school	Homeless and with relatives
Oscar, 19	No	Part-time work; sporadic	No GED/HS diploma; attending community college	With parents
Peter, 23	No	Unemployed, troubles with citizenship status	Earned GED; no current school	With wife in mother's apartment
Sara, 18	No	Unemployed, looking for work	No GED/HS diploma; attending school for GED	With father
Shawn, 22	No	Full-time employment	Earned HS diploma; no current school	In apartment, independent
Steven, 24	Yes	Full-time, but temporary employment	Earned HS diploma; no current school	Renting a room, independent
Tyrone, 20	No	Unemployed, not looking for work	No GED/HS diploma	Transitional housing

Note: All categories reflect first interview status unless otherwise indicated.
[a] Had second child during study period.
[b] Had first child during study period.
[c] John was the one participant to our knowledge who used community college credits to enroll in a four-year college.

incarcerated during what would have been his entire senior year of high school. Yet while trapped inside the halls and camps, Shawn made good use of his time; he earned his GED, worked at the camp laundry facility, and participated in additional job training programs. For these reasons, he described himself as a "model resident" at the camp, which he believed had set him on course for a successful reentry.

When Shawn returned home at age 19, he moved in with his mother, who was unable to work and was receiving disability benefits—a situation that limited the overall household income. His first major task was to find a full-time job. He worked temporarily for a packaging company, and when he was unexpectedly laid off, he remembered the words of a kind probation officer who had suggested that he contact him if he ever needed help finding a job. Remarkably, Shawn was able to locate the name of the company owned by the probation officer's family, applied for a position, and at the time that we met him, he had been working at this same company for nearly three years. Working 40 hours a week at $10 an hour, Shawn made just enough money to be able to buy his own car and move into a studio apartment. To him, these were the markers of having arrived at adulthood, moving from boyhood to manhood. He stated:

> [When I was released] I just wanted to go out and just go on with my life and really become a man. 'Cause my whole thing was like, "I'm 19, I'm an adult." My mom used to always tell me like, most of the guys that in high school they used to think they cool and they used to be the class clown, after high school, those gonna be the losers. And I never wanted to fall into that category. . . . 'Cause even though I used to mess up in school, once I was grown I wanted to be able to be cool and drive nice cars and like, have like my own apartment. I stayed with my mom a little bit after I was grown, but you can't really say you're grown and you don't have your own apartment, you don't have a car. . . . All that type of stuff . . . you just wanna become a better person. Stand on your own two feet.

Shawn's version of adulthood was clearly associated with economic independence. And despite the obstacles presented by his lengthy incarceration, he made sure to prioritize employment immediately upon his release. For Shawn, economic self-sufficiency was integral to his version of adult manhood.

Like many young men his age, Shawn had some ideas, but was not exactly sure about what his future career path might entail. However, with his work taking priority, Shawn had not had time or energy to pursue any college courses, and he expressed little interest in higher education. As far as the future, his major goals were to be able to buy a nicer car and a house, and down the line, perhaps to have a family of his own. He believed he could achieve his goals by staying loyal to his current company. He saw that some of his co-workers made a decent living, and he hoped he could do the same. Shawn explained:

> Yeah I can move up. Right now my co-workers, like, in a few years they gonna be running the company, and they like my friends, they my boys. And they told me as soon as they, as soon as they get in, they'll put me on salary, making 100 grand a year. I can stay there. . . . I don't make a whole lot, but I don't wanna leave. Cause they treatin' me good. Like they gave me a job when I really needed one, so I kinda wanna stay loyal to them, and just work there. . . . And eventually I wanna have real estate and stuff like that. Like my first house might be a duplex so I can rent one out and live in the other one so the rent can be paying for the mortgage and stuff like that, so eventually I don't have to work.

By traditional markers of independence, Shawn's situation was one of the most successful among all of the young men in the study. He had a full-time job, was able to pay for his own apartment and buy a car, and had some concrete ideas about the life he wanted to build for his future. However, while certainly optimistic and hard-working, Shawn did not appear to have a clear path about how to make the income that he desired. This idealism may not be all that different from other youth his age who have not fully thought through the steps that may be necessary to turn their dreams into realities. Yet Shawn's lack of postsecondary education may leave him without the ability to significantly increase his earning potential. His scenario illustrates some of the difficult choices regarding work and school that these young adults faced in attempting to carve out their pathways toward self-sufficiency.

Mario is another example of a young man who was making ends meet after spending most of his adolescence behind bars. Four years prior to meeting him, Mario was confined in adult jail, facing the possibility of a seven-year sentence for a drug crime. Throughout his adolescence, Mario was heavily involved with an organized gang, and like so many of his friends, he experienced numerous stints in juvenile hall and probation camps beginning at age 13. He got used to the experience of confinement, even feeling that he was safer at times when he was detained. However, spending time in adult jail represented to him a loss of his personal freedom. It also served as a period of intense reflection that prompted him to think about cutting ties with his gang. At that juncture, Mario came face to face with his future and his greatest fears. He reflected: "I already lost all my friends [to death or prison], not cool. And I didn't want to be the next." His financial situation also influenced his thought process, once he realized that his gang-related activities were not generating the same level of income that they had in the past. For all of these reasons, Mario made a conscious choice to pursue a different path upon his release.

Mario was similar to Shawn in that he placed great value on the notion of responsibility, and on a vision of adulthood that stipulated economic self-sufficiency. However, Mario had the added pressure of providing for his family. When we met him, he was the sole breadwinner for his growing family, which included his long-term girlfriend, her son from a prior relationship, and their two biological children. His girlfriend was also pregnant with twins at that time, and soon they would be a family of seven. In order to make ends meet, Mario was working two part-time jobs and attending a trade school. Maintaining these responsibilities required a great deal of discipline, structure, and self-sacrifice; he had to keep a taxing schedule beyond what most people could reasonably sustain. He explained that each day he wakes up at 5:00 AM to be at his first job by 6:00 AM. He stays there until noon, sometimes runs home for lunch, and then leaves for his second job where he stays until 6:00 PM After the second job, he drives to trade school, takes classes and studies, and then doesn't return home until after 12:30 AM. Both of his jobs are located fairly close to his house, so he is sometimes able to come home during his lunch break to "change a diaper or two" and occasionally pick up some of the children from school. On the weekends, he tries to catch up on sleep and spend a bit of time with his family, hopefully offering his pregnant girlfriend some reprieve from her taxing parenting responsibilities. Nearly all of his monthly income of just $1,500 goes toward rent, utilities, and diapers, with just a tad left over for entertainment. His immediate goals included earning his trade school degree so that he could obtain a higher paying job and moving his family to a larger home, likely out of Los Angeles because rent is so expensive. As the sole financial provider for his growing family, achieving his goals was essential to his family's survival.

Mario and Shawn had some interesting commonalities in their journey toward economic self-sufficiency. Both were extremely motivated to find and keep a job, in part because they believed that was what responsible men of their age should be doing, and in another sense because they knew that stable employment was their ticket to avoiding time behind bars. Another similarity was that their views on adulthood reflected the importance of hard work, responsibility, and for Mario, being the breadwinner for his growing family. These views contrast with contemporary trends of delayed independence for emerging adults, such as shifting gender norms, delaying marriage, and living with one's parents for an extended period of time (Furstenberg, Rumbaut, & Settersten, 2005). In many ways, their experiences likely resemble those of other young adults who forgo college for work and who may be providing for a family at a younger age. The main difference between these two young men and those without histories of incarceration is that their motivation to stay on course was at least partially informed by the examples of their former peers, as they knew that many of their old friends were either living the street life, dead, or in prison.

Mario and Shawn were actively forging their identities as responsible young men and fathers in contrast to others who were less mature even despite being a similar age. For example, Jerry was at the older end of the group (23 when we met) and was also a father of two young children, but he did not share the same sense of responsibility or place a high value on steady work. He grew up in a northern, more remote part of the county with his parents who had migrated to the United States, one from Mexico and the other from Central America. His parents were small business owners who worked "round the clock" during Jerry's childhood to move him and his three siblings out of the housing projects and into a safer suburb. Despite their efforts to shield him from negative influences, he started fighting with other boys in third grade and as a result, earned a solid reputation as a troublemaker. Fighting soon progressed into more serious delinquent activities; by age 12 he was stealing cars and selling drugs with his friends. He experienced his first arrest when he was 14 for strong-arm robbery, for which he was sent to juvenile camp placement for more than a year. Two months later he returned to juvenile hall for another felony charge, and it was during this stint that he decided to join a gang. He spent his remaining adolescent years in the juvenile justice maze, including four camp placements and some time fighting his fitness to be tried as an adult for a carjacking charge. While he was locked up, Jerry participated in a fathering program and eventually received his high school diploma. He exited camp at age 18 to find most of his friends either dead or behind bars, including his older brother, who was serving a 50-year-to-life sentence in state prison.

Since his release, Jerry had lived sporadically with his family and at times with the mother of his older child, then five years old. As Jerry had two children to support, he first tried to find a legitimate job at an amusement park. But as he described, his own attitude as well as his penchant for illicit activity led him to quickly lose that position. He explained:

> I was working at the amusement park and they liked me and were trying to promote me because I was the main guy, there were three guys and I would be chilling even more and make them work harder. I guess people were hating on me and I guess people that had the flash pass tickets, for 4 you pay 25 dollars and at the exit I would sell them for 5 dollars and I would have hundreds extra. And people that were cool that didn't look like a snitch, I would be like "hey I have passes here, 5 bucks take them all" and they would do it. And I guess the fools started noticing that I would be making money and some-one snitched on me. But they didn't have evidence and I know my rights. And they have department of security and they took me over there and questioning me of "oh we have reports selling flash pass tickets." Give me proof you got the wrong guy, because they had no cameras. They were like "oh don't let it happen again, just sign this paper," and I wouldn't sign it, my lawyer has to see it. He came at me disrespectful so I was disrespectful back to him. And he was like oh

no just sign it and you go back. And I was like I don't need this job and threw my nametag and didn't even finish my shift and didn't go back after that.

After that experience, Jerry returned mainly to the underground economy of marijuana harvesting and sales as well as work at a tattoo parlor. From these enterprises, he claimed to be making a great income; enough to support himself and two children, buy expensive cars, and place a down payment on a house. While we weren't sure if he was fabricating this reality, he definitely boasted to us a great deal about this financial prowess. His version of adulthood was definitely carefree compared to Shawn or Mario; as Jerry was staying connected to the underground economy, which he described as "treating him good" and barely evading trouble with the law. In addition, he claimed that his mother and father were always there to support him, even helping him to buy his house. This safety net, coupled with not yet getting caught for illegal activity, we believe contributed to his cavalier attitude about work, career, and his future.

"Be Aware of Your Next Move"

There were several young people who, although they had temporary jobs, were susceptible to certain triggers that could disrupt their tentative sense of stability. These included barriers such as substance use, turbulent relationships with family or significant others, and housing instability. For example, Steven was 24 when we met him, his last jail stint occurring about two years earlier due to driving under the influence of alcohol. Like Shawn and Mario, Steven had a strong work ethic that he associated with becoming an adult man. His motivation to work also stemmed from his love for his six-year-old daughter who was living with his parents at that time, about five miles away from the room that he rented in a larger house. Despite having strong intentions to support his daughter, he had difficulty sustaining employment and stated that he had held more than 20 jobs since he turned 18. When we met, Steven was working a temporary job on a night shift doing freeway construction, a job that was frequently dangerous and that kept him working from 9:00 PM to 4:00 AM, five nights a week. He described his intensive schedule:

Monday I will sleep in, wake up at 12 (noon), play basketball, go run, eat, take my protein shake, take a shower, chill, watch the news, I love the news. Wait 'til my daughter gets out from school, go to my daughter's house, pick her up, get something to eat, talk to her. "what did you do at school?'" She tells me she played. . . . She's in kindergarten but it's amazing the education at that age, so I try to teach her, read a couple books, have her practice writing, then have dinner like 7 or 8, 9 I go to the yard, then I go home, do meditation, pray, get my prep up. I am that type of guy where at every job I get nervous and scared, not knowing what's going to happen. I am very cautious, incarceration made me be aware, be aware of your next move. I don't want to cry, don't want to go to jail, don't want to get pulled over. I pray, I get pumped up, take my vitamins, proteins, pack my lunch, go to work. At work it's a different mentality. . . . I do what I got to do. Hustle, hustle, hustle. Then come home at 4 AM and work out again and then go to sleep.

While the demands of the night shift and taking care of his daughter are exhausting, Steven also believed that a career was essential to reaching his adult life goals: "I want to get an apartment. Why? Because that's where I want to live, a key to my place. And this job I am working so hard so I can earn a permanent spot. After this freeway job I want to work and they know that I am a hustler. . . . I want to stick with the company. The wages are amazing. I am blessed."

When we met Steven, he was clearly passionate about taking care of his daughter and took pride in his ability to perform taxing physical labor. However, with his extensive history of substance use and no college credits, his current success was tenuous, which made him also very nervous about his future. He had no concrete career plan; at that point, his life was simply hanging in the current balance that he had found in working nights, staying sober, exercising twice a day, and caring for his daughter. In Steven's view, his work was important, yet impermanent:

I just wanna learn, be with this company for as long as I . . . well my dad says for the rest of my life. It's just the fact that everyone drives on the freeway. It's gonna need repairs constantly. They do out of state jobs, so I'm like, I pray you know, that I get onto another project. I mean, we're not gonna be done 'til hopefully Christmas. And I get scared, like my dad goes, what are you gonna do when the job shuts down? When the job's over? I'm like fuck, like my dad right away, throwing me another little riddle. Like what do you mean? He goes, "Go to school." I'm like "Oh. My dad has his bachelors." I'm like "Fuck, I only got my high school diploma."

In addition to the tentative nature of his work and lack of time to pursue college, Steven also experienced ongoing problems with the mother of his child, Jessica. Like Steven, Jessica had a history of struggles with drug addiction. And, because Jessica had been in foster care when she gave birth to their daughter, at one point DCFS had tried to put their daughter up for adoption. Steven is extremely grateful to his parents for stepping in and taking custody of his daughter, and he had high hopes that he and Jessica could one day parent their daughter together. The problem was that helping Jessica stay away from drugs was a difficult burden for him emotionally; he felt enormous pressure to help her achieve sobriety, yet he was still fighting his own addiction demons. He explained:

Sometimes I feel like my baby mama still does meth, all the people she stays with or hangs out with . . . all her symptoms showed what meth does. She left me because she said I wasn't providing for her, I left her, I abandoned her, I wasn't man enough. Because she came from a foster home, she's traumatized by all that shit but now I am trying to be a man, be there like you know what I put my cards on the table like what can you put now. Because I am trying to do the best that I can, let go of the childhood shit, forget about the past. I am willing to do anything to have her as a family.

Despite all of these complications, Steven was holding out hope that the three of them could become a family while he was working all night, getting little sleep, responding to his parents' demands, and caring for their daughter. All of this, he explained, kept him in a state of constant stress about his next move.

"Too Stressful for $8.75 an Hour"

While the young fathers such as Mario and Steven had other people in their lives (partners and parents) to perform much of the heavy lifting in the care of their children, the two mothers in the study had sole or primary responsibility for their very young children. As such, they were not able to find a way to combine work and parenting in a similar way as the young fathers. When we first met Desiree, a nineteen-year-old African American mother of a two-year-old daughter Kianna, she was unemployed and surviving with the help of public benefits. Desiree lived in a subsidized independent living program for youth who had aged out of foster care, and she maintained her income through the federal Temporary Assistance for Needy Families (TANF) program (CalWORKS in California), which gave her a small monthly cash stipend, food stamps, and health insurance. During her second interview, Desiree shared that she was anxious about timing out of the CalWORKS program (recipients can only receive benefits for two years) and was feeling pressure to find a job. However, she wasn't sure how she would possibly juggle work and childcare.

Five months later, Desiree was working at a fast food restaurant earning minimum wage. She was nervous about applying for her first job, but she was happy she got the offer. She explained:

> I didn't expect to get the job at the restaurant. I just applied—I was just like "whatever." I was like "no nose rings, no facial jewelry, no facial piercings and no tattoos where they're visible." And I was like "I don't want to take my nose ring out and they're not going to hire me, but oh well." And then they emailed me back like an hour later: "oh, I'm scheduling your interview." I went in and I was just myself—this was my first group interview. And I was like so scared but I was like "oh well—it is what it is. Either they accept me or they don't." And I got the job. I was so excited. This was my first real paying job.

Desiree enjoyed the feeling of responsibility that came along with her first job. She was happy to have time to talk with other adults after being home with Kianna. But in order to keep this job, she also had to find childcare at odd hours. To do this, she would wake up around 9:00 AM with her daughter, feed her, and get ready for work. She would leave with Kianna around noon, giving herself five full hours to make it first to the home childcare and then to work, all by bus. Then she would work from 5:00 PM to midnight and travel back by bus to the childcare facility, returning home with her daughter around 2:00 AM. At times she and Kianna were so weary from this schedule that she would leave her at the all-night childcare so that her daughter could have a better night's sleep. She also felt very unsafe arriving home so late by bus and then walking the few blocks back to her home. She started to question whether this was ultimately the right choice for her daughter, who was her main priority.

This untenable schedule was short lived; she stopped working within a matter of weeks. When we met with her four months later, Desiree said that even though she had planned to quit, she ended up being fired for reasons she didn't fully understand. She explained:

> They didn't really give me a reason. They were just saying I wasn't a fit for the company and I don't know what was going on. Actually, it wasn't just out of nowhere, but 10 dollars out of my register came up missing. So, I think that, that was what it was. It was my first three weeks of work. But, I didn't understand about the ten dollars, I don't always pay attention, but I was trying to like perfect it. The first time my register was over .75 cents and then it was over five dollars the day after that. So, then if it's five dollars or over they'll talk to you about it, but they didn't say nothing about it being over and they'll just be like, "Hey, be careful." So then I started counting the money twice—like everybody does. Well, that's not what everybody does and that's why I didn't understand how my register was 10 dollars short. . . . So, I told them that I would pay them, but I don't know if you've ever worked with anything like that but that didn't work. So then they didn't fire me. I thought they would. They fired me a week later. They kept scheduling me late night. So, they kept scheduling me till like 2 o'clock in the morning and Kianna had to stay at her daycare, so that wasn't working out. So, I told them to give me some time to work things out and then they fired me the next day.

In retrospect, Desiree felt that that the job was "too stressful for $8.75 an hour" (California's minimum wage at that time). The reality of having to work such long hours for such low pay with the expense and difficulty of the evening childcare wasn't worth it to her anyhow.

In the interim, she enrolled in some community college courses, which helped her to extend her CalWORKS benefits period. But all of that stability was about to be disrupted, as Desiree was also about to term out of her independent living program. When we conducted our last interview with Desiree, she was preparing to move in with a relative, continue to take classes at a community college, and find another part-time job. All of this was in the works, but Desiree was used to frequent moves and disruptions, as she had endured multiple transitions throughout her entire life.

Amber was the other young mother in our study. At age 18, she had not yet completed her high school diploma due to a history of suspensions, expulsions, and stints in juvenile hall. Amber's history included a great deal of conflict with her mother and a brief period of abuse at the hands of her mother's ex-boyfriend. Yet when we met, she was relying on her mother for financial support and housing. So while her mother allowed her to live at the house with her children, Amber also applied for CalWORKS and food stamps to pay for basic living necessities. Like Desiree, Amber could not figure out how to work while raising young children. She described in more detail how she was getting by on a very limited income:

DIANE: Since you have had September [her second child], what would you say has been your biggest change in taking care of two kids instead of one?

AMBER: I be broke by the end of the month. I don't get income. I don't got no job. All I got is the county.

DIANE: How much do you get per month from the county?

AMBER: $516 and spending on diapers and wipes and lotion and body wash and clothes, I be broke. I be like oh my god. But you know I gotta do what I gotta do, cause I got two kids.

DIANE: Do you get food stamps too?

AMBER: Yeah. They give food stamps, cash aid, and Medi-Cal (public health insurance).

DIANE: Devon [the babies' father] helps out sometimes too right?

AMBER: Yeah, he gives me money from his disability and I buy the things for April and September.

County welfare benefits provided Amber enough money just to buy supplies for her children. Although Desiree was on her own and Amber received greater support from family and her partner, neither could manage to work while raising their small children. A minimum wage job would barely pay for childcare costs; and as single mothers, they also wanted to enroll in school in order to secure a brighter future for their children. Unlike the fathers in this study whose children had other primary caregivers, the mothers were clearly in a greater bind with work, leaving them much more vulnerable to poverty.

On the Margins

Many of our study participants were experiencing considerably greater marginalization and instability than those who were making ends meet. Part of their alienation from the mainstream labor force was related to high unemployment rates for their age group. It was also due to spotty work and educational histories, as well as self-perceptions, perhaps internalized through years of institutionalization, that they were not in fact "normal enough" to get a job. Those living on the margins had to cobble together public benefits, transitional housing, or the generosity of friends and relatives in order to find a way to survive.

"I'm My Own Worst Enemy"

For some of the young men in particular, an overriding sense of defeat led them to stray far from the mainstream workforce. Greg, the only white young man in our study, was 24 at the time that we met him. He frequently described himself as someone "living on the margins"; with tattoos running up and down both of his arms, long hair, and cutoff shorts, he seemed to fit the part at first glance. Greg's childhood was significantly colored by addiction. Both of his parents were addicted to methamphetamines during his early childhood, his father served time in jail for selling drugs, and his mother and grandparents raised Greg and his two siblings while actively using prescription and illegal drugs in the home. Greg began smoking marijuana in the fifth grade, and he used marijuana, cocaine, and ecstasy extensively throughout his adolescent years. During this time he started skipping school and fighting. It was a particularly violent fight in high school that led to his arrest and sentence to a juvenile probation camp.

Greg had worked on and off since he turned 18 but rarely held a job for more than a few months. His drug habits made him increasingly unable to keep a job. When we met him, Greg was temporarily physically disabled due to a car accident, and was surviving from the generosity of a roommate as well as General Relief and food stamps. In Los Angeles County, General Relief paid about $221 per month on a time-limited basis. He explained in the following conversation why it was hard for him to even apply for what he labeled a "normal" job:

GREG: I think that I've had a lot of people help me out. Getting me jobs. Nick [friend he lived with] helped me out with two or three jobs. I've gotten like one job on my own which was working at Safeway. And that sucked. I think my main thing is that I'm really shy and I really don't see myself being good at anything that *normal people* would be good at. So I don't go apply for jobs like Walmart or anywhere like that. I don't think I'm going to get the job. No one's gonna like me. Plus I have hand tattoos so it's like they see that and they think "oh this guy's weird." So I'm my own worst enemy. I judge myself more than people judge me. So that's what's hard for me. Just trying to get over that little hump. (Emphasis ours.)

LAURA: You kind of see yourself on the outside. You keep saying "normal."

GREG: Yeah I don't fit in with the norm, which is why I wanna go to mechanics institute and work on bikes for the rest of my life. That would be fine. Tattooing would be fine. I don't know. I just don't like the whole . . . I guess a nine to five deal. I don't like waking up in the morning. I don't like taking orders from anybody but myself. . . . There's something I wanted to do too when I was in [juvenile] camp. I wanted to work with either kids or animals. But I looked at the animal program in a nearby city and they don't allow you to have any tattoos. So that's kind of weird. It's not like these animals are gonna judge me!

Greg's only real work experience was when he was employed within a detention facility as a counselor for troubled youth. He liked the job, but admitted that he was fired for not showing up on time. During his second interview, he shared that, although he enjoyed the freedom to stay up late and not be confined to a routine, he found himself unwilling to fulfill the commitment of what he viewed as a typical job for more "normal" people. His emotional barriers compounded this belief in that he still saw himself as existing on the fringes of society. He believed that no one would likely hire him because of his tattoos and his nonconformance to a traditional image of a "working man." Even with his racial privilege, Greg's history of drug abuse and system involvement contributed to an overwhelming feeling that a normal job was unattainable for him.

Other young men, whether due to visible tattoos, lack of work skills, or the general marginalization and stigma associated with having a criminal record, shared a sense that they would simply not fit into the mainstream workforce. Evan, a tall and visibly tattooed African American young man, was a bit intimidating upon first sight. Yet underneath the exterior, he was a polite young man who shared many insights about his past. For several years, Evan was an only child, living with his mother while his father was incarcerated. When he turned ten, his mother and her boyfriend had two more children, and he sensed that they had unrealistic expectations for him to care for his new half-siblings. Around that same time he started to act up in school and received harsh discipline. He joined a gang in the sixth grade because he was "living life the way I wanted." The gang eventually led him into more serious crimes, such as selling drugs and burglary, and he spent the next several years in and out of the halls, probation camps, and eventually adult jail.

When we first met Evan at age 20, he was on adult probation that included mandatory drug testing and had prioritized completing his high school education above getting a job. Since he had no steady income, he was surviving on a very limited budget of General Relief and food stamps. He had no housing of his own, so he stayed with his grandmother on and off and at times slept on his friends' couches. Evan had worked hard to earn his high school diploma, and he was proud to walk the stage with his family there to witness this significant milestone. After graduation he said that he wanted to enroll in community college for a welding degree, but he missed several key deadlines, as he explained: "Oh, I'm going to enroll. I had waited too late and then I would've had to wait for financial aid and all that. So I didn't want to wait because I wanted to get it for when school first start. So I can get transportation and everything figured out. I wanted to go but I didn't want to go unprepared." Evan tended to miss his appointments for job interviews, job fairs, or other opportunities to submit applications. He was worried that an employer wouldn't give him a chance, based on both his appearance and his adult criminal record. As he said in the quote that opened this chapter, he feared that he wasn't going to get called for an interview based on his criminal history and appearance. To fill his time, he was doing odd jobs for his grandmother, "just chilling and watching TV," and trying to "stay out of trouble."

At face value, one could view this story as a 20-year-old young man being carefree and having fun. But realistically, without any true anchor, Evan was quite vulnerable to homelessness and was losing hope for a successful future. The momentum and good feelings he had built in getting his diploma were gradually dissipating. In the following dialogue below, Evan expresses how getting his hopes up for finding a job essentially would lead him to a sense of greater disappointment in his own life.

DIANE: When you picture yourself in five years, what do you think are any challenges that may stop you from getting there?

EVAN: This life is an obstacle period. I live it day by day. I don't even think about tomorrow like that.

DIANE: So you're living life day by day?

EVAN: To plan leads to disappointment sometime. I don't think about my future like that because, I mean, things change and you can never expect things to go as planned all the time.

Both Greg and Evan were surviving mainly on very limited public benefits, had temporary places to stay, and had little direction or momentum for their futures. Although Evan had taken the initiative to earn his high school diploma and Greg had not, they shared an overriding sense that they would not be considered in the traditional job market, so it was not so important for them to even try.

"It's Complicated": Rebuilding after Foster Care

Having a home, whether through relatives, public benefits, or work, played a significant role in establishing a stable base. Tyrone was one of the young people in the study who was insecurely housed and had very limited income or work prospects. When we met Tyrone at age 20, he had been out of probation camp for nearly two years. Yet navigating his life since becoming a legal adult was a constant struggle. He experienced numerous bouts of homelessness and "couch surfing," which usually led him to start stealing and selling drugs in order to survive.

When we first met Tyrone, he had recently moved into a transitional living facility for former foster youth that provided him with housing, food, and clothing vouchers, as well as counseling and independent living skills programs. Despite this support, he was having a difficult time carving out concrete plans for his future. He knew that he needed to finish school and find a job, but he encountered numerous setbacks every time he tried to move forward with these goals. For example, he had been unable to earn his GED because every time he moved residences he had to change schools, which often meant losing track of the credits he had earned along the way. He also encountered barriers in his day-to-day life that made it difficult for him to accomplish smaller, yet equally important tasks such as obtaining a valid identification card. He described these challenges: "I used to have my documents all in nice folders along with my poetry that I kept around from camp periods from like three years. I had a lot of documents—my certificates from classes. I misplaced some of 'em slowly over time. But I have some left. So I still have my birth certificate and that's it. But I just got on Medi-Cal, which I had lost, but I got that back. And I just went down there and got my replacement for the Social Security Card and my ID should be on its way. So it's almost like a circle 'cause I had those things." Tyrone frequently referred to these types of setbacks as "running in circles" (a theme we will explore further in chapter 5) and he was noticeably frustrated about his lack of progress toward achieving any concrete goals. He had no significant work history, had not lived independently, and he was acutely aware that in less than one year he would likely age out of eligibility for these critical housing services. Further contributing to his problems was his use of various substances; he admitted to smoking marijuana on a daily basis, and he had also dabbled with cocaine and other hard drugs in the past. His marijuana use specifically resulted in him being kicked out of several housing facilities, and it had hindered his ability to find employment. Yet he had not stopped smoking weed nor did he think he needed professional help. This was especially troubling for Tyrone given that the facility he lived in mandated that he stay sober, and they reserved the right to drug test the residents at any given time if any suspicion of drug use arose.

Despite the fact that his drug use could jeopardize his housing and limit his future employment prospects, Tyrone continued to smoke weed on a daily basis while promising himself he would one day stop. His stubbornness may have reflected a certain youthful agency; he had spent the majority of his life under the control of foster homes and correctional institutions, and smoking marijuana seemed to be one of his only outlets for fun and relaxation. However, the constant loss of his housing as a result of this habit had contributed to a loss of some essentials, such as bus vouchers and food. To comply with his current transitional housing program, Tyrone had applied for General Relief and food stamps, and he also had to provide a portion of these funds to the housing program. He had just one dollar in a bank account merely to "keep it open," and without the transitional program, he would have become homeless again. He knew that this program was a temporary safe haven, and based on his past instability he did not take any type of assistance or support for granted. Rather, he labeled his current situation as "complicated," meaning that "the complications is just you have to go out and you have to gather responsibility." While he really wanted to get a GED or learn a trade, he instead would spend his days looking at want ads, wandering the city, and trying to comply with his program rules to make sure he didn't end up homeless again.

"I Never Thought It Would Be So Hard Out Here"

For Tyrone, his past foster care experience, the absence of a stable housing plan, and his drug use posed major barriers to achieving self-sufficiency. Several other participants did not have the same substance use challenges, but found themselves similarly without a solid foundation from which to launch into adulthood. When we met Maria, a 19-year-old Latina young woman, she was hoping to complete her high school diploma. Since her release from a juvenile correctional facility, she had moved to a number of cities with relatives and friends. This was basically a continuation of her entire childhood, as she was never able to stay for long periods of time with her biological mother due to her mother's drug addiction. Maria was jumped into a large street gang at age 13, which eventually became her sense of belonging since many of her family members had belonged to the same gang. Gang membership led to fighting, arrests, drug use, and dropping out of school. By age 17, she was convicted of assault and spent time in a correctional facility.

Upon exiting the juvenile justice system, Maria did not find any new sense of stability, and once again was tossed around between relatives without finding a place to call home. She explained: "I was talking to my aunt and she was like 'ok, you can come stay with me' and I was like 'ok.' So I came down here and I was staying with her for almost like two months and then she told me that the landlady said no one else can live here and I was like 'fuck, what am I going to do?' I was like 'I guess'—my uncle lived down the street—'can I call my uncle?' I was like 'can I stay with you because I can't stay with my aunt no more.' It's like so confusing—I never thought it would be so hard out here." Maria was accustomed to transience, but now she had no place to live, no income, and no high school diploma. She was essentially homeless. When we went to contact her a week later for her second interview, she had already moved out of the area; her grandparents had decided to send her back to the Midwest to live with her mother. Although Maria and her mother had a very contentious relationship, she still held out hope it might work out this time. She wrote to us via email about her plans for the immediate future (spelling unchanged from original email): "Well i want to go back to indiana to try and help my mom out since my sister and her 3 kids left to mexico so its gonna be stress free but shes got bills to pay so ima help her out . . . and actually im not goin out there to be in the stuff i was before ima be straight in mind and attitude . . . also yes ima finish my degree out there because walmart actually pays for your school if your willing to go back and well im at work at walmart becasue thats the only place i can really get hired because of my mother working there as well."

Maria's story was disheartening not only because of her history of instability and neglect, but also because she seemed to lack confidence that she could find a way out of her current situation. On the one hand, Maria talked about her mother as her worst influence, as someone who had never truly been a mother to her. Yet she still held onto a dream that one day they could be a family again and help each other out. While we lost touch with Maria at that point, it seemed unlikely that moving back in with her mother would provide her with a pathway out of a seemingly self-destructive path.

From these narratives, we find that existing "on the margins" resulted from the interplay between logistical and emotional factors. Being temporarily housed or without a job left some of these youth feeling unanchored, which in turn contributed to an overarching sense of marginalization and hopelessness. The sense that they would never truly be able to get ahead regardless of their efforts then served as a barrier to put their best foot forward, which then began the cycle all over again. While social safety nets and other informal resources were temporarily able to keep them fed, it was quite uncertain how long these tentative situations might last. Those living on the margins were indeed one step away from homelessness and bottoming out.

CONCLUSION

In this chapter we portrayed the everyday realities of these young adults as they forged ahead with their lives after adolescent incarceration. As they became legal adults, we saw these men and women experiencing some of the trials and tribulations of young adulthood, including getting their first jobs, figuring out how to afford an apartment or move out on their own, and balancing work and school; experiences that are fairly common for individuals in this developmental stage. However, these young people were not afforded the opportunity or a great deal of time to ponder their futures, as most had to provide for themselves and take responsibility for their lives upon turning 18 or even younger. Given the high unemployment rates for young people in Los Angeles County at that time (Matsanuga, 2011), it makes sense that their most significant concerns revolved around making ends meet, becoming independent, and providing for themselves, their own children, and sometimes other family members as well.

Some of these young men and women were managing to stay above board financially and to secure jobs and housing. However, this achievement required an extremely dedicated sense of personal and familial responsibility, an intense level of structure and discipline in their daily lives, and the decision to forgo higher education. In order to keep moving forward with such intensity, they held onto the hope that everything would somehow work out for the future. And, despite their successes, they were still often vulnerable in the sense that if anything fell out of place in their very carefully planned lives, they could lose everything they had worked to achieve.

We also found that many of the young people were just barely skating by, being far more removed from the mainstream workforce. For some, this position stemmed from a lack of housing or caregiving responsibilities; for others, the cause was drug addiction, emotional scars and traumas, and lack of family support; or a blend of many of these factors. For those who were indeed removed from employment, the public social safety net filled in some of these gaps. These young adults were savvy about applying for social welfare benefits and using them to survive. Yet one had to wonder for how long they could remain on the margins before turning to illegal activities for survival's sake. The next chapter will delve deeply into how the young men handled temptations to participate in criminal activity in the context of these economic concerns and related struggles.

CHAPTER 5

Dangers and Decisions

NAVIGATING DESISTANCE AS A YOUNG MAN

> Sometimes you're gonna get tempted. And you might
> do it. But as long as you're handling your business,
> that's the way I see it . . . I never was out in the
> streets gang banging and this and that. 'Cause I knew
> my standards. I knew my limits. I knew what I had to
> do and what I couldn't do.

> —Cesar

TO CESAR, DESISTANCE MEANT "handling your business," knowing your limits and moral standards about what crimes are acceptable and which ones are not. Other men had entirely different definitions of desistance that evolved over the course of their transition to adulthood. In this chapter, we paint a nuanced picture of what it means to navigate criminal desistance for formerly incarcerated young adult men. We focus on how these young men navigated decisions around criminal influences and temptations in their day-to-day lives. In doing so, we hone in on an array of barriers to criminal desistance, including even minute mistakes that threatened to return them to the criminal justice system and derail their sense of stability. In chapter 4 we saw that the challenges associated with finding work, housing, and a secure pathway to adulthood left many of these participants on the margins, struggling to meet even their most basic needs. Here we continue to explore the tenuous position of being a formerly incarcerated young adult, more specifically in relation to the process of criminal desistance. Our goal is to provide greater insights into the ways that young men navigate challenges to achieving a law-abiding lifestyle as they are situated within the risks and opportunities of their everyday social contexts. As the process of desistance appeared to be quite different for the young women in our study, we center the next two chapters specifically on the young men and focus on the young women in chapter 7.

UNDERSTANDING DESISTANCE

As we noted in chapter 1, no simple explanation exists for how or why criminal desistance occurs for some young adults and not others, and our interviews reflected the very complexity of this concept. There are myriad factors that can facilitate desistance among young people who have committed crimes, including improved maturity and reasoning that appears to result from getting older, adopting new life roles and identities, finding internal motivation and hope, and accessing opportunities and resources (Mulvey et al., 2004). Pinpointing which of these factors or how much of one element is needed to truly make a difference in someone's life is near impossible. Measuring desistance, including when it ends and begins, presents an equally difficult set of challenges. Empirical studies tend to rely mostly on official accounts of criminal activity (i.e., through archival data such as police court records), yet these records do not allow one to take into account biases and disparities in arrest and incarceration trends based on race, gender, or age. For this reason, some scholars have advocated for the use of more subjective reports that allow individuals to narrate their own desistance progress and experience (Massoglia & Uggen, 2010).

Our analysis is grounded in the participants' perspectives on their own process of desistance, including the time points when they felt ready to change their lives and the steps they took to initiate this change. We found that nearly all of the participants felt motivated to become more law-abiding as they got older and took on more adult responsibilities. However, they did not use the term "desistance," and most were unable to isolate a specific day or moment in time when they officially decided to, in their terminology, "go straight." Moreover, the young men had different visions of what a crime-free lifestyle actually looked like, and as such, they employed various strategies to enact these visions in their everyday lives.

For all of these reasons, part of our analysis included a restructuring of the concept of desistance that more closely aligned with the participants' narratives. As we detail in the appendix, we purposively recruited young men into the study who had had a range of experiences within the criminal justice system, including those who had been arrested as adults and those who had not. However, after meeting with the participants several times and reflecting on their narratives, two points became clear: (1) arrest or conviction histories did not sufficiently match the extent to which participants were or were not still involved in crime; and (2) arrest or conviction histories did not capture efforts the young men had made to work toward desistance. For example, one young man who was very committed to desistance was re-arrested simply for missing an appointment with his probation officer, while another had frequently committed crimes but had not yet been caught. It seemed unfair that on the basis of having a record, the former young man might be categorized as a recidivist, while the latter would be considered a success story. Thus, rather than using re-arrest histories as the marker of desistance, we grouped the young men into typologies based on shared thoughts, behaviors, and strategies that facilitated their movement toward or away from criminal activity. The conceptualization of desistance as an ongoing process involving the gradual diminishing of criminal activity over time is grounded in the literature and also in the reality of what we heard from the young men themselves (Kazemian, 2007).

Overall, this chapter illustrates what the process of desistance looks like as it is individually enacted, how young men navigate and make decisions about criminal activity in their everyday social environments, and how micro-level (meaning day-to-day) decisions and environmental context work together to produce a set of desistance processes and outcomes. We focus on the desistance strategies they used during the specific period of emerging adulthood, when they may have outgrown some of their youthful behaviors but perhaps still lack essential tools and supports that would help them sustain a crime-free life.

Based on the young men's narrative accounts of strategies used to contend with criminal temptations, three typologies concerning desistance emerged, as follows: (1) "On the Road to Desistance," meaning those actively working to desist from crime altogether; (2) "Running in Circles," which included young men who had goals for a crime-free future, yet struggled to enact them based on other life challenges; and (3) "Still in the Game," referring to those who were still committing crimes and whose version of desistance generally equated to not getting caught. Table 5.1 provides an overview of the young men in each typology alongside their initial pathway into crime, time since exit from juvenile probation camp, and self-reported re-arrest histories. As we will illustrate, the young men's definitions and understandings of desistance framed their decisions related to criminal activity and their responses to the ordinary life circumstances that placed them at risk for re-offending.

Typology One: On the Road to Desistance

The seven young men who were on the road to desistance were actively working to remove themselves from criminal activity or situations that could lead to contact with law enforcement. They did not unilaterally decide to leave crime behind immediately after exiting the juvenile justice system. In fact, at the time of our first interview, three members of this group had been arrested as adults: Gabriel spent a weekend in adult jail after missing an appointment with his probation officer; Mario served time in adult jail for an assault charge, Steven had stacked up multiple parole violations related to substance use before he finally achieved sobriety. Oscar was later arrested as an adult during the study period, but was not charged with a crime. (See table 5.1.) However, as they transitioned further into adulthood, the young men in this group reached a point when they intentionally decided to change the direction of their lives. All were currently abstaining from crime during the time period we met with them; yet still, they continued to face situations that challenged their resolve. In this way, these young men were still engaged in an ongoing process of achieving desistance, which is why the term "On the Road to Desistance" best captures their experiences.

As a group, their perceptions of what it meant to be an adult played a large role in the desistance process. They equated adulthood with greater personal responsibility, a belief that served as motivation to establish basic aspects of independence, such as work or positive relationships that reduced their need and desire to engage in criminal activity. Ultimately their decision to change was facilitated by a series of concrete actions and a succession of internal and external identity transformations that further cemented a different life trajectory from their adolescence.

Typology Two: Running in Circles

The Running in Circles group included four young men whose experiences with desistance can best be characterized by a series of

TABLE 5.1.

Desistance Typologies for the Young Men

Typology	Name	Age	Race	Years out of camp/juvie[a]	Re-arrested since camp/juvie	Time since last arrest[b]
1	Oscar	19	Latino	1.5	Yes[c]	See note c
	John	19	Latino	1.5	No	—
	Eduardo	19	Latino	2.5	No	—
	Shawn	22	Black	3	No	—
	Mario	23	Latino	4	Yes	2 years
	Gabriel	24	Latino	5	Yes	4 years
	Steven	24	Latino	7	Yes	2 years
2	Tyrone	20	Black	3	Yes	1 year
	Cesar	23	Latino	5	No	—
	Greg	23	White	5	No	—
	Chris	24	Black	6	Yes	5 years
3	Carlos	20	Latino	2	Yes	6 months
	Peter	23	Filipino	4	Yes	1 month
	Jerry	23	Latino	4	No	—
	Mike	24	Black	6	Yes	3 years
	Anthony	20	Black	2	Yes	0 months
	Evan	21	Black	3	Yes	3 months

Note: 1 = On the Road; 2 = Running in Circles; 3 = Still in the Game

[a] At time of first interview.

[b] At time of first interview.

[c] Arrested but not charged with a crime during the study period, after the second interview.

starts, missteps, relapses, and re-starts. They were similar to members of Typology One in that they had initiated some positive changes in their lives since exiting the juvenile justice system; a few had found jobs and had experienced periods of time when they lived independently, and others had settled into family life. They were genuinely trying to envision futures for themselves that did not involve criminal activity, and expressed an end goal of ceasing all criminal activity. Moreover, each member of this typology could recall sustained periods of time where they successfully stayed out of trouble. However, as a group, they were not entirely ready or able to completely disengage from crime, mostly due to economic constraints. Many were still struggling to maintain stable jobs and housing, and they had less clarity overall about their future life plans. So while these young men had a long-range goal of abstaining from crime, they had not fully implemented the lifestyle changes to facilitate this goal. As such, they continued to have one foot rooted in the past and made fewer attempts to distance themselves from situations that posed criminal temptations or potential trouble with the law. Overall, the process of desistance for those in Typology Two involved lessening their participation in crime or in particular types of crimes, a strategy that left them susceptible to re-offending despite their intentions to do otherwise.

Typology Three: Still in the Game

The six young men who comprised this typology adopted a looser interpretation of desistance compared to the members of the other two groups. They emphasized a desire to avoid future jail time, expressed some inclination to reduce or eliminate criminal activities, and were often thoughtful and deliberate about their participation in crime. However, for these young men, desistance mostly consisted of "selective involvement" (Abrams, 2007), meaning choices that would mostly minimize their risk of getting caught and going to jail. This strategy included decisions such as committing crimes only when economically necessary, avoiding some situations that would tempt them to re-offend (while at the same time giving themselves permission if the need arose), or trying to avoid any possibility of contact with the police.

Most of the young men in this group were motivated at times to terminate offending, but they also were reluctant to follow through with internal and external changes that would support this end goal. Moreover, they did not readily separate themselves from their criminally associated friends or neighborhood contexts. For example, four of the six men in this typology continued to be active in their gangs as young adults. Further, the young men who were "Still in the Game" did not consistently seek out alternative identities or social roles in the same way that young men from the other two groups did. Despite all of these indicators, throughout their narratives, most insisted that they were taking steps toward desistance in their own way. For this reason, rather than categorizing them as criminal persisters, we viewed them as individuals who were perhaps not as determined or advanced in their desistance journeys as the members of the other two groups, but still fell somewhere on the desistance spectrum.

In the sections that follow, we highlight how the young men's internal transformations related to desistance unfolded within their community and interpersonal contexts. We specifically hone in on the issues that the young men felt had significantly influenced their desistance experiences, including their appearance and associations with family members and friends. We describe how each group navigated these barriers, and how a blend of micro-level thought processes, decisions, and environmental opportunities and constraints worked together to influence their trajectories concerning crime.

CHANGING APPEARANCE

The theme of appearance emerged frequently as the young men described their experiences of navigating life outside of a correctional environment. This was particularly relevant for the gang-affiliated participants whose outward appearances represented a direct link to their criminal pasts. Important aspects of appearance were quite consistent across typologies, and included choices concerning clothing, hairstyles, and tattoos. However, the responses to these choices were varied, all involving a blend of internal reflection, active decision-making, and then outward projection of their internal changes. This process was also ongoing, meaning that the young men found themselves analyzing their appearance at multiple junctures of their maturation as adults.

The men from Typology One were most motivated and willing to change aspects of their appearance as part of their ongoing commitment to staying out of trouble. The need to change their appearance did not occur immediately, however. In fact, after deciding that they were ready to distance themselves from their criminal pasts, most of the young men in this typology focused on completing more practical, concrete tasks associated with desistance; they began to look for legitimate jobs, enrolled in school, or sought out internships or other opportunities to occupy mainstream social roles. Over time, however, each of the young men underwent a series of changes, beginning with their thought processes and self-perceptions, that caused them to realize that changing their outward appearance represented an equally critical step in their transition. The stories of Oscar and Gabriel illustrate this journey.

Oscar was initiated into his gang around age 13, and over time, he had gained a reputation as one of the toughest, most respected kids from his neighborhood, one who was always ready to fight to prove his worth. By age 15, Oscar been in and out of juvenile hall more times than he could remember and had experienced his ample share of significant traumatic loss, including witnessing the death of one of his best friends. As he described, "Everything about me had changed. I wasn't Oscar. I wasn't the same Oscar that I was when I was 10 years old, 13 years old. I'd turned into an animal." Oscar experienced one of many arrests just before his sixteenth birthday. However, this arrest felt different to him because he was being charged with a serious crime that he insists he did not commit. The case was so severe that it single-handedly caused him to reevaluate his life. Interestingly, it was not the actual charge that left Oscar reeling, but rather the fact that one of his best friends from his gang had framed him for committing the crime. He described his shock upon learning of his friend's betrayal: "And my best friend, my ace, had turned his back on me. And not only that, he was trying to clean his hands off on me. So then he wrote a [police] report, giving dates, times, how, why's, and the where's." Spending a grueling year fighting his case, he struggled with depression and lost a significant amount of weight due to the stress. He was ultimately acquitted, but the experience of his friend's betrayal caused him to reexamine his commitment to his gang, the very people he considered to be family. The last day of his trial, he resolved to leave the gang life behind.

Oscar returned from juvenile probation camp fully committed to desistance, and he made a series of decisions to enact his goals. His first and most drastic decision was to completely cut ties with his gang; he stopped hanging around his old friends, stayed away from his gang territory, and enrolled in school. Next, Oscar made a conscious effort to shed aspects of identity that he felt branded him as a gang member. He described how he initially worked to change his manner of speech: "Just in my way of talking to people. I was more conscious of the things that I was saying and how I was saying them. What I was saying. Like the types of points that I was trying to make."

Despite making these initial changes, Oscar eventually came to a point where he realized that his outward appearance still projected a gangster image that he did not want to embody. He then took deliberate steps to alter his appearance, beginning with his clothing. Oscar described his thought process around his style of dress in the following conversation:

OSCAR: Yeah and I had to start accepting myself in these kind of clothes because it was hard for me to.

LAURA: Those look like nice clothes.

OSCAR: Just normal clothes I guess.

LAURA: What would you be wearing?

OSCAR: White t-shirt and probably some dickies or something.

LAURA: And that was your whole wardrobe?

OSCAR: Yeah I would wear black dickies or tan dickies or blue maybe.

LAURA: A t-shirt but not a button-down shirt.

OSCAR: Possibly a button-down shirt. It would probably be a dickies suit or a t-shirt and the t-shirt will go either black or any dark colors or white.

LAURA: And your shoes?

OSCAR: Those are probably the two biggest [the shoes] and your belt. The belt is probably more significant than anything. A guy can be from a Crip gang and wearing all red and you pull up his shirt and he's wearing a blue belt. The blue belt and shoelaces will tell you exactly where someone's from. Whether he is a Crip or whether he is a Blood. Not so much in the Mexican gang world but in the black gang world. Nine out of ten times you lift up someone's shirt and you see the colored belt, that's where they are from.

This excerpt illustrates the complex level of self-reflection that went into the young men's decisions about changing their appearance, even down to the most minute aspects of their clothing such as belts and shoes. In the same way that Oscar intentionally changed his thought patterns and then his manner of speaking, he had to take equal consideration to make sure that his appearance reflected the person he was becoming and not the self of the past.

Gabriel also sorted through a similar set of internal and then external transformations after deciding to "go straight." At age 17, after several years in the drug trade and the juvenile justice system, Gabriel realized that he was terribly unhappy with his life. Despite the large sums of money he had earned selling drugs, he was locked up inside a probation camp, felt constantly angry, had been a victim of gun violence, and had lost many close friends to street violence, drug addiction, and prison. Determined to change his life, he exited his final juvenile camp placement and enrolled in school. However, as a student without much money, he struggled with the temptation to return to the fast money of the drug trade. While sorting through his feelings, he found out that some of his former drug dealing associates had been arrested on federal charges and were facing very long sentences. Gabriel escaped prosecution, but coming so close to serving a lengthy sentence in adult prison served as a "wake-up call" that cemented his decision to change his life completely.

Despite making a series of concrete changes, including going to school, getting married, and cutting ties with his gang, Gabriel had to confront the prospect of changing his appearance. He had his first epiphany about the importance of his external identity when he had a chance encounter with some of his former gang associates. Up until that point, he had been pretty proud of his transformation. He was feeling happier with himself and believed that people were seeing him as a productive member of society. However, the chance encounter with his old friends triggered a deeper thought process about his external appearance: "The first thing that pops in my head was, they were all dirty. They were dirty, broke, on drugs. And I sit back and I think about it and I'm like, I used to look dirty. 'Cause most supposedly gangsters, most of them look dirty. There's those gangsters, those supposedly ballers that dress a little bit better. And then there's the pretty boys. And even though I used to wear new clothes, I sit and think like 'damn, maybe I did look dirty.' But I spoke to myself and was like 'nah, that's not what I want for myself. I wanna do better for myself.'" From that point forward, Gabriel became even more conscious of the ways that he continued to look "thuggish." He realized that until he changed the way he dressed, no one, including prospective employers, would be able to witness his transformed internal identity. In the following story, Gabriel offers his reflections on the image that he had projected to employers prior to making these important external changes.

> I had real short hair—almost bald. I had real baggy pants and a t-shirt. See right now I'm wearing a t-shirt 'cause I'm going to the gym in a bit. But yeah, I looked young. I still looked immature. And then with my tattoos it doesn't help. And so she just didn't wanna give it to me. And it's funny cause I'll say about four months ago, we needed a forklift driver so they told me, well do you know any staffing agencies that we might get somebody from? I'm like "yeah, I used to work for this agency" and they're like, "well go ahead and find us the contact and we'll go ahead and we'll set it up." So I ended up showing up. And I'm well dressed you know, shirt and tie and slacks. I sit down and she looks at me and she's like "I know you from somewhere." I'm like "yeah I used to work for you guys." "Like, how long ago?" "Like a little bit more than a year ago." . . . So then we started discussing history and she's like "I know who you are. How did you get this job?" And I ended up mentioning the way that I got it and she started laughing and she's like "I'm just proud of you. You did a good job. I'm just proud. I remember the first time that you walked in I was scared of giving you a job 'cause you looked so irresponsible."

Despite the careful steps Gabriel took to alter his appearance and break his gang ties, he also made a conscious decision *not* to remove his extensive gang tattoos that covered parts of his body. He was still somewhat conflicted about this decision. He wanted to remove the images of the life that he was no longer living, but at the same time he believed that the tattoos represented a part of his history that he could never fully forget or leave behind. He explained, "It's something that I would like to hide and just throw it in the back of the closet and just never let it out. But you know, my history, and just . . . my history doesn't let me."

Both Oscar's and Gabriel's narratives illustrate the complex struggles around internal identity and external projections of self involved with the desistance process. These young men had figured out the basic mechanics of desistance; leaving their gangs, avoiding contact with old friends, and pursuing school and work. Ultimately, however, both reached a point where they realized that it was imperative for their outward appearance to similarly reflect their internal desires to change.

Participants who were "Still in the Game" voiced similar concerns about barriers to desistance associated with their appearance. However, their inability, or in some cases, their lack of willingness to disentangle themselves from crime influenced how they responded to these barriers. For example, by the time he turned 18, Carlos left juvenile camp with the intention of staying out of trouble, and to his credit, he did just that. He enrolled at a local community college and obtained a part-time job at a business near his home. However, one day the sheriffs showed up at his home charging him with a vandalism felony that had lingered from his past. He figured it was best to be honest, so he confessed. This moment of honesty landed him in adult jail for 30 days. And because of his prior record and status as a known gang member, if convicted, he would earn a strike on his record, along with a gang enhancement charge that carried additional jail time. Carlos did not want to risk going to trial and losing, so he took a plea deal that earned him three years on probation and an automatic ten-year sentence for any future probation violation. He was released from jail on probation a few months prior to our first interview.

Carlos's post-jail lifestyle differed dramatically from the young men from Typology One in that he maintained connections to his gang and participated in gang-related activities when he felt they were necessary. Even with his ongoing gang involvement, he viewed himself as someone who was working toward desistance because he was making decisions to gradually disengage himself from some illegal activities, particularly those that were more likely to get him in trouble with the police. He was earnestly seeking employment in order to pay his monthly probation fines. He had stopped smoking weed, and he tried to focus his time and energy on more positive activities such as playing basketball, drawing, and writing rap lyrics.

Despite taking these positive steps, Carlos remained committed to his gang. He was proud of its history and he spoke at length about its reach and impact in the area. When he talked about his daily interactions, it was clear his continued gang membership provided him with a network of friendship and social support. On the flip side, his ongoing gang involvement made his day-to-day life difficult. When he was with his friends, he looked and dressed according to gang norms, which caused ongoing problems with the police and rival gang members (to be discussed further in chapter 6). He spoke extensively about the problems that arose based on his appearance. Of note, Carlos was the only member of Typology Two who had put serious thought into how and why he should make efforts to change the way he looked, and thought about how his appearance contributed to his frequent encounters with the police. He was also the only member of this group who had appeared to put more effort into desistance, even if ultimately these efforts did not completely stop him from engaging in criminal activity.

One of the more challenging issues for Carlos was his shaved head, which, in his words, made him look like a stereotypical member of a Mexican gang. During the times when he was most serious about staying out of trouble, he changed his image by growing his hair out and pulling it away from his face. He also tried wearing glasses so that he looked less suspicious and recognizable. Carlos was reluctant to maintain these changes, however, which reflected his overall conflict about the extent to which he was willing to alter key markers of his identity. In the following exchange he explained his reluctance to wear his hair in a less conspicuous style.

LAURA: So why not grow your hair out?
CARLOS: I don't know. I don't feel right when it's out. I feel, I don't know. People are always telling me it makes me look older, so I just cut it.

LAURA: But if you do, that would save you some harassment. It's not worth it to you?

CARLOS: Yeah, I mean. I let it grow out when I go to school or something, I'll let it grow out. But I don't have to do nothing right now. I don't have a job. I kinda like being bald, not to lie.

This excerpt highlights the central tension between desire to change and adaptation to a particular external environment. Carlos was most willing and able to overcome barriers associated with his appearance when he was pursuing activities outside of his gang such as going to school or work. These more mainstream and responsible activities then served as motivating factors toward desistance. On the other hand, he was much less willing to change aspects of his appearance during periods when he was unemployed, as he would then spend more time with his gang friends. In this way, his choice of hairstyle could be seen as a strategy for adapting to the specific environment in which he was operating at any given time.

Carlos was similarly conflicted about removing his tattoos, especially the one that was on his face. Despite his resistance to getting these marks removed, he was fully aware that having a gang-related tattoo in such a visible area greatly hindered his ability to get a legitimate job. He explained:

DIANE: What kinds of jobs are you looking for?

CARLOS: Anything. I like whatever. Hard work. Use my hands. Hands on, hands off, whatever. Supervision is very easy when I used to do that for the Boys and Girls club. But now that I have my three dots [pointing to three-dot tattoo next to his eye] on my face and stuff, I can't get those jobs no more.

Carlos had at one point received laser treatment to remove the three dots. However, he re-tattooed his face one year later with the same marking, and was hesitant to have it removed a second time. It was clear to us that his indecision about his external appearance reflected his larger internal battles about desistance as a whole.

While many of the young men, particularly in Typologies One and Three, were very concerned about their appearance, this sentiment was not universally shared. Those who were not prior gang members (across all typologies, but particularly in Typology Two) or who, like Carlos, wished to stay involved in their gangs, were far less concerned about their appearance. Greg, who was not a former gang member, represented one exception in that he was concerned about how he looked to the outside world. Part of the "Running in Circles" Typology, he had a number of visible tattoos on his arms, neck, and other parts of his body. Although these markings were not gang related, he had learned over the years that they still hindered his job prospects, particularly when it came to jobs involving caring for children and animals (the occupations of greatest interest to him). Despite this recognition, he did not have any real desire to remove his tattoos. In many ways he viewed himself as an outsider, and he was comfortable with this idea of himself as someone living on the margins; altering the symbols on his body would thus mean changing a core part of his identity.

Greg's reflections concerning the outward projection of his appearance are not all that different from the thought processes of Oscar (Typology One) and Carlos (Typology Three). Yet because he had no past or present gang ties, he didn't share the same set of fears about being targeted because of his tattoos or other aspects of his appearance. Moreover, Greg was not actively looking for a job when we met him, which made his outward markings less of an immediate concern. Despite the fact that the young men in Typology Two had held jobs since exiting juvie, none were employed at the time that we met them. Accordingly, as we detail in the next section, the struggles they faced related to criminal temptation had much more to do with friendship ties, neighborhood risks, and economic need.

NAVIGATING FRIENDS AND FAMILY

Navigating peer and family associations was an ongoing negotiation process for all of the men, as they were keenly aware that these associations with could either help or hinder their efforts to stay out of trouble with the law. Relationships with old and new friends, significant others, and family members all presented a set of important decisions relating to desistance. In this section we present two different strategies the young men used to navigate their relational lives, including "cutting ties" and "selective involvement." While they all adopted diverse strategies as situations arose and as time moved forward, nuanced differences in these strategies between typologies were also apparent.

Cutting Ties

Many of the young men experienced shifts in their friendship ties in early adulthood as a result of changing lifestyles and interests, people moving away, or because they had lost friends to gang violence, drugs, and lengthy prison sentences. Three of the young men from Typology One had deliberately cut ties with their old peer networks and limited their associations to just a few close friends and family members. They came to this decision after acknowledging that the people who they had previously considered to be close friends were still involved in behaviors or networks that directly threatened their own desistance goals. This was particularly true for the young men who were former gang members and whose survival literally hinged on completely separating themselves from their pasts. The decision to sever ties with friends altogether may appear to be an extreme one, but proved to be necessary in facilitating their movement toward desistance. At the same time, this strategy came with its share of drawbacks and required ongoing negotiation and recommitment.

Gabriel was one of the young men who adopted the strategy of cutting ties. After he left his gang, he severed his relationships with nearly everyone he knew outside of his family. Gabriel stated bluntly: "I don't have any friends. I don't have any friends. There's people that I know and might speak to, but I don't consider people friends anymore . . . My only friend is basically my wife and that's it. My wife and my family; those are my friends." At times, Gabriel longed to see some of his old friends, but he knew that he couldn't take that risk. During one of the interviews, Gabriel explained his strategy for dealing with his former friends when they approached him about making plans:

DIANE: So when they ask you when are you going to come hang out, do you just put them off?

GABRIEL: No I usually say, "yeah, yeah." Make up a date and I tell 'em where we're gonna go, and I get them all pumped up, and they're like, yeah we'll do this and we'll do that. And you know, it's like, at the end you know, my wife even turns around and says, "are you gonna hang out with them?" And I don't respond. I would like to hang out with them and say, "you know what guys, let's go to a pool bar. We'll play pool, have one or two drinks. Everybody goes home." But they're not about that. They always wanna be out there just causing trouble. That's who they are. And I'm not cool with that.

Gabriel would perhaps enjoy a chance to go to a bar, play pool with his old friends, and drink a few beers. However, he was very aware that the risks associated with participating in what would appear to be a benign outing were simply too great to take. Even beyond the risks imposed by just being around these friends, he shared that despite all the changes he had consciously made, he feared that his old friends might tempt him to return to his old life. He said, "I try to avoid it as much as possible because I think of a fear of going back to what I used to be. I think that I'm scared of turning back into who I used to be." For all of these reasons, Gabriel instead chose to skip the social invitations and remain in the safe haven of his home. For Gabriel, it was clear that his past left him with very little wiggle room to make any mistakes, which included seemingly innocuous social events such as playing pool at a bar. However, he had reached a point where he was very committed to the idea of fully abstaining from situations and people that might cause him to re-offend, or as he stated, to revert to an older version of himself.

Like Gabriel, for those who were On the Road to Desistance, cutting ties altogether helped to concretize their commitment to avoiding situations that could tempt them to revert to old patterns. While cutting ties was effective in facilitating desistance, this strategy did carry some disadvantages. A few of the young men who had severed their relationships with former friends acknowledged a deep sense of loneliness. When these young men left their gangs, they also left behind the people who provided their primary source of friendship and support. As a result, they often felt isolated and out of their element, even years after finalizing these separations. Moreover, they also acknowledged that it was difficult for them to forge new friendships and struggled to identify new social support networks. Some of this void was filled by their relationships with their significant others; in the early stages of their desistance journeys, four of the seven young men from this group became involved in serious romantic partnerships, some of which led to marriage. They also acknowledged that these primary relationships provided encouragement and motivation to adhere to their goals and make decisions that would benefit them in the long run.

We also learned that the process of cutting ties is not necessarily a fluid one, and much like the desistance journey itself, it can involve starts and stops while working to figure out the best balance for building a social support system. Oscar, for example, was another young man who initially decided to cut ties with his network of friends when he left his gang. When we first met him, he had been out of the system for a little over one year, and he remained in contact with just a few of his old friends who were also trying to "go straight." Oscar was open to making new friends, but he purposefully sought them out in alternative spaces. He dated a woman who lived in a part of town that was far removed from his old neighborhood. He also enrolled in community college in a different part of the city, where he specifically sought out friendships with people from diverse racial groups and life experiences, with whom he did not have to share his past. He viewed each of these steps as critical to his goal of abstaining from crime.

However, over the course of the next couple of years, Oscar gradually started to loosen his stance on his friendships. He had experienced such success in changing his life that he may have felt he no longer needed to live by the same set of stringent rules. An equally likely explanation, and one that we observed in the lives of many participants, was that despite their complicated pasts, these young people were experiencing the risk-taking and adventure that is typical of emerging adulthood. In most of our interviews, we noticed how juggling desistance along with survival needs did not eradicate their desire to simply have fun and be free from worry and fear. For those who weren't yet married, they were dating, socializing, and engaging in typical young adult activities: clubbing, movies, and going to the mall. Most received numerous texts and phone calls during our interviews, and a few brought their friends or significant others to our meetings to wait for them outside. Social activities and young adult spaces were clearly important to all of them. However, while the developmental stage of young adulthood manifested in these ways and many more, the desire to be a "normal" young adult—one who might be willing to take some risks—also carried the possibility of real life consequences. Because of their criminal histories, engaging in what might be assumed to be typical young adult behavior had the potential to disrupt their already tentative sense of stability.

We saw this process unfold when we met with Oscar about one year after his initial interview. During that time, he had remained determined to turn his life around and had the will and the supports to do so, including great support from his family, co-workers, and new friends. Oscar was dealing well with temporary setbacks: a failed relationship, his parents' potential separation, and even the prospect of eviction. These issues were disruptive and hard, but they did not necessarily compromise his mental resolve to take his life in a new direction. Yet still, his prior record and gang affiliation, along with living in a community that was over-policed, made Oscar susceptible to being arrested even without committing an actual crime.

One Saturday night, Oscar went to a party where people were drinking beer and listening to music. Yet this seemingly ordinary evening with friends ended at the police station because the house where the party was taking place had stashes of marijuana inside and guns for sale. And while he was just there to have fun and barely knew the hosts, he was arrested in a police raid. He described: "We were at a studio type thing. All of the walls were like this [pointing to wall]. Nothing too sophisticated. Then there was a hole in the wall that I didn't see where apparently all the marijuana was. I was being charged for fifty pounds of marijuana. Two gun possessions. Apparently, I was within twenty feet of five different guns." Simply for being at the wrong place at the wrong time, Oscar faced felony charges and had to serve a brief stint in county jail, and due to his record, he became a prime suspect in the crime. He described the hoops that he had to jump through in order to clear his name:

> Luckily with all my paperwork from school and all the proof that I had been working and that I don't have fucking time to be sitting there growing marijuana, I was able to prove that I had nothing to do with it and they had all the fingerprints. Everything came back negative. They only found my fingerprints on the beer. They said that if I had fought the case, that the DA was going to try to charge me with conspiracy because I was there. What was offered to me was

a class, where it was a guilty plea for having an ounce of marijuana and I take a deferred drug treatment class.

In the course of getting to know Oscar, we came to understand that working part-time, going to community college, and having the support of mentors and family members still did not shield him from the consequences of benign mistakes. This experience shook him to his core and even made him temporarily question his own identity as someone who was trying to do better with his life. He conveyed his emotions when he described the sobering experience of being admitted to adult jail:

> I was in shock for a whole week. When they gave me the bag [of jail clothing], I looked at it and was like wow. Like I'm really in these county blues [blue jumpsuit typical of LA County jail]? Like this is the conversation that I had . . . was so proud to say, like that I never had to wear county blues. I was like "man now I lost that right. I lost the right to say that I've never been to County Jail. That I've never been arrested as an adult and that's the part that hurts the most because well then it's like 'he was arrested as an adult.'" And that's forever going to be on my record. So that hurts. That really hurts because it puts me in this category that, I didn't really want to be in. It was already bad that I was arrested as a juvenile and a former this or former that. Like, that shit bothers me, that I'm a "former" this or "former" that, you know "ex-offender." Now that I've been in this adult system, it really strikes me in my heart.

In just one night, while just perhaps letting down his guard just a tad, a trip to jail made Oscar feel that he had shattered the positive lifestyle changes he'd worked so hard to achieve, and that he had let down numerous family members and mentors after years of trying to regain their trust. Oscar had clearly internalized the stigma of the "county blues" even though he had not committed an actual crime. The only positive outcome of the experience was that it made Oscar realize just how careful he had to be if he truly wanted to stay his course. In retrospect, he felt that he had been a bit careless with some of his decisions—going to parties, smoking weed, and failing to verify that there were no potential risks for him in a given social scene. It is important to remember that the average 21-year-old person does not have to make these types of decisions before going to a party, but for someone in Oscar's position, not thinking through these decisions ended up nearly jeopardizing his freedom. In the end, this experience grounded Oscar and strengthened his resolve to associate only with people who shared his desistance goals.

Oscar's resolve was tested once again just a few months later, when rival gang members murdered two of his extended family members. One was gunned down right in front of him, and this derailed him emotionally as they had shared a very close relationship and frequently encouraged each other to stay on the right track. To make matters worse, Oscar believed that he knew the identity of the killer, and for the first time since leaving his gang, he was tempted to retaliate. In the following excerpt, he describes what the next month of his life was like as he struggled internally with this decision:

OSCAR: It was a mixture of feeling inside of me. I wanted to seek revenge and I knew that I couldn't. I didn't want to be at home. I just wanted to be away from everyone. I wanted to cry. I wanted to go somewhere and cry without anyone seeing me because I knew that I was going to cry hard. I left the house and I was gone for two weeks. I had cried for two weeks straight.

LAURA: Where did you go?

OSCAR: I was at a park for about two weeks. I just sat there. I had money so I bought myself alcohol and was just drinking and drinking.

LAURA: Did you sleep in the park?

OSCAR: Yeah.

LAURA: You were really just letting yourself have it.

OSCAR: I was letting myself have it. Finally by the second week I got sick of all the alcohol. My stomach was swollen. I couldn't drink anymore. So then I slept for two days. I woke up and all of a sudden, I had this nightmare. I remember it very well. The nightmare was that these trees were chasing me. I would run and hide behind the houses and then the arms of the trees would come around and they would find me and then I'd run and I couldn't get away from the tree. For me I took it as, I'm not going to be able to solve my problems like this. I can't run away from my problems. I can't hide behind this bottle with my problems. I sat in that garage for two days and I wrote. I wrote and I wrote. I had a stack of papers this big of what I wrote. I just wrote everything that came to my mind—of everything that I ever saw, from everything I ever did, and how I felt about it. Then I read it all and that kind of brought me to peace. Then I was like "okay, I'm gonna stay here for another week and then I'm going to go home." During that week I felt that I was going to get stronger every day. The day before I decided to go home, I went to my cousin's grave. I napped there. I went into this sleep where you can still hear everything around you. I was laying there. All of sudden I could feel something was all over my arms and legs like my whole body was being squeezed but not tight. I could feel something was wrapped around me and I could feel a tiny bit of pressure. Then I woke up. That's when I knew that I was not going to do anything.

To us, this part of Oscar's story was one of the most chilling and vivid illustrations of the desistance obstacles that come from external pressures and circumstances, but end up manifesting in complicated internal battles. To feel something so powerful on the inside—the anger and rage of his cousin's murder—and yet not to act, showed incredible restraint. Even with these setbacks, we believe that Oscar is one of the young men who has and will continue to change his life in positive ways. He had maintained consistent employment, was working toward a college degree, and he remained committed to full desistance. However, as his narrative shows, even with all of these elements in place, the process of change is not straightforward, and is laden with emotional obstacles and setbacks, even for those who were the furthest along on the journey toward desistance. The circumstances that led to his arrest as an adult still served as a jarring reminder of how fragile his freedom could be. For, even when a person has taken careful steps to become a law-abiding citizen and establish a secure base for himself, one slip-up can potentially destroy everything he has worked to achieve.

Selective Involvement

Most of the young men in the study, including a few from Typology One, maintained a peer network comprised of a mixture of friends, including some who engaged in criminal activities and others who did not. This required them to make conscious decisions about how, when, and where they would interact with certain friends. This strategy allowed them to maintain their peer networks but scale back on their socializing during times when their friends might get them into some trouble. Ultimately, selective involvement helped most to abstain from criminal activity, but for some, it also led to some self-defeating choices. This strategy was particularly prevalent among young men in Typology Two, as we highlight in the narratives below.

Chris, who was a member of the Running in Circles group, is a good example of a young man who struggled with managing relationships with friends and family members. Chris was incarcerated four times as an adolescent beginning at age 15. He had sold drugs, made lots of money, robbed people, and gotten into numerous fights with the enemies of his local crew. By the time he served his final stint in a juvenile camp, he finally felt ready to change his life around. He could not pinpoint exactly what triggered this decision; he just felt that "something clicked" during this particular placement, causing him to become more focused and responsible than he had been in the past.

When Chris returned from camp, he was motivated to achieve his goals. With the help of a reentry program, he enrolled in a community college outside of Los Angeles, and he seemed poised to start a new life for himself. Unfortunately, Chris became easily distracted in his new school environment and found it difficult to develop the habits needed to support his newfound goals. He also felt very racially isolated as one of just 15 black students in his entire school. He provided details about what it was like being away from home with no real structure:

CHRIS: [I was] Partying, kicking it with females, smoking and drinking, getting in trouble. Doing stupid things on campus. Being bored out there in the middle of nowhere.

LAURA: Did you have any fun?

CHRIS: Fun? Yeah it was a lot of fun. Yeah that's the problem, it was too much fun.

LAURA: So do you feel like you weren't prepared to take college seriously at that time?

CHRIS: I wasn't. I probably thought I was. Or I probably didn't even think I was. I just wanted to get out of here. But like I said, I ain't never applied myself 100 percent really to anything, honestly. But especially to school. Ever.

While at the school, Chris eventually formed friendships with a few guys and they started stealing items from dorm rooms such as laptops, IDs, and wallets. He soon got caught, arrested, and sentenced to six months in the local county jail. After serving his time, he exited with no plan and no place to call home. He soon found support from a woman he had started dating just before his stint in jail. Within a few months of his release, the two got married and started a new life together. He found a job at a local fast food chain, and over the next few years he worked full-time at various restaurants in order to support his wife and the two children they had together. However, their situation took a turn for the worse when they moved back to Los Angeles to the community where Chris grew up. He and his wife had already had tension between them, mainly because of his infidelity, and these sour feelings moved with them. Shortly after their return, Chris's wife left him and moved back up to northern California, and he found himself divorced and without the family unit that had provided him with his primary sense of stability over the past few years.

Like many men of his age group with a criminal record, Chris struggled to maintain steady work in Los Angeles. By the time we met him, he had experienced significant bouts of unemployment over a two-year period. He tried to start various businesses to generate an income, such as a taxi service, but the earnings were inconsistent and did not allow him to live independently. As a result, he wrestled with the temptation to return to selling drugs:

LAURA: You haven't been in any trouble since the burglary charge, right? Have you been tempted to make money in ways that are easier than working?

CHRIS: Yeah. Yeah I've been tempted. But that's when I created this business. That's why I created the business. 'Cause I don't wanna do that. That's why it took me so long to come back out here in the first place. 'Cause I didn't wanna get caught up in the same things I was into when I was out here last. So I coulda came back out here. A lot of times, when I was up there in college—when I was homeless. I could have either went to Vegas with my cousin, or come back out here. But I didn't wanna do either one. So I stayed out there.

Moving forward, Chris had no clear plan for financially supporting himself and his two children. His main source of income at that time was his personal car taxi service, but he was forced to put the business on hold when he had to sell his car for cash. He had other business ideas in the works, but there were questions around the legitimacy of some of these ventures, such as his idea to start a female escort service. When we asked him about the possibility of returning to jail, he said that he was not completely confident that he would stay out, precisely because of the nature of some of his business plans.

Further complicating his situation was his feeling that he couldn't rely on anyone else in his life for financial support. He was extremely appreciative of his grandmother, who allowed him to live in her house after he and his wife divorced. However, when his grandmother received an unexpected eviction notice, none of his other relatives were able to offer him money or a place to stay, and he ended up having to move into a low-cost motel. He was disappointed that he could not count on his family to help him when he needed it the most. He said:

CHRIS: Don't nobody just look out. Just look out, look out.

DIANE: So when you realized you needed a place to stay, you didn't call your cousins?

CHRIS: Yeah I did. I put it to use. I said let me see if you know, see how it really is. And I asked everybody. And people promised things like "Oh yeah, I can do this if this happens," and then not follow through. And then say, "well I said I can do it." Things like that. Like my other brother, he helped me out in the past.

DIANE: What kinds of stuff has he done for you?

CHRIS: If I was short on my phone bill or something, he helped me out on my phone bill. He'll look out. But I just don't really depend on nobody. I don't really like calling on nobody. But when I needed rent I did call everybody. I called everybody and ain't nobody give me nothing but my grandmamma.

Despite these setbacks and the limited number of people he could count on for tangible support, Chris remained adamant about not wanting to return to jail. To stay out of trouble, he knew that he had to limit the amount of time he spent with friends and family members who could negatively influence him. He admitted that most of the guys he knew in the area continued to get into trouble with the law, which is why he kept a safe distance from them. Similar to Gabriel (from Typology One), Chris shared that he rarely socialized with anyone, preferring instead to stay home and away from potential trouble. However, later in the same interview he backtracked on this statement, suggesting that he did still have relationships with his network of family and friends despite their criminal ties: "'Cause I didn't cut everybody out of my life. They still, I'm still accessible to them. But it's limited. Because when we kick it, we cool. They know we close. But they just also know that I'm not that type to . . . that like a lot of company, that depend on you or have you depend on me. None of that." For all of these reasons, it was unclear to us how committed Chris was to desistance. Overall, he seemed to be straddling a fine line in terms of avoiding outright criminal activity, but relying on potentially illegal means when economically necessary. He mentioned that the conditions of the neighborhood posed numerous criminal temptations, yet he continued to stay put, mostly because he lacked any financial options to move. He was selectively involved with people and activities that helped him to survive, but that could in the blink of an eye also land him in the arms of the law.

Like Chris, Tyrone adopted a loose interpretation of what it meant to desist from crime, yet he had not experienced periods where he had cut crime out of his life altogether. Tyrone had committed petty crimes throughout his adolescent years to earn some cash while living on the streets. As he entered early adulthood, he realized that he wanted to establish some sort of stability in his life in terms of having consistent housing and employment, and he knew that having felonies on his record would hinder his ability to achieve his goals. While he expressed a desire to stop participating in criminal activity, he never fully committed himself to this idea, and instead he adopted the mind-set that he could avoid jail by engaging in smaller illegal acts such as selling drugs rather than committing more serious crimes.

Tyrone was different from the other Typology Two members in that he never experienced any significant life events or relationships that may have triggered a change in his thought processes or his behaviors. He continuously acknowledged in his interviews that he needed to change, but he did not quite know how to get there. As a result of his vague and undefined perception of what it meant to desist, Tyrone spent most of his late adolescent and early adult years drifting in and out of a criminal lifestyle with no real plan of how to establish a different life for himself. Similar to Chris, Tyrone perceived his family as unable to provide him with tangible forms of support. As a result of growing up in the child welfare system, he lacked the benefit of a close family that many other participants relied on for help with their post-incarceration needs. He had tried to build relationships with his biological siblings over the years, but they were limited in the amount of help they could offer him due to their own financial and other life struggles. Tyrone described the nature of support he received from his family:

DIANE: So are there people in your life who you feel like you can call if you had a problem and you just needed someone to talk to?

TYRONE: Yep. I'll call my sister, or I'll call my brother, or I could call my other brother.

DIANE: And what would they do? You call them and?

TYRONE: I think we'll just talk. I just do things by myself. I'm telling you. 'Cause they have no way to get over here. I just have myself right now. I need to only worry about myself, 'cause I'm gonna be the one on the bus. I'm gonna be the only one handling my business. I'm gonna be the only one—I need to do me. So I love everybody from a distance.

He further explained that even though he knew he could call upon his siblings if he had a major problem, he rarely did so because he did not want to burden them with bad news. For this reason, he chose to contact them only when he had positive life updates to share. Sadly, he still identified his biological family members as the most supportive and central to his life, even though his narrative conveyed a sense of distance and cautiousness in his relationships with them.

Tyrone also used selective involvement with his friendships, but he was different from many of the other men in that his dependence on his friends was due to a pressing need for survival more than a desire for friendship. Throughout his interviews, he referenced having an extensive informal support network in his life consisting of people from the past who would invite him to sleep on their couches or help him find ways to make quick money. Although he did not provide a great deal of detail about these individuals, it was clear that they did not positively influence his desistance journey. He explained that over the years, these people had involved him in drug dealing, gangs, and even pimping at one point. He was reluctant to describe these people as friends or to identify them as part of his support network, despite the fact that they had played a critical role in his survival over the years. Both Chris and Tyrone thus similarly struggled over how exactly to cut negative influences from their lives, when these same influences could potentially help them to stay afloat financially. This dilemma sheds light on why both held onto the belief that they were in their own way taking steps toward desistance; they perceived themselves as making the best of a bad situation while at the same time still trying to maintain some hope for the future.

CONCLUSION

In this chapter, we described a set of everyday circumstances that the young men navigated related to decisions around criminal activity and desistance. We attempted to paint a detailed picture of the overwhelming set of challenges that they faced despite even their best intentions to forge their lives in a positive, crime-free direction. The young men in Typology One had experienced the most success in moving toward complete desistance. They had stayed out of trouble for the longest periods of time and they had also taken intentional steps over the years to ensure that key aspects of their lives and identities matched their desistance goals. Additionally, most had found external support from people and places that further facilitated their movement away from crime. What we learned, however, was that none of these elements completely shielded the "On the Road" participants from facing obstacles or from the lingering remnants of their pasts. In other words, wanting to change and working really hard to do so did not ensure a smooth and worry-free desistance journey.

Participants from Typologies Two and Three also professed some degree of desire to be free from crime, yet they struggled to define and enact their goals. Their stories were interesting in that most perceived themselves as making progress toward desistance; a crime-free life

represented a milestone that they could see themselves attaining one day
in the future. However, the fact that they defined desistance as a cutting back or gradual cessation of crime led to repeated stumbling blocks
in their journeys. Specifically, we saw that, compared to Typology One,
they made very different sets of decisions when confronted with dilem-
mas related to their appearance and negative influences, which further
hindered their desistance progress. However, we are hesitant to consider
these young men chronic offenders, as this label fails to capture the ways
they felt motivated to change their lives, and some of the steps they had
taken to enact their goals. Some of the missteps they made along the way
are no different in some ways than what the young men in Typology One
also made before finally "getting it right."

These narratives also illustrated how the daily challenges related to
desistance vary depending on one's background and present needs. It
was clear that the young men who had been involved with gangs (from
Typologies One and Three) faced a particular set of desistance challenges
related to their appearance, families, and peer networks. Meanwhile, the
young men in Typology Two were running in circles largely because of
their inability to find and sustain stable housing or work. The young men
in each typology had to have some willingness and determination to
overcome the obstacles in their path, but the type of resources needed to
support their efforts were not necessarily the same.

Regardless of typology, all of the men were figuring out how to deal
with their interpersonal relationships with friends, romantic relationships, and family members. There was not one cut and dry approach to
dealing with this set of relational challenges. Cutting ties clearly helped
keep these young men out of trouble, but it resulted in a great deal of
loneliness, and was not necessarily a realistic or sustainable decision for
all. On the flip side, cutting ties afforded these young men an opportunity
to re-establish their lives with new friends and surroundings. As Oscar
explained, his new friends at community college "knew nothing about
my past or me being part of a gang" and he felt no need to disclose that
information to them. In this sense, these young men, while experiencing
loss of community, were also able to cautiously test out new social settings and identities that conformed more to their internal views of their
changing selves.

The majority of the young men across all three typologies chose not to cut ties, and instead employed the strategy of selective involvement. This approach was most successful for participants who had made a clear decision to desist from crime for two important reasons. First, they were very clear about the types of people they needed in their lives to help them succeed; so while they may have had some friends around them who were not committed to desistance, they were careful not to allow their negative actions to influence them. Second, most of these young men shared a perception of adulthood that included being responsible, which meant earning a legal income and establishing some foundation for their future. This perception encouraged them to build lifestyles and friendships that were consistent with this vision. However, selective involvement was a much riskier strategy for participants from Typologies Two and Three when certain friendships represented a constant temptation for them to be involved in illegal activities. In the next chapter, we further examine how these strategies played out in the young men's lives with regard to their interactions with former allies and enemies as well as the police.

CHAPTER 6

You Can Run but You Can't Hide

We are all marked. Forever. All of us. No matter how
much the transformation.

—Oscar

THE ROAD TO DESISTANCE does not necessarily lead to
a complete sense of freedom. From prior enemies and friends to the
police, the young men in this study were challenged to contend with the
markings of their histories. This chapter delves into the various layers of
meaning associated with Oscar's profound statement noted above. One
of the most important lessons that these young men taught us was that
no matter how much internal or external change they had achieved, they
could not fully discard the sense of being marked. From the young men's
worldview, being marked was partially related to the stigma stemming
from appearance, age, and race, but was also tied to navigating the urban
environments of Los Angeles as former gang members, drug dealers, and
those who law enforcement viewed as criminals.

ORDINARY FEAR

As we presented in chapter 2, Los Angeles has a host of troublesome
problems with policing and racial profiling, particularly in geographical
spaces that are notorious for gangs and gun violence. These risks are concentrated in poorer areas with high densities of African American and Latino
populations (Advancement Project, 2011), the neighborhoods where most of
the young people in our study were raised and often still resided. Figure 6.1
illustrates where the young people resided at the time of their first interview
in relation to county poverty rates. One can see that several were clustered
in the South Los Angeles area, and all but a few resided in areas with poverty
rates that exceeded 25 percent of the total population.

All participants, including the women (who we will discuss in chapter 7), were acutely aware of the risks associated with simply traversing
their own neighborhoods by foot, bus, or car, even in broad daylight.

Several young men had survived being shot or stabbed—some multiple times—and nearly all had witnessed friends, neighbors, and/or family members who had been severely injured or murdered by rival gangs or enemies. These experiences heightened their everyday fears about their own safety as well as the safety of their loved ones. Gabriel, who had made great strides to fully change his criminal trajectory, was one of the young men who had survived multiple incidents of violent victimization. His narrative provides deep insight into living through the trauma and aftermath of fearing for one's life.

I always woke up with a feeling like I was gonna get killed that day. I used to have so many nightmares where in my dreams I was dead. I used to dream about it all the time. Yeah I used to have nightmares about it. About getting killed. There's one specific nightmare that I had all the time. Me being outside my house and I was outside my front porch smoking a cigarette, and a white car passed by and started shooting. And I remember I turned around to grab something and as I turned around they shot me. I remember me laying down on the floor, and all my family standing around me. It was one of the worst nightmares. And it seemed so real.

So when I actually did get shot, I thought I was gonna die. I remember we were at a fair. And I remember that I was armed. I wasn't trying to go but my friends kept pushing me, so I ended up going. But in order for me to feel safe, I grabbed a gun and I was carrying it with me. And I ran into one of my ex-girlfriends, and we were talking, and when she hugged me she felt the gun. So between her and my best friend, they took it away from me. They told me that I was crazy, that I was just delusional, that nothing was going to happen to me. So I let them take it from me. They put it in the car. At the end of the night, all of a sudden, some of my friends started getting into an altercation. I didn't pay much attention because I was still with my ex-girlfriend. And so then I'm over here talking to her, and all of a sudden she tells me, "turn around, turn around." And as I turned around I heard a gunshot. And I felt a sharp . . . I don't even know what it was. I don't even know how to describe it. It was like as if they had put a firework in my back and just slit it. It was just bad. And as I felt it, I'm like wow, I got hit, I got hit. And as I turned

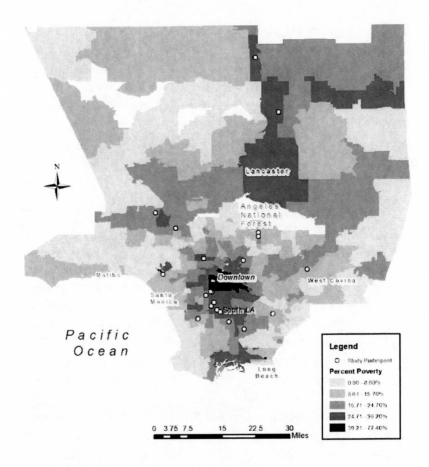

FIGURE 6.1. Participants' Residences at Time of First Interview by Poverty Rates. Map created by Christina Tam. *Data Source*: US Census, American Community Survey, 2013

around this dude was still shooting at me. So he must have shot about two, three times. I remember all of my surroundings. And I could see this guy shooting at me. And out of all the shots, he only hit me once. And I remember that I turned around and looked at him, and he turned around and started running. And I remember that I even checked my waistband to see if I had my gun with me. But I think if I would have had my gun, I'd still probably be sitting in jail. 'Cause I think I would have killed him. I think I would have.

I turned heartless after that. I lost it after I got shot. Like that's when I was real paranoid, and wherever I went I took a gun with me, thinking that something was going to happen. I used to sleep with a gun under my pillow. I had an automatic pistol under my pillow, and I had a shotgun at my door just in case anything happened. And it was like that for a while. I remember that I'm sitting in a hospital room and they're doing CAT scans on me, and they have me stripped down completely. And the doctor is trying to figure out why I'm not bleeding. 'Cause I wasn't bleeding. He was trying to figure out where the bullet came in from. They finally found the bullet hole . . . They said that if it would have been just a little bit more to the side, I would have probably ended up paralyzed. So I'm sitting in the room and I'm in so much pain. And all of a sudden through the emergency doors I see my mom run through the room. And she runs to me and I remember that she looked at me, and she said, and her exact words, she said: "Pendejo [Stupid], look what they did to you. Stupid! Look what they did to you! Look where you are! I told you. I told you." And she turned around and she just slapped me. And right after she slapped me, she gave me a hug and started crying. That's something hard you know? When she said, "that's what you want? That's what you want is that one day I receive a call from the detectives saying you're dead? You're laying on the pavement and to go pick your body up? Is that what you really want?" And I didn't answer. I put my head down and a couple tears came down my face and that was it. That was it. But I was just . . . I was just so caught up. I was just so ignorant at that time. I was just so ignorant.

With raw honesty and emotion, Gabriel was able to articulate exactly what he felt living in constant danger, taking a random bullet in his body, and nearly losing his life, as well as the long-lasting imprint of those moments on his psyche. This experience, and his mother's emotional response to his near fatal condition, could have propelled him to change his life and get out of the game. Yet, as he so poignantly reflected, nearly losing his life actually made him a bit more "heartless." At that crossroads, Gabriel became even more ensconced in his gang and prone to carry a weapon for protection, even sleeping with a gun under his pillow. While in retrospect he chalked up his response to this event as "ignorance," his story also illustrates how the trauma of being victimized by violence can make one feel paranoid, vengeful, and numb to emotion and empathy.

Now 25 years old and looking back on his former self, a high-ranking drug dealer and someone capable of murder, Gabriel was extremely committed to complete desistance. He was married, was holding down a well-paying job and was far removed from his past life. To facilitate his desistance process, he routinely avoided any potential trouble from his former enemies as well as former friends. Although not all of the young men in this study were on the same road to desistance as Gabriel, they nevertheless employed a variety of strategies for handling threats to their personal safety. Within the narratives, we found three primary strategies that the young men used for contending with daily risks: (1) *avoiding dangers*, meaning that they assessed what activities, routes, and people they could engage with in order to avoid most aspects of trouble, yet still made some selective decisions about their risks; (2) *running and hiding*, a strategy that was the most successful in avoiding all situations amounting to trouble; and (3) *calculated risk-taking*, which meant making conscious and rational decisions to involve oneself in troublesome situations when deemed important for survival or to maintain respect from peers or family members. As we shall discuss further, these strategies also loosely corresponded to desistance groupings, as those who were "On the Road to Desistance" and who were "Running in Circles" tended to use the strategies of "avoiding" or "running and hiding." On the other end of the spectrum, the young men who were "Still in the Game" tended to rely mainly on calculated risk-taking to skirt the possible dangers associated with their illegal activities.

AVOIDING DANGERS

From a young age, all of the men were accustomed to anticipating and adapting to the dangers of their neighborhoods, schools, and local hangouts. Several talked about growing up hearing the nightly sounds of the "ghetto birds" (meaning police helicopters) hovering over them. Or, like Gabriel, they recounted memories of being shot, stabbed, or subject to community violence, as both victims and perpetrators—emotional traumas that they carried with them through nightmares and paranoia. All of these experiences influenced the way they handled themselves as adults, using strategies to navigate potential risks of violent victimization and potential trouble with the law.

Greg, the one white participant in the study, lived in a densely populated housing project area controlled by a Mexican gang. He felt that he stood out because of his race, and based on his outlier status, was noticed and targeted by his neighbors from the day he stepped foot in the projects. The first week he moved into his apartment he had to hide in his closet due to a massive shootout between rival gangs. He recalled:

GREG: When I first moved in to this apartment over here, I was at work and my roommate about noon he gives me a phone call. It was the third day we lived here and he was like panicking like crying. . . . He's like, I don't know what to do man. Go in your closet and lay down for a little bit you know? I'm like this is not good. We just moved here. There's already people getting killed? Later that day when I got home from work he's like yeah man one officer got shot, two of the gang members got killed.

LAURA: Is there anything you do in your immediate neighborhood to hang out?

GREG: Seriously no. I hate this place. We've been trying to get out of here for like three years.

LAURA: What don't you like about it?

GREG: Like it's 3:30 now. If you were to stay for another four or five hours, it gets infested with gang members everywhere. Drug dealers, gang members, there's cops all the time. There are helicopters all the time, at least two times a night.

Greg repeatedly stressed that he would like to move to a safer neighborhood. Yet without the financial means to do so, he instead developed various strategies to preserve his personal safety. He recounted in detail how he comes and goes from the car to his apartment, protecting himself from potential crossfire or more direct targeting of him as an individual:

I usually have to park like back here or like right here [pointing to map]. And I'd come home and it'd be like 9:20, 10 at night. I'd always have my skateboard in my car, and I'd always have my Dodger bat. I'd put on a hoodie or something and I'd skate up to where I needed to be which was home. And I always thought a skateboard would be faster. It sucked. I used to hate parking my truck. 'Cause there's no parking on the street ever. . . . So I always had to pull back here which is like a mile away and then trek up this way. Once I hit like, 'cause there's an apartment right here, and there's a dude at ten every night, there's a dude from 10 to 5 in the morning and he just stands there and sells crack out of his gate all night. So I would always like, skate up this street and then hang into here and come back out this way and go down, just to get off the street.

As Greg discusses how he wears a hoodie, takes various back routes to his apartment, uses a skateboard, and avoids certain people and times of the day, these strategies were all carefully planned to avoid the pitfalls of potential community violence. Since he had a history of drug use and selling, he also felt that his neighborhood potentially compromised the small steps that he was taking toward desistance.

All of the young men had developed a set of conscious and unconscious strategies to navigate their personal safety, which they detailed on maps that reflected their daily movement in their neighborhoods and surrounding communities. Some went out of their way to shop for groceries or clothes at locations far from their homes or former gang territories; others made sure that they were never alone at a bus stop, or didn't go out of the house after a certain time of night. Laying out these strategies on actual maps, we were amazed at just how far the young men had to travel, sometimes without the luxury of a car, to navigate their way around potential safety hazards or hotspots of criminal activity.

For example, Steven resided in a relatively safer neighborhood than Greg's housing projects and was more firmly situated on the road to desistance. He had a full-time job and a daughter to care for, and as we profiled in chapter 4, was one of the young men who was financially making ends meet. Yet despite these gains, he spoke in depth about being on alert at all times. The following interview excerpt illustrates his tactics for avoiding dangers:

DIANE: So do you feel pretty safe in this neighborhood you live in?

STEVEN: Depending on the time. Say if it's like past 10, 11, 12, I won't be in the streets. Unless I'm driving. But walking, hell no. Why? Because there's just guys that's "where you from?" and just wanna hit you up.

DIANE: Are there a lot of gangs by where you live?

STEVEN: Yes. Well basically hell yeah there's a lot of gangs.

DIANE: Where would you say they are?

STEVEN: Oh all over. All over. 'Cause this area has at least six or seven cliques.

DIANE: So is that a pressure for you?

STEVEN: No. Because that's why I dress different. I try not to cause attention. I don't socialize with those or hang around with those. So that's why my networking is more about being business. Or recreation. Like we're gonna kick it, do something chill. Not like "let's go pick up drugs or pick up somebody." It's more about, like I said if it benefits me, I'm cool.

DIANE: Well it kind of helps that you have a car. You can avoid whatever drama is around you.

STEVEN: Yeah before, remember when I said I used to live down the street? I used to walk. I used to hate it. 'Cause people wanna walk around with their muscle type shirt and they just bother me. I'd be walking and they'd be like "hey" tryin' to say stupid shit or throw stuff at me. Hell yeah it helps having a car.

DIANE: So if you had to say any particular streets by you, are there any particular streets you would try to avoid?

STEVEN: Yeah, this one. King Street. That's gang. King Street and then Berry. That's all gang territory. [Note that the names of streets here were changed to protect confidentiality.]

Although Steven had no prior gang involvement, he was acutely aware of the cliques, gangs, and unsafe areas surrounding him. He was very cautious about where he traveled, what time he drove along certain routes, and where the hazard zones might lie. In avoiding dangers, Steven is also clearly using very specific strategies related to desistance in that he says he is "dressing differently" and "not causing attention."

Those young men who were "Still in the Game" also had some fear of bumping up against potential enemies, but they expressed more bravado than fear when talking about their personal safety. Anthony, who still associated with gang members in his neighborhood, was aware of dangers surrounding him, but claimed he was not afraid to walk anywhere. Unlike accounts from Greg and Steven, Anthony stated that he regularly made use of public transportation and freely traversed through his own neighborhood and what he identified as rival areas. He reported having friends that were scattered in different locations, which made him able to travel more freely. He knew that risks of harm and gunfire were always present; and not having pledged himself fully to a gang, he was an open target. However, he expressed a sense of resolve that this was just his way of life, and that the conditions surrounding him were unlikely to change. He stated, "It's the same everywhere. You have enemies, you have to watch yourself. Just because you aren't in a gang doesn't mean you can't get banged on: dying is a chance you take by living . . . you have to die from something." What we might identify here as a fatalistic outlook on life was also Anthony's lived reality; he had seen many of his friends fall to violence and he was willing to take his own chances.

Like Anthony, Jerry frequented his old stomping grounds and neighborhood and had not removed himself from the possibility of putting himself in danger. Yet in Jerry's case, he was protected from harm by virtue of his gang allegiance. After turning 18, Jerry had moved out of his old neighborhood in order to try and settle down with his girlfriend and children, yet he was still involved in illegal activities, including selling drugs. So to conduct his business, he still traversed his old 'hood on a near-daily basis. Here is how he described his sense of safety:

LAURA: Tell me about this neighborhood now. Is it still unsafe?

JERRY: It's calm. It's calmer. But it picks up and dies down.

LAURA: Do you consider it a place that you like to be?

JERRY: Hell nah. I like to get in here and then leave. You have to watch your back.

LAURA: From the police or people?

JERRY: From everybody. Police. People that recognize me from the streets, that know me.

LAURA: So would you say that even though you're protected here, it's still not safe?

JERRY: Nah, they'll come in here.

LAURA: It's still not safe for you.

JERRY: I feel safe, yeah. But they'll look—oh, there they go. They know where to find me and they'll come here to find me.

LAURA: So who's your biggest threat?

JERRY: I don't know. I'm not worried about no one. We're the kings. We're on top. We're on top of the game.

It was interesting that Jerry began the conversation by talking about feeling unsafe in his old stomping grounds due to rivals and the police. He also clearly relayed the sense of being marked, as he was aware that people would always recognize him, both the police and his enemies. Yet he still ended the conversation by claiming that he has little to fear due to his position of power—as the "kings." By still being involved in his gang, he was protected in a way that others, like Anthony and Steven, were not.

RUNNING AND HIDING

The young men who had extensive gang histories faced very real and serious risks of violence from former or current enemies. Yet for those who had left their gangs behind, they carried the additional burden of living in fear of their estranged gang friends. One journalist has described the process of leaving a gang as follows: "Getting out of a street gang in LA is about like getting a tattoo removed: slow, painful, scarring" (Smalley, 2009). The young men in our study had mixed views about this idea. Some concurred with this assessment, claiming that you never really "leave" a gang, but you can become inactive after you have served your time. Others disagreed with this notion, arguing that you can leave or deescalate your involvement at any point. Still another set more actively dissociated themselves fully from the gang by cutting ties altogether; yet knowing still that by leaving, they could become the next target. To make matters worse, by leaving the gang, these young men were also not afforded any protection from their former enemies. We had no way to verify the young men's claims, including the extent of their prior involvement in their gang, the potential dangers (or lack thereof) associated with leaving their gangs, and differences in leaving gangs across neighborhood and racial lines. Thus we took each participant at his word about feelings of safety and risk regarding this topic. For those who shared their grave concerns about being targeted, we asked them to paint a picture of the dangers they faced in their day-to-day lives.

When Oscar was released from probation camp, he knew that his gang had turned against him by framing him for a crime, so he was not able to rely on them for any further protection. As such, he had to live with the threat of a "green light" on him by his previous enemies, meaning that they had the go-ahead to kill him if discovered. He said: "I guess they say you can run but you can't hide. That's the saying. I live with— this is the big fear of mine. I can change my name, but I can't change my face." To contend with the green light, Oscar had taken several steps to conceal his whereabouts, particularly when he had initially taken residence in his old neighborhood following his release.

LAURA: But that green light follows you in the streets?

OSCAR: Everywhere I go.

LAURA: Do you feel like people are watching you or no?

OSCAR: The good thing is that I moved away from my old house. That takes a lot of the pressure off. Because now I am in a different area. So if they were looking for me, they're looking for me in the wrong places. My mother changed location also. So even if they did find out where I lived before, they would still be in the wrong area.

LAURA: You have unlisted numbers?

OSCAR: The number I have is not under my name.

When we first met Oscar, he had been out of camp for more than a year, working hard to reestablish his life, maintain his safety, and still reside in his neighborhood with his family. The green light and lack of protection haunted him daily, causing fear, stress, nightmares, and paranoia. As we got to know Oscar over time and he became more integrated into his newer life, the intensity of these feelings gradually dissipated. However, as he reflected back on his experience during our final interview, Oscar admitted he had to go through a certain amount of negotiation with his former gang in order to remain safely housed in his neighborhood. After about five years post-juvie, he eventually felt free—although not 100 percent—from the target on his back.

When we met Gabriel, he was a few years further removed from his gang than Oscar. Yet because of economic constraints, he still lived and worked near his former gang territory, and due to this proximity was still vulnerable to his enemies. With his prior experiences of being nearly shot dead at the county fair and living in the throes of gang warfare, Gabriel was still concerned about his safety. Using a blend of strategies, including avoiding as well as running and hiding, he was conscious of his daily travels by car or by foot. He avoided driving down what he called the smaller residential streets and instead stuck to the main roads. He also explained that he always did his shopping and socializing in areas that were far from his current residence. Putting this much thought into his daily travels and activities was stressful for Gabriel and his wife Carolina, as he explained: "There are still places that I can't walk. There are still places that I can't pass through. There are still people that I avoid even though I have changed my life. And my wife she turns around and she looks at me like, 'But you're not in it no more.' Just because I'm not in it and I'm not a part of it, doesn't mean that they still don't like me." Although Gabriel did not believe that any of his old enemies were actively seeking him out, he recounted instances where friends of his had left their gangs and were later murdered because they had not moved away. Thus, to keep himself and Carolina safe from potential harm, he took these precautions in his everyday life. When we asked about how he copes with this daily stress, his response was also quite chilling, because even someone as committed to a full life transformation as Gabriel was did not experience the comfort of feeling free from violence. He said: "I'm used to it. And sometimes my wife tells me, oh, 'cause the other day there's a new restaurant around my old neighborhood. And she's like, 'oh baby we should go there.' And I'm like 'no.' She's like, 'well you see if you would have never got in so much trouble, we'd be able to go everywhere. But you can't go anywhere.' And I just didn't know what to tell her. I wish I could say everything is fine. *But it's not.*" [Emphasis ours.]

Akin to Gabriel's avoidance of certain public places, John also had to run and hide because he literally feared for his life if discovered. When John was released from probation camp, he found himself at a serious crossroads between his life with the gang and the woman he had always loved. He realized that he couldn't have both. Ultimately, he decided to leave his gang; quite simply, he wanted to be with Raquel more than he wanted to be with his gang. Still living in his old territory due to logistical necessity, John spent the next year hiding out from enemies and from members of his own gang who he believed would try to attack or kill him because of his decision to defect. This was a dangerous and complicated move, especially because the only place he had to live upon his immediate return home from camp was his family's apartment right in his neighborhood. To avoid running into people, he rarely left his house in daylight hours and stopped returning calls and visits from his friends. He explained:

> There were points in time where I would stay at my mother-in-law's house, and they would be like, knockin' on the window, whistling and calling Raquel out. Asking her like "oh where's John at?" And she would have to lie and be like "oh I broke up with him a long time ago. I don't know what happened to him. We just broke up. . . ." So they would show up and ask for me during that month and a half . . . And I would like stand on the stairs and like put my ear to the window, and I would be able to hear them talking in the alley. And it was just so fucking strange, cause these people are the people that were like having my back and I was willing to die for them and shit. And now they're in my alley looking for me.

John was still filled with fear of his former friends even two years after he left the gang, feeling that he had to continue to conceal both his identity and location for the foreseeable future. He regularly checked the online county inmate locator as well as social media sites to monitor which of his old gang members were incarcerated, released, or deceased. He changed his name on social media, his phone number, and public listings. He was constantly on alert to protect himself and his family.

Eventually John took additional steps toward starting a new life, including moving out of the state for a period of time and marrying Raquel. At a certain point, they moved back to their old neighborhood, hoping that time and distance would protect them from harm. Yet even with that time and space, John soon found that trouble could find him at any point, such as the time he was spotted by one of his old gang associates one day while working at a retail store. In the following story, he detailed this chance encounter:

> It was like the day before Christmas, and I was standing at the front of the store right there by the door. Luckily, and usually it's only one person up there, but luckily it was busy . . . And I always like to make sure I'm looking out, just to see who's coming in, just because I'm real nervous about that in public places. I like to know everything

that's going on around me. And I noticed that they were already walking in. There are two sets of doors, and then there's like a little foyer kind of thing, and then there's another door. They were already in the first door. It was a guy named Kiki and his girlfriend. And I had looked to my right and I seen him and I was like, "oh fuck!" And I don't think he saw me at first, but I totally made it awkward because I turned my back completely and was facing this way, while he was talking to the other guy. And so my back was to him the whole time and I was like just trying to keep my face away from him. And I was able to hear them talking, so was able to hear when they started walking this way. So each time he took a step, I would start turning myself like this so he couldn't see me.

Eventually as soon as he got over to customer service, I told the guy next to me, "dude that's one of the people from my old gang. I gotta run. I gotta get out of here or something." And I started running to the back of the store, and I looked over. And as soon as I looked over, he was staring at me the whole time. So I was like "fuck!" And so I ran over to like the video game section. I was just hiding there, thinking that he wouldn't try and look for me. But then I like walked out in the aisle and I looked over, and he was walking toward the video games. And he had seen me and he went like this, he like waved me over! So I ran into the warehouse and I hid in the warehouse and then that was when my manager first found out about me being an ex-gang member. And he just told me not to worry about it. He's gonna make sure they get out of here. They got 'em out of there pretty quick. They didn't kick him out or anything. They just put a rush on their service to get him out of there. But since then he came back twice. The second time he came back, I was on lunch and I was able to see him coming in his car. So I called my job and I was like, I can't really come back in. I know I'm on lunch but I can't go back in there. And then the third time he came back I wasn't there. I was supposed to be there that night but I traded shifts. And so I got lucky again.

He was one of the hot heads. So he would have definitely swung at me. It would have been physical. But I don't think he necessarily would have tried to kill me in the store. Yeah. The only thing I'm nervous about is just when I leave after work, especially at night, is just making sure what cars are around in the parking lot. Just kind of making sure, keeping an eye on the rearview and the side view, just making sure that nobody's following me or anything. 'Cause then it would be like ten times worse if they knew where I lived.

This encounter, which he described in vivid detail, made John even more hyper-vigilant about his surroundings. From that point forward, he explained, "it's always in the back of my mind." He was mindful of not being alone in public spaces such as bus stops and parking lots, and he regularly scanned his environment for people who might recognize him. He checked his rearview mirrors constantly to make sure that no one was following him home. John had not been able to shake the markings of his past; running and hiding were the only way that he could protect himself, his wife, and later his son (born during the study) for the foreseeable future.

In chapter 5, we emphasized how wanting to change, and even taking necessary steps to enact change, does not preclude one from continuing to experience desistance-related challenges in many settings. The accounts provided in this section, of living in a state of fear of being targeted by former friends and enemies, highlight some of the very real challenges of survival that can ensue, even after one has made the decision to get completely out of the game. Public opinion may hold that individuals should move away from people and places that will become a hindrance to attaining a crime-free lifestyle. However, not everyone has the option to simply pick up and relocate, and they may not want to separate themselves from the surroundings where their families and friends reside. These narratives thus also shed light on the emotional costs associated with running and hiding from one's past life.

The Perils of the Police

The police were an ongoing source of risk and fear for these young men. Many felt marked by the police due to their appearance, race or ethnicity, tattoos, criminal records, or past gang ties. As sociologist Alice Goffman (2014) described in her ethnographic book *On the Run: Fugitive Life in the Inner City*, marginalized young men of color in urban spaces develop a range of strategies for avoiding police contact, particularly when they have a criminal record, warrants, or are on probation. This held true for the young men in our study as well.

The "Still in the Game" and "Running in Circles" participants spoke at length about the harassment they encountered from local law enforcement because they were known gang members. As they remained connected with their gangs to varying degrees, they had devised specific strategies to avoid police contact and detection altogether. For example, Carlos explained how evading the constant scrutiny of the police in his neighborhood comprised a large portion of his daily routine, thoughts, and actions. When we first met Carlos, he was on adult probation and also had a gang injunction imposed on him by the courts. The gang injunction increased the daily risk of being arrested for simply being on the wrong side of the street or with any members of his gang, or with other men who looked suspicious to the police. When Carlos wanted to get together with his friends, he had to make calculated decisions about which streets he would walk or drive on because being seen with his friends was a direct violation of his probation. He was very aware of the potential for him to be picked up for a probation violation, and as a result, evading the constant scrutiny of the police in his neighborhood occupied a large part of his everyday routine. He preferred not to walk around his neighborhood at all, as "it feels stupid to walk 'cause I'm putting myself in the position to get shot at or pulled over by the cops, or anything could go wrong."

Carlos also felt that he had to be very careful about not spending too much time at any particular location, so as to avoid police who might be looking for him and to lower his risk of being involved in a police raid of a given home. He provided details about the strategies he used to still be able to associate with his friends despite the gang injunction that made his hanging out with them a crime:

CARLOS: I'm allowed to be in my neighborhood, but I can't be around none of my homies.

LAURA: So even if you're caught with one person then . . .

CARLOS: They can send me back. That's a violation.

DIANE: But you could be at the store or something, like if you were by yourself?

CARLOS: That's fine. That would be fine.

LAURA: But like if I was one of your homies?

CARLOS: If you were one of my homies I'd tell you to walk across the
street and walk on that side ahead of me while I'm on this side . . . I
just tell them, if they pull me over, you just get out of here and run
if you have to. 'Cause I'm not trying to get busted you know? That's
what I would tell them.

LAURA: So how do you negotiate hanging out with your friends?

CARLOS: If I were to do it, I'd rather do it in a place, like a house or something. And it wouldn't be for long though. Like an hour or so, and
then I'd take off to the next spot. You don't want to be somewhere
too long, you know?

Still protected by his gang, Carlos feared the police far more than he
did his enemies. As such, when he and his friends did get together, por-
tions of their daily conversations were spent discussing the activities of
the local gang unit and which sheriffs had been seen in their neighborhood. He explained:

My only focus and I believe like, all my homies like we don't really
trip on the enemies. Like we talk about them a lot, you know on certain days like when we have our carnival and stuff, we know they're
gonna come through . . . But on a regular day, who cares about
everybody else or them. It's just like one of the sheriffs who's gonna
come and raid us. "Where are the sheriffs?" "You saw the gang unit
pass by?" That's the talk of us. As soon as, like if I'm walking and I see
the gang unit, I go the other way. Go to my friend's pad, "Hey the
gang unit's around. You saw the gang unit?" "The gang unit's around.
The gang unit's around. The gang unit's around."

Although his experience of being marked caused Carlos a great deal
of stress, his keen sensitivity to the whereabouts of the gang unit also
helped him to avoid trouble with the law. In this sense, his navigation
skills enabled him to avert some of the many possibilities of his re-arrest,
a scenario that might cost him seven years behind bars due to the terms
of his probation.

Peter's story also illustrates how young men who were still involved
in gangs handled the looming threat of police surveillance. He was still
actively associated with his gang when we met him, but he explained that

he had recently toned down his activities in order to avoid serving more jail time. Yet still, Peter admitted that he committed crimes on occasion to make money such as stealing and then selling car parts. In fact, the same week we met him, he was facing criminal charges for two separate offenses.

Peter was quite vocal in his complaints about the police harassment he had experienced. Although he no longer lived in his territory, he visited often and was aware of ongoing police surveillance. In his view, their presence contributed to recidivism for himself and his friends in that any contact with the police usually resulted in some type of probation violation for a petty cause, such as an expired license plate tag or a broken taillight. Peter had thought hard about how to contend with this problem. To start, though he visited often, he made sure to limit the amount of time he spent in his old neighborhood on any given day. He also explained that living outside of his gang territory enabled him to scale back his activities and behaviors when he wanted to avoid the police, or when he was simply more serious about wanting to stay out of trouble. In his words, this allowed him to "not be on the streets too much, stay indoors as much as possible, not put myself out there." In this way, Peter experienced a certain level of freedom in choosing when to be involved with his gang and when to run and hide.

By contrast, Carlos lived in much closer proximity to his gang territory, so separating himself required more complex and deliberate solutions for avoiding the police gang unit. Peter's ability to limit contact with his territory presented a key difference between these two young men who were equally struggling daily with their desistance goals and criminal temptations. It also sheds light on the difficulties that can arise when a person may have some inkling toward desistance, yet is constrained by his or her proximal environment.

Cesar offered a different opinion about the police, one that stood in contrast to those of most of the other young men in the study. Cesar was in many ways embodying multiple dimensions of the desistance journey. He had taken steps to move away from Los Angeles and go to college, but was not comfortable in that environment, so he moved back home. He was also very involved in community service activities. Yet, despite his newfound work and persona, he had not fully separated himself from his gang. He was proud of his neighborhood and saw no reason to leave it all behind. Cesar made it clear that he was no longer actively involved in the gang or violence on a day-to-day basis, and instead enjoyed his position as someone who had put in enough work over the years and could now serve as a positive role model for the younger guys. He said that many of his friends honored his decisions and were proud of his educational and community accomplishments. In this way, he had established a new version of himself as a respected young man with both street knowledge and success.

Despite his standing in the community, Cesar was aware that his ongoing gang ties opened him up to police contact. Different from almost all of the other young men, he did not feel threatened by the police scrutiny he often received. Rather, he felt knowledgeable enough about the law and empowered to challenge the police if they were to falsely accuse him of wrongdoing. He explained:

LAURA: So moving away, some people say that you can never escape the marks of your past. Do you feel that way?

CESAR: No. I don't feel like that.

LAURA: So what's different for you?

CESAR: My tattoos are not gangs. They have different meaning to what I am and what I've become. I would never mark me as a target for the police because now I have something that I can rely back on. When I speak to police officers, I come at 'em straight up. I know my rights. I have my bill of rights and I know that I don't have to say nothing to you. All I have to do is show my ID and then I don't have to say nothing, just wait for you to say something and if you wanna search me, go ahead. I don't have a problem with the police like that. I don't feel scared. There's nothing to be scared of. You're just a person in a uniform. And they're trying to do their job. And there are some cops that can be assholes, that can be ignorant, and do certain things they're not supposed to. But then that's when you gotta step up, and go up there and start making the cops go for what they done and make them go to court as well.

Here Cesar felt empowered to challenge police harassment by know-ing his rights and asserting them. Although being stopped by the police may be inevitable in his neighborhood, his awareness his rights made him feel safe from unfounded harassment or a false arrest. Cesar's knowledge and confidence around issues of policing were definitely not the norm among the rest of the young men, who tended to express that they were still unfairly targeted and profiled, but were far less equipped to feel that they alone could fight the harassment they received. More often than not, the young men had an overriding sense of fear of the police as well as knowledge that they could wind up dead if they caused any trouble.

It's How I Look

Embedded in these stories around police interactions is the experience of racial profiling. Anthony, who is African American, discussed how racism impacted many aspects of his life, including not being hired for jobs, being a target of prison violence, and being profiled by the police. During our second meeting with him, he was confined in county jail for a breaking and entering charge, which he felt he was picked up for because of his race rather than any actual crime. In his words, he attributed his recent arrest to "being black in a Mexican neighborhood." In his account of the incident, he was on his way to his cousin's house in a predominantly Mexican community when some gang members tried to approach him. He ran away and ended up jumping a fence into someone's private yard. The resident contacted the police and he was caught further down the block. When the police officers caught him, he had a screwdriver in his pocket because he was going to help fix his cousin's bike. Yet the resident reported him for a possible breaking and entering. Since the officers who arrested him were Hispanic, as was the resident who placed the phone call, Anthony felt that the officers took the resident's word over his because of their shared race. Although we were not able to confirm the actual circumstance of the crime or the charges, it was clear that Anthony truly believed he was racially profiled and charged for being black.

Mike also shared the experience of being marked by the police because he was a young black male. He explained how, regardless of where he traveled in Los Angeles County, the police profiled him as looking suspicious. Although he was reluctant to describe this treatment as racism, he definitely felt targeted on account of his race even when he wasn't engaged in illegal activity. He tried to explain this dynamic:

LAURA: What makes the police so suspicious of you in particular?

MIKE: Just how I look, how I dress.

LAURA: Which is what?

MIKE: I don't know, I guess how I look.

LAURA: Is it racism?

MIKE: Yeah. I don't think it's just really like racism, it's just I am black and "he might be up to something."

LAURA: That's not racism?

MIKE: No, I don't know. It's kind of racism. I don't know. It's just because of how I look.

It was not only the African American men who had experienced racial discrimination or profiling; Carlos explained that whenever the police pulled him over, they were harassing him because he was "bald and Mexican." In the following conversation, Carlos talks about his own experience of racial profiling:

CARLOS: And when I'm bald headed I could be dressed however, like even casual, but if I'm bald headed, there's something about the way that I look when I'm walking down the street, and there's not one time that a cop would pass me up. They'll always pull me over. Always. Always.

LAURA: Because the bald is part of the look?

CARLOS: If I tell them something like why are you pulling me over, 'cause I'm bald and Mexican? Then, "yeah, cause you look suspicious" Every time they just say "put your hands on the hood," you know? And while they have me put my hands on the hood, then they'll ask me if I'm on probation or something, which I usually am, so they're like "oh."

LAURA: So can you get rid of this target on your back, do you think, ever?

CARLOS: From the cops or what?

LAURA: From the cops, yes, let's start there.

CARLOS: Yeah, I mean. Cause if I'm off probation that would help a lot, 'cause they can't really hassle me when I'm in the streets. I started carrying around a camera.

LAURA: You do? For what reason?

CARLOS: The cops.

LAURA: To film if they do something?

CARLOS: Just to film myself if I see them. They have only pulled me over three times since I lived here. But the sheriffs, those are the ones that always always always around me. I can't blame them. Because I'm always always always in their territory where they patrol at. And usually I'm up to no good, so I can't say that's harassment, you know?

The discussion here with Carlos represents a mixture of his own views. On the one hand, he is aware that the police have the potential to misuse or abuse their authority and to target him based on appearance and race; but on the other hand, he knows that being "up to no good" can amount to the police being rightly suspicious of him. Either way, carrying a camera is one way that he tried to protect himself against police misconduct.

Both Carlos and Mike resented being targeted by the police, yet at the same time, they seemed to understand these experiences as a routine part of how young men of color are handled and monitored in neighborhoods like their own. While not directly labeling these experiences as racism, the notion that "it's how I look" cannot be disentangled from race. In fact, research has found that police officers have implicit and explicit biases that cause them to react more suspiciously to people of color, particularly young men, and to shoot more readily when they feel threatened (Correll & Keesee, 2009; Fridell, 2008).

For both Carlos and Mike, the perception that the police would likely stop them because of their race or appearance encouraged them to either reduce their involvement in crime or to take extra precautions to ensure that they did not get caught doing illegal activities. Having experienced adult jail, they knew that the stakes were high; they were no longer willing to take so many casual risks of getting caught. Nevertheless, they also shared the belief that no matter what their precautions, the chances were great that they would be stopped and considered suspicious based solely on their appearance, including their skin color, age, and gender.

CALCULATED RISK-TAKING

While all of the young men in the study made very deliberate decisions to avoid contact with the police, several were more willing than others to walk headfirst into risky situations. These situations included hanging with old friends, entering dangerous rival gang territory, or exposing themselves to the possibility of police contact by virtue of either hanging out with legally banned gang associates (as Carlos described) or actually committing crimes; all of these were situations that led most of these young men to adult jail or prison at some point. With knowledge and awareness that they were putting themselves in dangerous situations, the young men who took calculated risks did so for what they considered to be important and justifiable reasons.

One of the main rationales that the men offered for taking calculated risks was economic survival. For those living on the margins of the mainstream economy, such as Mike and Tyrone, they periodically faced tough choices: Engage in illegal activity, or go without food and shelter. More often than not, they chose the former option. Tyrone, the young man who had been emancipated from the foster care system, had several rough years before landing in a transitional home where he was able to stay for two years. While couch surfing and living day by day, he risked taking part in low-level drug crimes in order to make some money for food and shelter. He acknowledged the decision that he made to sell marijuana rather than other more serious drugs: "I can't afford to get no felonies. So I avoided getting felonies, even though I took risks. But I would try to be conscious of what I'd be doing." Tyrone's calculated decision to sell marijuana was that a low-level offense would likely not result in a felony charge, which would amount to less potential jail or prison time. This is a textbook example of a calculated risk, one that would prevent him from getting a felony strike on his record, but that would allow him to survive.

Mike, whose initial foray into crime was also based on poverty and need, likewise had struggles with homelessness as an adult. From the first interview through our fourth meeting more than a year and a half later, he had stayed with many relatives, been kicked out of these same relatives' houses on a number of occasions, and had very sporadic work, partly due to not having a permanent address. The last time we met with him he told us that he was living in his car most of the time and selling drugs to provide some financial help for his seven-year-old son, who lived with the child's mother. In the excerpt below, he explained his philosophy on calculated risk-taking:

DIANE: Has it [drug sales] picked up because of your homeless situation?

MIKE: Yeah, 'cause I be out more. I just need to figure it more because I don't want to keep doing the same stuff but I need to find something I can do—like legal but I need money so right now I got to continue to do this.

DIANE: So being out more means you are more at risk for getting caught.

MIKE: Yeah, but I don't be moving a lot. That's how I got caught last time. Like, always moving and now I just stay in one place.

DIANE: I know you've always lived in this neighborhood. Do you feel unsafe at all?

MIKE: I do think about it, but it's normal. You don't really be scared. It just be normal stuff that can happen so you just try to avoid stuff, but it ain't no avoiding the police. As long as you around here you gonna get bumped up. You could stay out they way but every now and then they gonna get you. I just try to have nothing on me.

Mike was aware that police contact is inevitable in his neighborhood, but he also had to take risks of getting caught in order to survive. Without a "legit" job, he still had to find a way to make ends meet. Over his many years of living on the margins, Mike had clearly figured out ways that he can live out of his car, continue to sell drugs, and still try to stay safe from other drug dealers and the police.

Lack of geographic mobility also led some of the young men close to situations that could land them in trouble with the law, where they had to take risks with gang territory or with the police simply due to where they were able to find a place to sleep. Gabriel told us a story about a friend who wanted to leave his gang, but wasn't able to relocate. He soon ended up dead.

All he was trying to do was change. He was gone in the blink of an eye. He was gone. When I got that phone call and they told me, "oh, he's dead," the first thing that I said is, "I told him. It's not easy. It's not easy." I think it's harder for a person out there gang banging, trying to get drug money, it's harder for them than what it is for a regular person that has a nine to five job, making a certain amount of money, living a regular life. Yes, we feel it difficult 'cause we have obligations and we have duties. But the person that is out there in the street is at risk all the time. If it's not with the government, it's with the streets. . . . The thing is that he lived in the middle of the trouble. I think that was his problem. You see? Living in the heart of the trouble. It's where it's bad.

Here Gabriel's description of his friend's death, and his inability to escape his surroundings, gets to the heart of the matter of this chapter and the experience of being marked. Having to live with this constant fear is inevitably much more taxing and tiring than living, as he called it, a "regular" life. Most people in this situation don't have the money to escape their surroundings, so like Gabriel, John, and Oscar, they had to use many other strategies to leave that life behind.

As in Gabriel's description of his friend who lived in the "heart of trouble," Evan was one of the young men who ended up stuck in his neighborhood without other possible living arrangements. When we met him he was on adult probation, so his risk of police contact was heightened. He explained that even if he wanted to leave his neighborhood, there was no other imaginable place for him to go where he would feel safe. He said: "I don't go over to other people 'hoods to go hang out though, 'cause can't nobody, that's a no-no." As he was staying with a relative in his own gang territory at the time of the interview, he felt protected. And although he was trying to cut back on his criminal activity because he is tired of being sent to jail, he still puts himself in precarious situations simply by hanging out with his friends. As Evan explained, he doesn't necessarily want a way out of the "'hood" as "this is my whole life. It's normal for me." Like Evan, some of the young men from Typology Three didn't see a whole lot of other alternatives; and as Gabriel witnessed with his friend, this put them at risk of getting into trouble, encountering police, and possibly being shot dead by their enemies.

A VICIOUS CYCLE

Peter, who was struggling with unemployment and fighting several current court cases, took calculated risks for all of the reasons mentioned above—for economic survival and to reap the benefits of informal social supports that could help provide him with an income. He needed money to clear his current petty charges and his record in order to actually get a job. However, this led him into a cycle of illegal activity in which he felt essentially trapped:

PETER: The biggest challenge is funds. I need money to get all that shit off [my record]. There is no other way to make money unless I run around.

LAURA: So you need money to clear your record to get a job, but to get money you have to do something to get you in trouble so it is a vicious cycle. Is that correct?

PETER: Yes. I have to take a risk.

LAURA: So you take a risk to make money to get yourself out of trouble. That's a big problem,

PETER: Yeah that's a big problem.

When Peter needed to bring money home for food and other supplies, he went back to his old neighborhood because he knew that his friends would loan him money, fix his car, or bail him out of tough situations. They would also let him take part in dealing stolen auto parts so that he could bring some money home to his wife and mother. While still protected in many ways by his friends' support, the favors also heightened his own risks, because on the basis of these exchanges, he then owed favors to his "homeboys." These favors required him to carry a gun, which then posed risk for a police charge if pulled over. At times he even had to stay out all night to protect his friends, leading to questions and complications from his wife. Ducking trouble and often cleaning up his past mistakes, Peter wished he could break this cycle, but wasn't aware of, and not quite committed to, a clean way out of the game. He offered the following advice to other kids getting out of the system: "Get a legitimate job. Something you like, that you will stick around, not get bored and quit and get stuck in the cycle." This was an interesting piece of advice coming from Peter, who was one of the few in Typology Three who had actually had a job (although not a career) at a coffee shop when he wasn't locked up. His experience emphasizes the point that it's not just having a job, but rather establishing meaningful employment that formerly incarcerated youth need to fully get out of the game.

Overall, those who were "Still in the Game" took calculated risks of being targeted by violence or sought after by the police. The reasons for taking these risks ranged from economic survival to choices regarding social support or friendships. However, these young men also experienced time with friends that helped them to acquire informal social capital; to be part of a familiar community of people who could provide reciprocal types of exchanges of favors. The choice to remain in contact with these old surroundings was seemingly quite deliberate—in other words, worth the risk; even the risk of being discovered by their enemies or harassed by the police. The important points for them were to stay safe, protect their friendships and loved ones, and avoid getting arrested or going to jail.

CONCLUSION

The story of violence and fear is embedded in these young men's lives in ways that were both expected and unexpected. While we had assumed that formerly incarcerated young men would have stories about neighborhood and gang violence, we were unaware that the feeling of being marked would be so present for all of the men, regardless of their stage of or commitment to desistance. The experience of having to watch your every move was an underlying stress that characterized their travel, decisions around daily planning, and sense of safety on an ongoing basis. All had to work to avoid enemies and the police, even if they tended to downplay their own safety risk.

The experience of police harassment was also near universal, although not surprisingly was felt more intensively by those who were less committed to desistance. We were struck by stories from young men such as Cesar and Carlos, who carried cameras, or knew their legal rights—as signs of potential empowerment and fighting back against discrimination. Nevertheless, the stories of being unfairly targeted by the police based on race or appearance far outweighed any sense of empowerment that a few may have felt. For most, the police presence, like other threats to safety, were just part of the package of living "in the 'hood."

Last, the great lengths that men like John, Gabriel, and Oscar had to take in order to protect themselves, even years after leaving their gangs, struck us as a quite important finding to relay in regard to daily challenges of desistance. For, there seems to be a prevailing sense in public discourse that individuals can turn their lives around simply through sheer will. The narratives that we captured in this chapter illustrate just how much more layered the desistance process can be, particularly when one is trying to move on from the protection of a gang. In many ways, those who were still involved in crime or gangs felt most protected by their friends and allies. While this may be counterintuitive for some, it made sense within the composition of their narratives. For if we are indeed "*all marked, no matter how much the transformation*," does it make more sense to be marked and alone, or marked and protected? This is a question that each of the young men had to weigh in accordance with their needs for survival, social support, and to live a life that felt meaningful at their various stages of desistance.

CHAPTER 7

Finding a Net to Fall Back On

THE YOUNG WOMEN'S JOURNEYS

I already knew it was going to be hard for me, so I already had prepared myself. I wasn't scared, I was just more preoccupied with how to get home; the way. I don't even remember where the streets are at, how to get home. I hope I'm going the right way.

—Irene

THESE WERE IRENE'S THOUGHTS upon exiting the California Youth Authority after five years of incarceration; a twenty-year-old young woman with five dollars in her pocket and a small bag of belongings from when she was fifteen. Nearly all of her former friends were by then incarcerated, had moved, or were no longer reachable. She had no close family members to help with her transition, and no cell phone to connect her with people who could possibly provide her with support. How does a young woman in these circumstances survive? How will she resist the pressure to turn to crime if she finds herself without shelter or food?

In this chapter, we showcase the young women's experiences with desistance on their pathways toward adulthood. Prior research has found that young women are more likely to achieve desistance in young adulthood than their male counterparts in part due to the bonds they are able to forge with friends, family, and significant others. Whereas women's movement away from crime is often facilitated by social relationships, men appear to be more instrumentally or individually oriented toward their own successes (Benda, 2005; Salvatore & Taniguchi, 2012). Yet as we saw in chapters 5 and 6, social relationships, particularly with friends and family, were critical to the desistance process for young men. In this chapter, we probe how these relationships operated for the young women.

While the women in our study certainly shared struggles with the men in regard to becoming economically self-sufficient, they did not grapple with temptations to continue in criminal activity in similar ways, nor did they encounter the same set of problems in their interactions with the police, former friends, or enemies. However, stemming from a dearth of family stability, all of these young women were still teetering on the edge of solid ground, putting them at risk for criminal activity either for survival or through their associations with romantic partners and friends. For the young women, their sense of stability post-incarceration appeared to be dependent on their own resourcefulness as well as the generosity of the people around them. Many of their struggles revolved around finding a stable base when the very sense of home had been quite elusive to them throughout their lives. All of the women's stories are hence interconnected through the themes of finding home, breaking the cycle, caregiving, social bonds, gendered violence, and survival and resilience.

Irene: Finding a Family

When Irene was released from CYA, she had no family members to return to, no job, and limited concrete plans for her future. As may be all too customary, her parole officers had done little to prepare her logistically for her release. Irene was unable to return to her mother, as their relationship had not recovered from its contentious history, and her mother had not visited her even one time during her lengthy incarceration. By the time Irene was set for release, she had heard from a relative that her mother had moved out of state and was serving her own prison term. This news sent Irene into a bit of shock but also gave her motivation to change course, to steer clear of her mother's self-destructive path. She explained: "So, in reality now I see it as a big step that I don't want to see myself. When I look at the mirror I don't want to see my mom, right, I want to see me. Something else—break the chain at least."

Irene's sincere motivation to "break the chain" was compromised by her tenuous circumstances, particularly in finding a place to call home. When we first met Irene, we were impressed with her mature sense of understanding how her history of abuse and trauma had led her to criminal activity. Although she had largely committed crimes of economic survival, she sorely regretted the cost of these actions to her victims, which is one major component of desistance (Maruna, 2001). After five years of contemplation at CYA, she was mentally and emotionally committed to a new way of life. Notwithstanding Irene's emotional maturity and will to change, her circumstances were still very much in flux; she had been out of prison for seven months and was already on her fourth living situation. Irene described some of the difficulties that she had experienced in finding a stable home:

> I had a "so-called" friend that I called my aunt and I went to her house but after I stayed there for a whole week . . . She was a big girl. She had her boyfriend come over and stuff and I guess her boyfriend made a comment saying that "oh, I saw her naked when she came out of the bathroom. She did it on purpose"—when I *never* do that. So she started tripping, I started to leave and she called my mentor, and told her "she can't be here." So they found a halfway home for me and I didn't like it because they are racist. It was all black girls and there were elder people, too, so they were kind of jealous, too—this halfway home had girls and guys. So the guys would talk and they thought "oh, she's trying to take my man da da da," so that made me go "like, ok, I need to get outta here. I need to find a job as soon as possible." So I found me a job and then I moved.

Fleeing the halfway house due to the suspicions and threats surrounding her, Irene landed a part-time stocking position at a store and rented a room in an apartment for about $200 a month, which was still a stretch on a limited income. Yet soon she had to exit that situation because of a potential danger from the landlord. Once again, she felt threatened by her position as a woman in a world that she knew very well from her history—one with the potential for sexual exploitation: "males think that if I'm a young lady by myself they want something else." Fearing another problematic situation and with her survival instinct on high alert, she quickly moved on.

Seven months after her release, Irene appeared to have found a sense of stability. Now in her fourth home, she was renting a room in a house from an unrelated female landlord in a modest neighborhood and had obtained some part-time retail work. The apartment was fairly devoid of furniture and decoration, yet she had her own bedroom and seemed comfortable there. She mentioned that she was still a bit lonely living with a stranger.

Just four weeks later when we arranged to meet for her second interview, we were surprised that Irene had moved again, this time with her boyfriend Javier in his family home. Irene had met Javier at a bus stop just a few weeks after she was released from CYA. While she had not had many intimate relationships due to her history of abuse and a significant amount of time behind bars, she had found someone with whom she could finally feel "at home." She articulated how the relationship with Javier moved her from a space of being isolated in the apartment with a stranger to feeling loved and protected. She said: "We've gone through our ups and downs but it's just like, we have a similar background. We understand each other and he helps me out and he gave me his family because he knows I don't have no family." So several months into the relationship, she moved into his family home in a working-class neighborhood in South Los Angeles. There she and Javier shared a small bedroom with one of his other brothers.

Irene's immersion into Javier's large family fulfilled a deeply seated longing: a bonded sense of place and home. Initially, Javier's family appeared to be an ideal setting to find this sense of peace. During her lonely times of incarceration, Irene had "a vision that I was being on my own for all the time . . . alone." The loneliness of confinement had caused her to accept that she was always going to be on her own, so she was pleasantly surprised by her good fortune. Javier had a large family with seven siblings and many nieces and nephews. Moving into a family had broken her long-standing sense of isolation. She also finally found a mother figure that she could trust; a woman with whom she could cook meals and have intimate talks.

Despite all of these positive elements, living with Javier was not without its own risks. Irene knew that Javier was on parole and that some of his siblings, cousins, and friends were actively involved in a local gang and on probation or parole. Some also had a gang target on their backs with the police. With Javier, she frequently went to parties where trouble could emerge at any moment; yet she willingly took the risk because she enjoyed feeling finally free after so many years of institutionalization. She explained: "So, me and him, we're just alike. We work 'cause, like, we drink together, we hang out, we have lots of fun, you know, like, life of the party." These activities obviously placed Irene in situations where she could get into trouble with the police simply by being at the wrong place at the wrong time. For Irene, the benefits of being part of this family and in this relationship clearly outweighed the risks.

Four months later, Irene's life took another sharp turn when Javier was arrested for attempted murder. Although she fervently believed in his innocence and viewed the evidence against him as circumstantial, she worried that his past convictions might be enough for his lawyers to talk him into a plea deal that would carry a long sentence. While awaiting trial, Javier had also proposed to her, and she accepted his offer of marriage. Irene was emotionally torn about staying loyal to a man who was facing a long sentence. She was not sure he would get out of prison in the foreseeable future, yet she desperately wanted to maintain the sense of security that she had found with him and his family. So while he was awaiting trial, Irene continued to operate as a member of the family who cared for her as Javier's fiancée, as she explained, in the way that "a traditional Mexican family does."

Javier was a force in her life who simultaneously pulled Irene into trouble yet also protected her from criminal influences and past associations. One of the ways that he protected her was through his extreme jealousy. Although Irene was involved in many positive activities, such as job training and attending community programs for formerly incarcerated youth, Javier had asked her to cut back on these activities due to his fear of her meeting other men. On the one hand this deeply annoyed her, as it reminded her of years of being told what to do while she was confined; yet still, laying low and minimizing going out protected her from getting into any trouble. When Javier was locked up, she found herself with a degree of freedom that she did not feel she was ready to handle. Being only minimally employed, she also had time on her hands. So during his trial, Irene began to contact old boyfriends and gang-associated friends through social media but still tried to keep her relationship with Javier in the forefront of her everyday decisions.

A few months later, Irene had moved on, ending her engagement to Javier (even though he was acquitted and returned home), leaving the family home, and landing a new job, one that she believed had more potential for her future. This decision was not without significant turmoil, as she disclosed that she had survived some violence within the relationship. This maltreatment was understandably very emotionally triggering due to her history of physical and sexual abuse and difficulty with trust and intimacy. Yet Irene managed to find the emotional resources that she needed to feel whole, both within herself and through her outside support system. Many of the friends and networks she had developed, including the volunteer mentor she worked with at CYA, came to her rescue to help her find an apartment and move. She felt blessed with the outpouring of support from her community. During our final interview, she explained: "So, I'm just trying right now little by little to control myself and have back what I've built up before because I've lost myself. Because he [Javier] made me something . . . I really wanted to just turn around and ask him, you know that I've gone through so much and you didn't even make it easier for me . . . I feel bad because basically, I waited for a jerk that is just going to come back to me and abuse me. Use me and abuse me. But I'm doing better. I'm going to school and going to work. I'm about to get my license to get a car. Other than that, I have a nice spot." Despite having to contend with violence and sever ties with her post-prison family, Irene managed to find her way back to herself and was working to move forward. She relied on her social supports—mostly those who were new in her life—to get her to a better place and to interrupt the cycle of abuse.

Irene's story is distinctly her own; one of strength, survival, and emotional resilience. Yet it also touches on many of the young women's struggles post-incarceration: seeking to find a place to call home, contending with the threats of physical or sexual victimization by men, depending at times on others for economic protection, and enduring several moves, twists, and turns before finally landing on her own two feet. Among the eight women in the study, five moved at least once just during the course of our interviews with them, three moved more than once, and two moved out of state and became unreachable. And while Irene managed to move forward with her life even with these uncertainties and criminal associations, others were unable to gain the momentum needed to propel them toward a more positive and stable future. Lupe's story represents the latter of these possibilities.

LUPE: THE COST OF GOOD FORTUNE

At age 18, Lupe was in the process of transitioning out of both the juvenile justice and foster care systems. Wearing a backward ball cap and baggy jeans, she appeared tougher than her demeanor, which was quite open and soft-spoken. As we described in chapter 2, Lupe had a turbulent childhood that included an absent mother, paternal abuse, familial rejection based on her gender non-conformity and sexual orientation, and drug addiction. Her crimes of survival were quite common among the young women in this study, including theft, drug use, and running away from foster care.

We first met Lupe when she had been out of her juvenile camp placement for about seven months and was living in a home for women transitioning out of foster care. Lupe's few years prior to emancipation had been extremely unstable, both logistically and emotionally. She met the self-described "love of her life" while in a group home at age 16. With Lydia, Lupe felt that she could better control her compulsion to abuse drugs. So when Lydia was released from their shared group home placement and she was not, Lupe felt lost and started using drugs more heavily again. Although she was court mandated to live in her group home placement, she ran away to be with Lydia. Soon after she went AWOL she got caught and was sent back to a different group home, one of more than 15 placements she had lived in since age nine.

Three months later, Lydia was in her own apartment and pressuring Lupe to move in with her. Technically still on the run from the law, Lupe moved into Lydia's apartment in a low-income neighborhood in East Los Angeles, where they fit into the densely populated Mexican American community. They lived together in a relatively stable situation for about a month. However, the police soon picked up Lupe again, this time as a result of her brother's gang associations. This was her closest brush with the law as a newly minted legal adult. She recounted:

> I was there for a month until one day we decided to go to the movies. . . . I guess we got stopped because my brother was bald headed—he was banged out. It was like a white cop—a white old cop. What the fuck, why'd he have to fuck with us . . . They stopped us because of my brother. I had a warrant, so they ran it. They run my brother's name and they run my name, they run my girlfriend's

name and they're like "you, you have a warrant for your arrest."' I'm
like "oh, fuck." And my girlfriend's just like "you should have given
them a fake name." I'm like "you know what, I'm going to just get
over it. Do my time and get out." So they took me in, back to juvie
for 3 days. I had court the third day and I guess my girlfriend and my
brother showed up. So they showed up to my court date and I guess
they told him "she has a place to stay at," that my girlfriend would
help me look for a job and you know go back to school. And I guess
my judge was tired so he agreed to release me off of probation. I was
like "what!?"

Much to her surprise, Lupe finally had some unexpected good fortune; having reached the age of 18, she was dismissed from her probation, evaded a potential adult jail sentence, and was released from court
supervision.

Set free from dependency and delinquency courts, Lupe moved in
with Lydia. Without structure from the state for the first time in over
nine years, she did not know quite what to do with her time. She had not
completed high school due to her transience and she was unemployed.
She soon fell into a static place and began to smoke weed "around the
clock." She explained: "We had a neighbor, he smokes a lot and he would
like smoke us out. I didn't go back to school; I didn't attempt to find a
job—I just was smoking weed every day, and my girlfriend didn't like
that. She would hate to see me smoke. She hated it; she hated me at the
time. And at that time we were all living off of GR [General Relief] . . . so
like, I would spend it on her but the rest I would go buy some weed. She
hated it. Then I started drinking—like drinking a lot, a lot." The situation
quickly deteriorated as the apartment was crowded (her brother and his
children also stayed there) and they had very little money. Lupe spiraled
into heavier drug and alcohol use. By her own admission, she wasn't at
all prepared for the freedom of adulthood or absence of state supervision.
The relationship with Lydia had also descended into a negative cycle
to the point where Lupe was worried that she would replicate her own
violent victimization patterns. She remarked: "I thought to myself, 'you
know, I don't want to turn into my dad.' 'Cuz when my mom and my dad
used to be together my dad used to beat the fuck out of her, you know?
Like, I'm not going to do that no more, you know?'" Similar in many

ways to Irene's desire to "break the chain" of family cycles, Lupe wanted to make sure that she did not fall into the trap of becoming like her own abuser. Both Irene and Lupe had enjoyed few positive adult role models in their lives and they were determined to carve out more stable paths.

Although the relationship with Lydia stabilized to a more peaceful place, they eventually came to the realization that they needed the financial support of transitional housing. They applied to housing programs for former foster youth and were accepted at separate residences. When we first met Lupe, she was living in a transitional program where she had access to GED classes, case management services, rent, and food. She lived with 11 other young women in what she described as a "gang banging" and violent neighborhood that she despised. Despite the support of the transitional housing staff, she was feeling stuck about moving forward in her life. As Lupe stated, her major downfalls were always "drugs and girls." During our first interview, she was trying to refrain from using any substances without the support of Alcoholics Anonymous or any other program, remarking that she was proud to be three weeks sober.

Three weeks later, Lupe appeared a bit more disoriented, and we suspected that she might have been high during our interview. She was still living at the transitional home but had stopped attending her GED prep class. When asked why she had quit, she replied: "I don't know. I started getting high so I got lazy and stopped going." To fill her time, she often helped her brother with childcare, but since he was "slinging" (meaning selling weed), she would visit him and basically spend the day getting high. Also, since he was selling drugs, hanging around her brother put her at risk of police contact, a risk she was willing to take for the free drugs. At the same time that Lupe was slipping into a downward spiral, Lydia had found a full-time job and was bringing in a steady paycheck. Lupe felt a bit hopeless about her own future because she had no GED and feared "dirty drug tests." In comparison to Lydia, she felt worthless.

By her own admission, Lupe was unable to stop using drugs, was lying to Lydia about the extent of her use, and was trapped in a cycle that she knew was a slippery slope toward self-destruction. When asked about these patterns, she explained:

LUPE: Yeah, so I just stopped. This past week and a half I haven't smoked. I've had money on me but I haven't gone and bought some.

LAURA: But it seems pretty up and down for you?

LUPE: Yeah, it's like up and down, you can say. I can stay clean for a certain amount of time, but then I'll relapse.

LAURA: So what draws you back, do you think? Is there a trigger?

LUPE: The feeling, I don't know.

LAURA: Like, when you're upset.

LUPE: Bored, I guess, and when I'm mad, too, sometimes . . . Yeah. It makes me forget about . . . 'Cus usually when I'm upset it's because of my girlfriend. It makes me forget about her for a minute and then it just comes back to me—the problems and shit.

In the absence of a clear direction, Lupe had returned to the comfort that she knew from an early age: to numb herself from emotional pain by using drugs or alcohol. This cycle may have protected her emotionally but also prevented her from accomplishing any of her goals.

At the same time that she felt unable to move forward, Lupe also had made some important changes in her life. This was particularly the case around desistance. Similar to the "On the Road to Desistance" young men, Lupe had spent a great deal of time thinking about changes in her appearance and mannerisms that would project a more pro-social identity. All of this was part of her growth and transformation toward a law-abiding self. She explained: "The way I changed . . . The way I dress, the way I talk. A lot of my appearance, the way I treated people, 'cuz like, I go back and I read the letters I used to write to her and I think to myself like 'what? I used to talk like this? I used to write like this?' And just the things like I used to dress like banged out and I used to treat people like shit, you know. But now I have more respect for others, you know? I treat them just like everybody else, you know?"

In addition to her outward appearance, Lupe felt that a large part of her change was the way she treated other people. She saw herself moving from a disrespectful teenager to a kinder and more thoughtful adult. She explained: "I didn't care. I didn't care about nobody's feelings. I used to break cars and I didn't think about 'oh, it's going to come back to me one of these days.' Like, I didn't care. I'd tell you 'I love you' just to get in your pants. I was disrespectful to staff when I was in placement. I don't know, I just didn't care. I didn't care about nothing, nobody. But now I do." Hence, despite her lack of progress with regard to drug use and obtaining a career path, these two elements—appearance and respect for others—were a large part of her growth over the year since her emancipation from the system.

One of the lessons that we learned from Lupe was the role of good fortune in helping to pave the road for a more positive future. Just as in many ways Irene had stumbled upon the protective although temporary confines of Javier's family, Lupe also happened to come into a degree of financial security. As a child, Lupe was in a serious car accident that left her with a sum of money to receive upon emancipation from foster care. Using her resourcefulness, Lupe enlisted the help of an advocacy organization to retrieve the trust fund (she estimated at over \$200,000), which she received around her nineteenth birthday. Thus when we next spoke to Lupe four months later, she was renting a one-bedroom apartment with Lydia. These resources allowed her to finally make a clean break from public benefits, which also made her feel more confident about her future.

A lot had changed materially for Lupe as a result of retrieving this substantial sum of money. She could afford an apartment and furniture, and she was not pressured to get a job. She moved out of the group home right away. Christina, one of the project interviewers, remarked in her field notes:"The place was very clean, and I was half expecting the apartment to be less than furnished, considering they had moved not long ago. Her disposition was much more cheerful this time around. She led us into her bedroom where we could get some privacy. I noticed that the furniture in this room was matching and particularly new." As Christina wrote, the new furniture and belongings represented a huge change from our last meeting, when she was on General Relief and struggling to make ends meet at the group home. Lupe agreed with our assessment, stating: "I didn't have nothing, we didn't have nothing, you know—all we had was our clothes and a couple of things. Everything in here, we bought it."

Lupe explained her radically changed circumstances very openly. When she finally got hold of the trust fund, she quickly moved out of the transitional shelter and into the apartment. At the same time, Lydia moved out of her group home and quit her job. She was not entirely pleased with her new neighborhood, but she was relieved to finally have her own space and security. She explained: "I'm happy about it because

I don't have to worry about being homeless. Because I used to worry about that a lot, you know? Like, when I was in transitional housing, worrying about getting kicked out for smoking, you know? Right now I got no worries." Similar to what Irene experienced when she moved in with Javier, Lupe finally felt a sense of relief in finding a place to call home, creating her own comfort and family without being told what to do or how to spend her time. She also welcomed in her brother and his children to her apartment with open arms; she wanted to sustain a connection with her brother and her nieces and nephews as a whole family unit.

Lupe was also in the process of trying to gain custody of one of her teenage brothers, who was still in foster care at the time. She had applied for custody and was taking steps to seal her juvenile record. But to follow through on this reality, she knew that she needed to show that she had a stable income, and to do this she had to stop getting high. While she was admittedly still using drugs on a regular basis, she also wanted to become a good role model for her little brother. In the past four months, however, she had not been able to make a great deal of progress toward those goals, partially because of the freedom that the trust fund was providing.

While clearly the money made a world of difference for Lupe, she knew that she had spent too much too quickly. Not only had she furnished the apartment and bought expensive electronics, she also had taken her family members on trips to amusement parks and other places that she never got to enjoy in foster care. This produced both a sense of liberation and anxiety. She described: "Yeah, I get bored, I wish I had more stuff to do. I have to wait for this class [educational program]. That's all I have to wait for to get out. I don't really like to go out because every time we go out we spend. Now they're kind of used to eating out a lot. We used to not have the chance to go out to all these places and now that I do we just go." While Lupe relished in her ability to finally provide for herself and her family, she was also concerned about spending the money too fast. She, Lydia, and her brother were spending most of their time smoking weed and playing video games—a life that Lupe described as less than fulfilling. She said: "Next week I'm going to start going to job training stuff. I don't know—some class me and my girlfriend and my brother are all going to go to, to like get more help to find a job and to go to school. Because I'm tired of living like—not this life—but always buying stuff. It gets kind of boring." After this interview, we left feeling hopeful about Lupe's future. She finally had found a home, resolved some of her issues with Lydia, and seemed happy and more motivated. We were thus surprised when two months later, we found out that she had moved out of state and was living with a distant relative; we were unable to find out exactly why she left California or establish any further contact with her. The sudden moved seemed out of place and abrupt.

Lupe's story illustrates a few themes regarding the desistance process for young women. The desistance journey is clearly not entirely gendered. Lupe was battling some of the same demons as Tyrone, whose drug habits were also holding him back from making concrete progress in his life. She also had a similar script as some of the young men, such as Oscar and Gabriel, who felt that part of the desistance process involved the outward projection of identity to coincide with the newer person inside.

There was, however, a sense that we got from Lupe that she felt very compelled to care for everyone else, particularly her girlfriend, brothers, nieces, and nephews. It seemed easier for Lupe to focus on the well-being of others rather than herself, and within that paradigm of caring for those around her, she did not attend much to her own problems. Coupled with her drug use, this lack of attention to her own goals made her indeed vulnerable to staying stuck in a cycle of depression and addiction that was detrimental to her overall well-being. Although she was the only young woman in this study to struggle extensively with substance dependence, she was certainly not isolated in having others depend on her both financially and emotionally. Whether it was parents who depended on them, such as was the case for Carina and Theresa, or young children, such as in the cases of Amber and Desiree, the women had to balance caregiving with their own work toward desistance and self-sufficiency.

MOTHERING AND DESISTANCE

For Amber and Desiree, the challenges related to criminal desistance were overshadowed by their more immediate desire to provide a safe environment for their own children; a home and an upbringing that would look very different from the turmoil that had characterized their own childhoods. While Desiree was essentially on her own, relying on public benefits and occasional work to make ends meet (as profiled in chapter 4), Amber had family support from her mother and aunt as well as her boyfriend, who was also the father of her children. Both of their stories provide insight into how a balance of caregiving and perseverance factors into young women's journeys toward desistance.

Amber: Everything Changes as a Mother

At age 17, Amber gave birth to a baby girl, April, with her boyfriend of then about two years. She was nervous about having to provide for a child without the benefit of any work experience or a high school diploma, but she decided to raise April with the support of her family (her mother, aunt, and sisters) and her boyfriend Devon. To make ends meet, she and April moved in with her mother, while Devon lived about 50 miles away with his parents. She described her strained financial situation: "To tell you the truth, the County helps me but when I run out of County money I try to do chores around the house to earn money from my mama but she don't be giving me money like that. She's like 'you got a baby-daddy, so he's got to help you' so I don't even ask her for anything anymore. I don't tell her about needing no bras or panties or nothing—I just get it on my own."

Amber was not happy living under her mother's roof due to their ongoing conflicts as well as the location of the home, which she considered to be an extremely dangerous neighborhood. Like the young men described in chapter 6, Amber struggled with living in a neighborhood where "anything can happen at any time," including gunfire, violence, and crime. She described her sense of continuous fear: "It's just my neighborhood is bad, horrible. So I'm nervous. I'm stressing. When we're there [at Devon's home], I'm at peace. I love it. But once we come back to LA I start stressing. I don't know when he's coming, I don't know anything, you know? So it's like—'oh my God.'" While Amber would have much preferred to live with Devon on their own, neither had enough money for rent. She was in the midst of trying to finish high school, and Devon was unemployed and receiving limited state disability benefits. She was very unsatisfied with her living situation, but it was the only option that made financial sense at the time.

Although having a baby at a young age posed financial strains, April provided her with fierce motivation to move her life in a more positive direction. That said, Amber had not been to a juvenile hall or camp since her initial stay around age 15, mostly because she described it as a terrible experience: "When I tell people like—when people are like 'oh, have you been to camp before?' I tell them 'yeah' and they look at me like 'for real?' 'Yes, I've been to that horrible place before—it's horrible, horrible, horrible.'" So while Amber's original source of motivation to desist was a fear of being incarcerated, having a child had helped to solidify her goals and to "get my act together." Despite her intense motivation, Amber dropped out of school shortly after the first interview and, like so many of the other young women in the study, her life had changed dramatically in a short period of time.

Four months after our initial meeting, we were surprised to find that Amber had a three-week old infant in tow. She had not mentioned that she was pregnant at the time of the first interview, but now she had another baby girl who she named September. Both April and September were present during the interview, this time at her mother's home where she still resided.

Amber explained that just after our initial interview, her boyfriend's disability had worsened and landed him in the hospital, so she had dropped out of school in order to provide more care for him. She recounted: "He got sick and put in a hospital. He was in there for a month. And then his mom was always working, so I had always had to go to where he lives at and help him because his whole right arm had stopped working." Around this time, she also discovered that she was pregnant with their second child, which was quite a surprise to both of them. With a one-year-old daughter and another baby on the way, Amber was not able to juggle her caregiving responsibilities for Devon and April while also attending school during the day.

Once she gave birth to September, she began to realize how difficult it was to live on a limited public assistance income and take care of two children. She was still living in her mother's home and they were fighting frequently. All of this financial strain was weighing on Amber, who was trying to figure out how to care for two small children, get a job, and finish her GED or high school credits. Eventually, she wanted to become a nurse.

Nevertheless, the seemingly long and arduous upward climb to reach her goal of becoming a nurse made her propensity for fighting or getting into trouble with the law an invention of the past: "I was horrible. I was bad, fighting and all that. I just didn't care." Now as a mother, she has so much more to focus on. She explained:

> Yeah everything has changed a lot [as a mother]. Because I don't really be out like that unless, they somewhere I know that they safe. If they are at my auntie's house, like my auntie is obsessed with April. If I go out to party with my best friend, if we go out and people see us. I don't want to say they are hating on us but they will look at us up and down. They'll say stuff. I'll be like "you don't even know me and you're talking like that." They be like "what?" And then they be like "we can fight and all that." And I'm like "I don't have time for all that." It has changed. I haven't been fighting at all.

Amber had just turned 18 at the time of our second interview and was still trying to hang out with her friends on occasion and have a young adult life. However, with two children under two years of age and a great deal of responsibility on her shoulders, she could not afford to make silly mistakes or to run away from her problems as she had done in the past.

Similar to the situation that Irene faced with Javier, Amber's relationship with Devon was a complicating factor in her desistance journey. Devon also had a history of crime and gang involvement, but he, too, was trying to get his act together for the sake of the two children. She described the transition to fatherhood as sobering for him: "He's calmed down. He felt that when he was young, that was his time. Now he's older, he felt he has done his stuff and he don't need to do nothing else. So it's time to take care of my kids. He's got kids to live for so I don't got time to be, you know going after this person . . . going to jail." Despite her recognition that Devon was trying to make changes in his life, Amber expressed concern that he would not fulfill his promises and was not certain they would end up together in the long run. Thus, she hoped that they would eventually get married and live together but did not count on this as a sure reality. In the meanwhile, she was very focused on her immediate tasks: raising two young daughters, finding a more stable income, and trying to get along with her mother. Overall, with the support of her friends, family, and boyfriend, Amber appeared to be hopeful and energized about her future.

Desiree: Motherhood under Scrutiny

Desiree was similar to Amber with regard to criminal desistance in that she found her motivation to stay out of any further trouble with the law for the sake of her daughter. In many ways, her pregnancy was the impetus for closing the revolving door of running away, juvenile halls and camps, and group homes. However, because she was a single mother and still in foster care when she gave birth to Kianna, having a young child also put her at risk of police and child protection surveillance in a way that the young fathers and Amber did not experience. This type of over-policing was different from the young men's experiences, but nevertheless had some similar effects of mistrust, fear, and high stakes for small mistakes.

At age 17, Desiree found herself pregnant and very much alone, having been thrown out of both her mother's and grandmother's homes and waiting for a new foster placement. Like Lupe, she found out by chance that she was actually terminated from the juvenile justice system. Yet unlike Lupe, who was overjoyed about her sudden turn of events, this abrupt termination left Desiree in a serious bind. She explained:

> I'm telling the lady [foster home] "oh yeah, I'll be out of your house Tuesday—don't worry." Tuesday come—no. Wednesday come—she's like "ok, why are you not out?" So, Thursday—I called, I just happened to call the court and I was like "do I have court scheduled, you know, for Tuesday?" . . . And they were like "oh, you don't have court and your probation was terminated two weeks ago" and I was just like "what?" . . . So I found out I was off probation and was just crying, crying, crying. I had a PO [probation officer] that actually I used to give a hard time when I was at camp and I ran into him. He seen me; I told him I was pregnant . . . He was like "ok, keep in touch with me if you need any advice or whatever," so I called him and I was like "I don't have anywhere to go, I don't have any money. I don't have my birth certificate, my social security—nothing." And he was like "this is what you do, go to the county building and tell

them everything you just said to me and they should help you." I was like "I don't have money to get on a bus, like, I don't have anything."

Alone, destitute, and essentially homeless, Desiree used the last of her remaining resources to get to the county office to enter back into the child welfare system. This was her only option at this point besides a homeless shelter. She was one of the crossover youth in this study who was booted out of foster care and handed fully over to probation; but once her probation ended, the child welfare system was required to take her back because she was technically a pregnant former foster youth without a home.

DCFS placed Desiree at a group home for pregnant and parenting foster youth. Even with such horrible childhood experiences in foster care, she had high hopes for this placement and was eager to learn independent living and parenting skills. Yet when she arrived, she was very disappointed with the placement and particularly the group home staff, whom she felt were trying to control her every move. For example, the staff told her that she had to give birth at a designated hospital, but she had heard from the other women in the home that this specific hospital had substandard care. So Desiree communicated with her attorney and social worker to make sure that she could have the baby at the hospital of her choice. The staff did not relent in their decision, so she had to violate the rules to find the best care in her labor and delivery. She stated, "I had to AWOL when I was having contractions." Subsequently, every time she left the group home she was at risk of getting picked up by the police. Desiree explained:

> The placement was supposed to take me to get my birth certificate. They told the social worker, "we're going to take them, we go on trips every weekend, or every week" to get my social security, my birth certificate and my ID. I was like, "you guys are going to take me this week or next week, something. You gotta fit it into the schedule because it's supposed to be there." But I had to sneak out, and my baby was two days old and as bad as it may seem I was out there with her. I had like a pouch and I covered her with blankets and stuff. I took her everywhere. I had to AWOL to go to the doctor but I would tell my judge, who knew everything I was doing. My lawyer

knew everything I was doing. I was calling her constantly and my social worker knew everything.

Although Desiree was doing everything in her power to advocate for Kianna's care, she was well aware that she was also skirting the system and defying the staff's rules. In her view, because she had refused to follow the rules, the group home staff members were out to get her back by calling child protective services and reporting her for maternal unfitness.

After giving birth, by state licensing rules for foster homes she had to switch to her own room where she and the baby could have separate beds. Prior to that date, she had a roommate and a room with two twin beds. When she brought Kianna back to the group home, her new "mother and baby" room had been freshly painted, but the fumes were so strong that she refused to sleep in her newly designated quarters. She had to fight vociferously for her right to sleep in a room that wasn't toxic, and she moved herself back into her old room, sleeping with Kianna in her twin bed. Subsequently, her choice led to a call to DCFS for suspected child abuse:

> So they call the hotline because, what did they say? I was refusing to go into the other room and I was sleeping with my baby in the bed. But what I did was, everybody—the girls—had felt sorry for me—"oh, they're trying to take your baby." And I was like "I'm not scared of what they're trying to call." So they called the hotline on me. I got into it with the hotline lady because she was like "you're being defiant and blah blah bla" and I was like "you know what? I'm not going into that room until the 24 hours is up and if it still smells like fumes in the room I'm not going in there, period. Because if my baby catches pneumonia or something like that you guys are going to be at fault for it and I'm going to deal with that," and she was like "um, well you're going to go in the room and if not we're going to come out and you're going to have to deal with that later." And I was like "as a matter of fact, since you have a lot to say—you're going to come down here, you're going to go into the room, walk in the room, smell the room and then tell me that I have to go in there. That way if something happens you're going to be at fault for still

not going in the room." And she was like "I'm not going to do that so you and the staff are going to have to handle that on your own" and I was like "ok, I thought so."

Subsequent to that call, DCFS left her situation alone. However, a few days later, the group home called the hotline again to report her for sleeping with her baby in the bed. She explained:

> They had to call the hotline on me again because I was sleeping in the bed with my baby but I had woke up in the middle of the night and my baby had threw up all over her face and I was scared because I didn't see, I didn't hear it or anything. I just woke up—and she was in the swing—and she just threw up everywhere. And I was scared—if she had been in the crib she would have drowned in her own throw-up. So, she slept in the bed with me, on my chest. And they were all "oh, people have rolled over the baby and give the baby SIDS" and I'm like "I really don't care about any of that, I just experienced something that I don't ever want to experience again."

Maintaining her most remarkable spirit of survival and self-determination Desiree fought to get out of that group home, and she wound up in an independent living program. This program allowed her to get into her own apartment, which was subsidized for former foster youth, and to receive CalWORKS benefits for Kianna and food stamps. For the first two years, she devoted her time to being the best possible mother that she could be.

Yet still, her position of being an African American young single mother with a juvenile record and a history of DCFS control left her open to further monitoring and investigation. The second time we met with Desiree she had just moved to a different supported independent living apartment and was in the process of getting settled into her new environment. She had a stable place to live and, despite not having a job, she had the support of public benefits and a boyfriend, Chris, who often helped with Kianna's care.

Although Chris had provided her support in the past, Desiree did not like his overall attitude and particularly his jealousy, so she decided to break up with him. When she tried to get him to leave her apartment, he became physically abusive in front of Kianna, so she called the police. She recounted that the situation hit rock bottom when he punched her in the gut and then broke her cell phone, so she had to knock on several doors in the building to get help. To her shock and horror, when the police finally arrived, they called DCFS to file a report for emotional abuse because Kianna had witnessed her mother being punched and beaten by her boyfriend. This was a no-win situation, in that the very authorities who she called to help her in a time of danger were now threatening the one thing she had fought so hard to protect: her daughter. To prevent a DCFS investigation of her home, she had to file an official restraining order against Chris, which she did the next day. Still, her own experiences in foster care left her even more untrusting of the system that had essentially raised her, her mother, and her siblings. She explained:

> They came on the emotional abuse that one time and they're look- ing for if I got food in my house, or if she has somewhere to sleep— just stuff like that and I'm just like "you guys are dramatic and I don't want you here." No, seriously, I don't like DCFS because they're not looking for the traits in bad parents. There's a lot of kids I've seen that *should* have been taken away from their parents and they didn't. But the ones that shouldn't have—they take them and then they end up all screwed up. . . . So, they traumatize these kids and then they just give them back to their parents all messed up. . . . Like, they say they're trying to help—Department of Children and Family Services—it's not a department of children and family nothing. And I'm not just upset because of what's going on with my daughter, it's just never been right.

Desiree experienced being marked in a gendered and racialized way: being a poor single woman of color on public assistance. She was doing everything that she could to raise her child the best way she knew how, far surpassing the care she was ever provided in her own life. Yet still, she ended up with DCFS involved in her life at several junctures. At that point, she just hoped that they would close the case and she could move on.

Four months later, Desiree reported that DCFS dropped the case, but a short while later she let Chris back into her life. She needed the childcare help to look for a job, and also Chris was the one person that Kianna had ever called "dad." Desiree felt guilty about taking him away from Kianna. Soon after she let him back in, though, his violent behavior and jealousy escalated, so she had to kick him out again. This time, she relied on the support of her friends and her faith to get her through hard times.

> One of my other friends told me that certain people being in your life might block your blessings. I feel like every time he leaves everything works out smoothly. I didn't have childcare last time. I just happened to call this lady, said "yes I'll watch her and I'll watch her for free." God has been taking care of me . . . I know that I had appointments in the past couple of days that I had to go to and I was just making up excuses to keep him around and then every day God was sending me signs. Little signs, signs by signs and even after the fight he was begging—he called me like 40 times in the middle of the night. He came to the house and I was praying. She [Kianna] stayed up. She was scared. I was praying that she didn't hear him. She has little fits. But for the most part, I just don't want him to come because I don't want her to be bothered—I don't want to be bothered.

In the few months in between this interview and the subsequent one, Desiree had undergone significant changes in her life largely due to the community she was developing with other formerly incarcerated young people. Together, they had encouraged her to leave Chris for good and assured her that she would be okay on her own. They also helped to care for Kianna. Desiree had many new people in her life and a strong network of formerly incarcerated people that she called her family. She described her new way of love and support by her chosen family: "I'm just excited to actually have a family behind me to help kind of support that and knowing in foster care, it's not like that. You don't have people who really stand by you and a lot of support. People move in and out . . . We are a family; no one should be struggling by themselves. Everybody should be looking out for each other. I don't have much, but if someone needs help—I'm going to help them. We volunteer . . . So, that's another thing—I want to go and volunteer. At least give a little bit of my time to the schools." With the help of her community and relatives, she also had secured a part-time job, enrolled in school, and was planning to move in with her great aunt, who also ran a daycare out of her home. This was fortunate, as her eligibility for transitional housing benefits was soon coming to an end. Remarkably, after fighting the system for so many years, she seemed more than ready to be free of many of her past burdens: abuse at home and in foster care, mental health wards, juvenile justice, and then domestic violence. Desiree knew instinctively that she was repeating a cycle of trauma that she refused to extend to Kianna. Exuding self-confidence, she exclaimed: "I'm changing my life . . . I have wings, and I'm moving on."

CONCLUSION

The women's stories were replete with so many diverse experiences and triumphs that it felt to us more difficult (in contrast to the young men) to locate the areas of connection. However, through these narratives, as well as those not fully examined in this chapter from the four other women, we identified the themes of finding home, breaking the cycle, caregiving, social bonds, gendered violence, and survival and resilience as being critical to the young women's desistance journeys.

Finding home was not just a practical need for these young women but also an emotional one. Many of the young women had not actually had a stable space to call home for nearly their whole childhoods. Thus the search for this place of "home" had multiple layers of meaning, including a way to start over and break the cycle of the abuse or negative experiences they had witnessed in their own childhoods. This desire to break the cycle was not only related to criminal desistance, but also to be a better person, partner, parent, sister, or friend than their own family had been to them.

Caregiving and social bonds are intimately connected themes through close relationships with others, and both are associated with desistance (Salvatore & Taniguchi, 2012). Having strong social bonds and/or adopting a caregiving role is protective with regard to recidivism, particularly for women (Benda, 2005). In the case of these young women, they created meaning in their lives through providing care to others (boyfriends, children, friends)—clearly in the case of the young mothers, but also in the other stories, particularly Lupe and her care for her family and her girlfriend. Caregiving was important to them and something that motivated them to stay out of trouble for the sake of those who depended on them. At times, however, caregiving duties prevented them from tending to their own needs or well-being.

A bit more reluctantly than with caregiving relationships, they also relied on social bonds to support their own movement forward or at times to bail them out of difficulty. We use the term reluctantly here as these young women were used to relying on themselves, their own street smarts, and their ingenuity to create their own path forward. Yet still, we were struck that many formed bonds with groups, mentors, or friends that really came through for them in times of need. The young women spoke about these relationships as though they happened just in the nick of time to avoid a crisis, but they were also forged through their own deliberate involvement in positive social groups. From the stories of Irene and Desiree, it was quite clear that social support played a huge role in keeping them connected, committed to their goals, and feeling safe in the wake of breakups and crises.

One of the major threats to the young women's sense of safety was gendered violence. In some ways similar to the young men, the young women had to navigate risky neighborhoods, watch where they went at night, and steer clear of danger. Yet on top of the everyday risks associated with disadvantaged neighborhoods, the young women had to contend with fears or actualities of gendered forms of violence such as intimate partner violence, rape, and sexual assault. As many had already suffered trauma from these forms of violence in their own childhoods, this violence had the potential to emotionally and practically destabilize their progress toward their goals. Even when Desiree tried to protect herself and her daughter from violence, the police contact led to further complications with DCFS. Desiree's was clearly a no-win situation in which being the target of gender-based violence led to her being doubley targeted by the authorities.

Last, through all of the ups and downs in the search for a safe place to call home, the young women exhibited what we would identify as extraordinary resourcefulness and resilience. Reflecting back to Irene's narrative that opened this chapter, we must reflect back on the survival skills that weave a thread throughout these stories. Life changed quickly and dramatically in between each interview and many challenges remained, yet still, these women managed to find places to live, ways to support themselves, and mechanisms for growth and self-improvement. In the next chapter, we will offer our recommendations for how social policies and supports can be put in place to provide a more secure base for these young women and men not just to survive but also to flourish.

CHAPTER 8

Everyday Desistance

THEORY MEETS REALITY

THE CORE CONCEPT THAT we sought to unravel in this book was the everyday experience of criminal desistance during the transition to adulthood. Through life history narratives, we aimed to uncover (1) how the process of desistance unfolds for young adults in a particular urban context; (2) specific strategies used to navigate challenges related to desistance; and (3) gender differences in these experiences and navigation tools. Among the 25 young men and women in this study, all expressed some degree of desire to break free from the revolving door of crime and incarceration. However, there were key differences in their level of commitment to changing specific aspects of their appearance, identity, and behaviors, the progress they had made toward criminal abstinence, and how they responded to criminal temptations. Consistent with extant theory, we did not identify any one pathway or singular factor leading toward desistance. Instead, we found that a blend of internal and external factors contributed to supporting their desistance goals, with some factors playing a more prevalent role at different times in their lives than others. The combination and timing of these factors was situated in the constraints and opportunities of each individual's proximal environment.

Criminal recidivism was not necessarily a marker of the progress our participants had made toward desistance. Slightly less than one-half of the group had been re-arrested in early adulthood and yet, of these, only five were firmly "still in the game," or what we considered to be actively involved in crime. This is not to say that repeated contact with the police had no relevance to understanding criminal patterns. However, what emerged as more important were the steps each young person took in his or her own way to enact positive life changes in spite of the challenges they encountered. In this chapter, we look at how current theory can account for how desistance is defined, navigated, and enacted among people during this particular life stage.

WHAT IS DESISTANCE FOR YOUNG ADULTS?

For the young adults in our study, desistance was akin to what criminologist Shadd Maruna (2001) described as a "maintenance process" that involves drifting and zigzagging in and out of criminal activity. This conceptualization undergirds our theory of "everyday desistance": our assertion that formerly incarcerated young adults are consciously and unconsciously negotiating decisions around criminal activities, identities, and associations in their everyday and ordinary experiences. These negotiations had both positive and negative aspects, as these young people had experienced varying degrees of victories and disappointments in their journey toward adulthood. Bouts of unemployment and homelessness, family troubles, and careless decisions often went hand in hand with pursuits of higher education, establishing positive relationships, and achieving sobriety. In exploring the life history narratives, we were able to better understand why desistance is often a zigzagging process and to witness the incremental and arduous nature of making and sustaining behavioral change.

Honing in on these more minute, micro-level aspects of desistance was important given that we met these individuals at a time when their lives were very much in flux, and so desistance (or lack thereof) was not in any way fixed. Had we met these young people at another point in time, our conclusions about their typology or place on the desistance spectrum may have been quite different. For example, when we met Cesar, he had clearly been running in circles since leaving probation camp. He had enrolled in college but was still getting into trouble along with his gang and other neighborhood friends. Overall, he was struggling to reconcile his current self with the person he ultimately wanted to become. We have since had conversations with Cesar where we learned that he had finally managed to break the cycle he had been caught up in five years prior. Now, as a nearly 30-year-old man, he has a stable full-time job and is deeply committed to improving conditions in his community and caring for his family members. In his own words, he perceived himself as a completely different person from the 23-year-old young person who we initially met.

Cesar's journey provides support for our claim that no formerly incarcerated youth is necessarily doomed to a life of ongoing crime and struggle. The young people who are "running in circles" or "still in the game" in young adulthood still have the capacity to get on the road to desistance at some point in the future. When that happens, or what might trigger that shift, is still uniquely individual and unpredictable, and the shift in itself may not be a defining factor of future criminal abstinence. However, we find it important that theory and ultimately policy and practice make more room for young people to embody this "in-between" space where the journey may take different twists and turns before landing firmly on a particular path. Perhaps whether or not a young person can be considered a criminal desister or persister should not be the goal; instead the focus might entail accepting that youth may fall into this liminal space and equipping them with tools and strategies to help them navigate their way through these murky waters.

Motivation to Change

Our discussion of desistance would be incomplete if we did not acknowledge the importance of individual motivation to change. In the narratives of these young men and women, personal motivation resulting from "wake-up calls," formative relationships, or even from just being tired of the cycle of incarceration were quite important in triggering the internal and external movement toward desistance that ensued. Motivation on its own, however, did not always effectively sustain long-term change, particularly because these young people were over-policed and vulnerable to the weighty consequences of even very minor mistakes. We feel that this is an important point to make given that popular discourses and media images frequently portray formerly incarcerated youth in extremes: either as a "success story" who is able to overcome the odds by sheer motivation and optimism, or a "failure" who, by default, lacks the drive or character to break free from a criminal mentality.

The narratives of our participants suggest that in reality, formerly incarcerated youth represent neither of these extremes. By and large the young people we met were living lives that were hanging in the balance, in that their pathways to adulthood included successes and mistakes, triumphs and setbacks, motivation and indifference. Their histories of instability and lockup aside, they were simply in an exploratory phase of life that involved making decisions about jobs, relationships, school, identities, and future directions. These pursuits and interests fall very much in line with what other transition-age youth who have never been locked up or arrested experience during this life stage.

However, there is no skirting around the reality that the individuals in our study who had sustained the longest periods of criminal abstinence demonstrated a concrete commitment to changing their lives; desistance indeed started with a state of mind and a goal to attain. And we saw that this mind-set, combined with very persistent efforts, paid off over time. Intrinsic motivation coupled with external supports and opportunities led to tangible, positive outcomes, and eventually enabled them to translate the desire for desistance into comprehensive life changes. This doesn't mean that even the most motivated young people weren't prone to getting off track or zigzagging along the way, or conversely, that those who re-offended did not also aspire to change their lives. What it does mean was that the intent to change among those who gradually left criminal activity behind became more pronounced over time compared to their counterparts.

Given that young people are likely to have varying levels of motivation to desist from crime at different times, questions arise about the types of support that are necessary to engage youth around their desistance goals and the types of methods that can best monitor their progress. Answering these questions is difficult due to wide variance in how individuals respond to the internal and external circumstances at work in their lives. LeBel and colleagues (2008) raise this point in their "chicken and egg" inquiry about desistance, suggesting that subjective and situational factors work together to influence offending patterns, but that it's difficult to determine whether motivation precedes actual desistance behaviors or vice versa. Moreover, they noted that even when individuals are presented with the same challenges and/or opportunities, they often vary in their responses and ultimately in their desistance outcomes.

LeBel et al.'s (2008) theory helped us to interpret the range of desistance stories and experiences found among our study participants. The young men and women all possessed some motivation to change their lives, and had encountered people (mentors, family members, significant others) or places (advocacy programs, educational institutions, jobs) that offered sources of support toward desistance. However, they did not all respond to these factors in the same manner. In our understanding of the chicken or the egg, we would assert that in addition to motivation, one's definition of desistance played a critical role in facilitating the ability to take advantage of supports available. When we look at where the participants fell on the desistance spectrum, individuals who clearly associated desistance with abstinence from crime were better able to latch on to the support networks around them and navigate desistance obstacles. Moreover, possessing the internal motivation to change, along with the belief that they were truly establishing a different "script" for their future selves, further facilitated their movement toward a crime-free lifestyle (Bandura, 1989; Maruna, 2001). Again, we do not intend to suggest that others were failures or had made no efforts toward desistance; but rather, their motivations, definitions of desistance, and how they enacted these understandings reflected key differences from those who were on the road to desistance.

Catching Breaks and Making Mistakes

While it is clear that motivation played a critical role in propelling individuals forward in their desistance journeys, we also discovered perhaps a more untold part of the journey, that is, catching a break, or simple good fortune. For several participants, catching a break allowed them to change their environment in ways that were consistent with their desistance goals. Shawn for example was fortunate in that he was able to land a job just as he was reaching adulthood, all because he remembered the name of the company owned by his probation officer's family, and the officer's promise that he could get him a job there upon Shawn's release from camp. Although Shawn was already motivated to stay out of trouble and never return to jail, finding stable employment was instrumental in helping him to achieve his goals. Lupe also caught a break when she was able to tap into her trust fund left by her early childhood car accident. This break helped her rent an apartment, meet her basic living needs, and generally stay afloat while she figured out her next steps. However, since her internal motivation to change was not quite as present as Shawn's, this "break" did not result in her actually launching a career or more stability in her life (to the best of our knowledge). Extant desistance literature does a great job of describing the myriad of factors that come into play when young people are trying to desist from crime, which we reviewed in chapter 1. However, this idea of being able to catch a break and make the most of that opportunity is rarely discussed. For the young adults in our study, these breaks were just as important as any policy or program designed to assist formerly incarcerated youth with their transition-age needs.

On the flip side of catching a break was the notion of little mistakes, which are largely unaccounted for in current theory. We found that one of the major stumbling blocks for the young men and women in our study was small or uncalculated mistakes that put them at risk of police contact or other adverse consequences, such as losing their housing. Making mistakes and learning from these experiences is not particularly unique to incarcerated youth; in fact, it is a normative step in all young people's development (Arnett, 2000). However, for youth with criminal histories, mistakes can carry enormous, life-altering consequences. We know that well over half of all formerly incarcerated youth are likely to be re-arrested (Pew Charitable Trusts, 2015), ranging from minor, non-violent offenses such as missing a probation appointment or riding a train without a ticket, to more serious felony charges. Likewise, even when not directly involved in crime, we saw that our participants were susceptible to making mistakes simply when they let their guard down. For even the most motivated and determined individuals like Oscar or Irene experienced moments in which they just wanted to have fun and hang out with their friends without having to ponder their every movement or worry about each social situation they entered. Simply put, they grew weary of being marked and having to carry around the weight of the past.

Unfortunately, for some of our participants, making careless decisions nearly jeopardized their freedom. The narratives of young men like Oscar and Tyrone illustrated that the consequences for making mistakes were high, such as losing their housing or benefits, or for Desiree, risking child welfare oversight into her parenting life. Trying to recover from the losses associated with these types of penalties—finding a new place to live or a source of income, repairing relationships with family, and dealing with the psychological impact of having to rebuild—was a difficult and inevitably arduous process that often left them running in circles.

How can we better account for the missteps that formerly incarcerated youth are likely to make as they transition into adulthood? More importantly, what is the best way to help young people when they do veer off track, in a way that supports them yet still holds them accountable for their actions? We view the concept of mistakes as critical to any discussion of desistance. The notion of little mistakes, and the counterpart of catching a break, aren't easy to capture in research, but did appear to be salient in locating or losing the hooks for change that are so critical to the desistance process for this age group.

Gender-Specific Patterns

One rather open set of questions that we posed at the onset of this study concerned gender differences in the desistance process. Do young men and women have different motivations, setbacks, and points of engagement? What factors were likely to cause triggers for desistance for the young women and young men, respectively?

In the course of the study, we definitely found some gender-neutral processes at play in several aspects of the desistance journey. The young women and men shared housing, jobs, and related economic struggles, and they all were actively working to rebuild their lives after years trapped inside the juvenile justice system. They also had to juggle competing demands of school, relationships, and parenting, all the while exploring being a young adult. Their experiences were also parallel in that motivation to change and their own definitions of living a "different type of life" preceded a set of internal and external changes to facilitate desistance goals.

Yet some of the pivotal challenges and barriers to desistance did appear to be more gendered. One of the main differences that we found among the young women in our study was that they did not struggle with criminal temptations and being marked in the same way that the young men did. This finding may be attributed to the limitations of our sample and the younger age of the women. However larger and more representative studies have found that women are more prone to age out of crime than men as emerging adults (Piquero et al., 2014). While the young women were definitely more vulnerable in certain ways, in particular around housing, personal safety, and vulnerability to economic strain, they did not describe being as vulnerable in their relationships with the police, former enemies, or former friends.

Yet relationally and in regard to social support, the young women carried a different set of struggles that threatened to compromise their desistance goals. To begin, while men's relationships with their partners and wives appeared to very much promote desistance, the young women, with the exception of Lupe and her female partner, experienced the opposite effect. Gabriel and John both married women who were solid anchors for their desistance process and who provided them with motivation, unconditional support, and encouragement. By contrast, Irene's choice to be with Felipe, an active gang member, and Desiree's entanglements with her physically abusive boyfriend, led to closer contact with the police or other agents of the law (such as child welfare officials in Desiree's case). The young women seemed to struggle with finding romantic partners who mirrored their own goals and with whom they would be free from violent victimization of their pasts.

Another way that relationships were more strained for the young women was family ties. By and large, the young women in the study had experienced foster care, so finding safety in family was often elusive to them. Even the young women who did not have an experience in foster care described a great deal of family strife in their histories. Accordingly they were less trustful of their parents or relatives, and could not easily lean on them for social support, housing, or even emotional assistance to help them process or overcome hurdles they encountered along their journeys. Thus, for young women the relational process itself often posed a set of major vulnerabilities, whereas for the young men, ties to significant others and families were often anchors for desistance.

There were also gender differences in the connection between the economic margins and criminal temptation in that the young women who were by and large on the margins (unemployed, hadn't graduated high school) were not struggling with criminal temptations in the same way as the young men in similar circumstances. For example, Irene struggled with homelessness and unemployment, but never turned to selling drugs to make money. We speculate that this is perhaps because most of them had learned over the years how to survive; and how to access and utilize formal and informal supports—including friends and social service programs—to meet some of their basic needs. In early adulthood, we saw that they continued to do the same. In our interviews, they didn't express the same temptations to return to crime in the same way as their male counterparts.

With regard to questions surrounding gender differences, our findings affirm some of the gender-neutral aspects of desistance, such as how internal and external factors work together to facilitate change (Giordano et al., 2002). Yet we also found several important gendered dimensions of desistance, particularly in regard to sexualized violence and stereotypes for the young women, and being marked by the police for the young men. Here the intersection of race, class, and gender is salient for both genders. For example, being a poor young black or Hispanic man casts an immediate mark of being dangerous, particularly in the eyes of the police, with potential state intervention to ensue regardless of actual criminal activity. For a young woman in these circumstances, she may not be marked in a similar fashion. However, she may have the police but also other agents of the law, such as the child welfare system, to view her with suspicion or a parallel "blaming the victim" when targeted by sexualized violence, as Desiree experienced. Hence, for formerly incarcerated youth in the transition to adulthood, we would argue that gender indeed played a role in shaping their experiences, stumbling blocks, and the desistance process as a whole.

A NOTE ON CRIMINAL PATHWAYS AND DESISTANCE PATTERNS

Through our life history approach, we are presented with the opportunity to examine whether the earlier pathways to delinquency had anything to do with their desistance process as young adults. For example, did the early starters have different patterns than the late starters? Did the crossover youth end up in worse circumstances than others? In reexamining the stories and patterns, we found that the relationship between the pathways into crime and the challenges involved in early adulthood were complicated and not necessarily predictable. Nevertheless, there are a few observed patterns that warrant discussion and future consideration.

To start, the connection between early delinquency and more persistent and severe adult criminality is a well-established point in the literature (Thornberry et al., 2004). In our study this association was present but by no means definitive. The 11 individuals who we classified as "early starters" were quite polarized in the desistance patterns they exhibited in adulthood. They tended to be very firmly secure on the road to desistance, such as Oscar and John, or still in the game, like Carlos and Peter. However, one could not have necessarily predicted that an early starter like John, who was deeply entrenched in a gang, would now be graduating from a four-year university and pursuing graduate school. Could Peter or Carlos find similar landing points in the future? Perhaps yes, and perhaps no, as there is no way to be certain that Carlos or Peter will find that same mix of motivation and opportunity that John did. Nevertheless, we find hope that even those young people who were deeply entrenched in their youthful criminal identity can mature into successful, thoughtful, and productive adults. This is not necessarily a new discovery, but it does provide a sense of optimism at a time when popular discourse presents a narrative of gang members as destined to be dead or in prison by the time they are 25. Indeed, the most successful youth in our study were aware that they have indeed achieved beyond anyone's expectations of them, including their parents, the school system, and agents of the law.

Among those in pathway two, the late starters, we found no discernable pattern of desistance in young adulthood. Granted there were only four young men in this category, and among this group, all seemed to eventually wind up on the road to desistance (even with some starts and stops) except for Anthony, who was awaiting trial in county jail the last time we met with him. Moffitt's (1993) theory of age and crime argues that late starters by and large tend to desist in early adulthood; but why is this the case? What we can say about individuals such as Shawn, who was definitely a late starter, is that despite some bumps in the road, the absence of an entrenched criminal identity caused him to more closely appraise himself in relation to those who he encountered in juvenile camp. In Shawn's case, he felt that he should set himself apart from the highly criminally entrenched youth who he viewed as aimless and destructive. This sense of being different, combined with the work opportunities that he found, appeared to make it easier for Shawn to get out of the game entirely. His case is just one, yet still emphasizes the real relevance of internal identity shifts, and in particular seeing oneself as "not a criminal" as one component of desistance in this particular life stage.

Movement toward the road to desistance seemed to be the most challenging for the young people in pathway three, particularly the young men in this group, whose forays into crime stemmed from family troubles, poverty, and childhood maltreatment. With the exception of Gabriel, the young men in this group were all running in circles or still in the game. For the most part the young women were not involved in crime, but were often facing difficulties such as unemployment and homelessness that may have placed them in the "running in circles" group had we applied these same typologies to them. Relatedly, most of these young men and women were also struggling to achieve markers of stability as young adults; with one exception, they were all living on the margins during the time that we met them, finding it difficult to sustain themselves economically, live independently, or find meaningful career or schooling paths. The association that we can make here is quite clear: the heavy disadvantages in childhood, whether through poverty or child maltreatment, greatly hindered the ability to land in young adulthood. In turn an inability to land threatened desistance goals.

It is also important to acknowledge here the uniqueness of the crossover youth group, who had the most severe instability in adolescence. The drift and disconnection that they experienced post–juvenile justice system was very connected to their histories of maltreatment and foster care, rather than any entrenched propensity toward crime. Out of all the youth in the study, they struggled the most with establishing a secure base as young adults, and with little family support to fall back on, it is not surprising that they faced continuous cycles of economic and social instability. We view the connections between child welfare involvement and young adult drift as critically important, and in chapter 9 we will offer some particular policy directions to address these concerns.

In sum, in looking at the life histories from childhood through young adulthood, we see some associations between early criminal pathways and desistance in young adulthood. Many of our observed patterns are consistent with established life course research (Thornberry et al., 2004). In particular, we saw that the early starters had more criminal entrenchment (although an equal number in this group rebounded to a clear desistance pathway), the late starters had a somewhat easier time desisting, and poverty and child hardship led to disadvantage in young adulthood, but did not necessarily determine desistance patterns. We offer these patterns as conforming uniquely to our study in the context with which we have situated these stories, and note that more extensive research would be needed to continue to examine these pathways from childhood to young adulthood in the future.

CONCLUSION

The task of pinpointing exactly what criminal desistance entails is no doubt an arduous one. As changes in the larger social context continue to unfold, such as delayed age of marriage for young people, juvenile justice reform, and educational policy, we must continue to refine theories of what desistance means and how it is enacted. While available theories offer a framework to understand desistance, our intention was to more firmly situate this process within the transition to adulthood period and in a large urban landscape.

As the narratives of these young men and women in this setting reveal, the road toward disentangling oneself from past criminal behaviors and patterns is not linear, but it does share some common characteristics including internal motivation and identity shifts, external shifts that mirror this internal movement, and opportunities that facilitate the embodiment of desired social roles. Yet within this journey, there are many starts and stops, zigzagging, and drifting that can occur. It is precisely within this drift that we find the core of everyday desistance: decisions around transportation, events, relationships, appearance, friendships, and other seemingly innocuous moments that actually have great relevance to these young adults. It is easy to look at only the outcomes of the journey: if someone is re-arrested, has a job, or other official markers of success. One point that we hope to add to this conversation is that these outcomes do not adequately or accurately reflect the journey itself.

It is clear that no one leaves the juvenile justice system unscathed. No doubt there were individuals who could be considered success stories in the traditional sense; some have earned college degrees, others have transitioned into social justice advocates, and a few others have become loving parents who were extremely committed to their families. Yet these accomplishments did not shield them from experiencing their own share of trials and setbacks in their journey toward adulthood. Ultimately, our analysis pointed to a set of interpersonal and structural barriers that, unless systematically addressed, will continue to place limitations on young people's ability to thrive after spending their adolescence in the juvenile justice system. Failing to remove these barriers may also potentially leave these young people trapped in a cycle of setbacks as they enter adulthood. In our final chapter, we will provide suggestions for policy and practice reforms that conform to our emerging theory and findings.

CHAPTER 9

Policy and Practice Reforms

SUPPORTING THE PATHWAY TO ADULTHOOD

IN THIS BOOK, WE have situated the life histories of 25 formerly incarcerated young adults within the parameters of Los Angeles County institutions (i.e., education, child welfare, and juvenile justice) and additional layers of the social, political, and economic landscape. Through this contextualized approach, we can see the many ways that social institutions and systems have shaped these young people's opportunities, barriers, and life chances from early childhood to adulthood. Completing this analysis led us to one of the most challenging aspects of the project: laying out what this study can contribute to social policy and practice reform.

To this end, we held several fruitful discussions, some with the study participants, and others with colleagues, friends, family members, and each other, to organize our thoughts around policy and practice implications. We came up with a broad range of ideas, but tried to keep this discussion as close to the data as possible and not to reinvent the wheel. After much deliberation, we decided to divide this chapter into three major sections associated with the flow of the book: prevention (chapter 2), the juvenile justice system (chapter 3), and the transition to adulthood (chapters 4–7). Through each of these phases, we wish to emphasize how social policies and institutions can be more responsive to the needs and experiences of children who are growing up in conditions that give rise to delinquency and juvenile justice system involvement.

It is important that we recognize that this study is focused in one urban space with a small number of participants and was not intended to be generalizable. We did not randomly select a representative group of young people in this study. However, through our methodology, we purposively sought out individuals who were not experiencing the more extreme ends of success or failure in order to capture likely a more typical, nonlinear experience. In this way, we were able to look at starts, stops, and missteps that might characterize a process of desistance for young people emerging from similar circumstances. Moreover, we found that many of the young people's stories in our book resonated with ethnographic accounts of formerly incarcerated and criminalized youth in other urban areas (Fader, 2013; Goffman, 2014; Rios, 2011). For these reasons, although our sample is not generalizable, we have crafted our policy and practice implications to apply more broadly than the Los Angeles region.

PREVENTION

In our discussions with study participants about the findings, they overwhelmingly emphasized prevention as the best way to address the problems that they encountered from childhood through young adulthood. This idea was a bit daunting for us, as prevention can lead to many vast directions. Despite our initial apprehension of tackling this topic, we came to the realization that the idea of prevention typically comes into play when discussing solutions for more privileged youth, such as the emphasis on mental health services for white men who perpetuate mass shootings. With youth of color, the answer to problems of violence is typically to discipline or incarcerate, rather than to prevent them from occurring in the first place. Although prevention may lead us a bit further from our data than we would prefer, we believe that these youth are equally deserving of these strategies as their more privileged peers. Hence, based on the "how we got here" chapter, we will hone in on three prevention strategies: (1) family supports and safety nets; (2) the school to prison pipeline; and (3) crossover youth and child welfare systems.

Family Supports and Safety Nets

One of the major pathways to delinquency among the participants was family poverty. In identifying poverty as a main factor in contributing to delinquency, we are aware of the risk of oversimplifying the mechanisms leading to troubled youth behavior. There are many parents without economic resources who are loving and encouraging and whose children grow up to be successful and engaged citizens. Conversely, there are wealthy parents whose children wind up becoming career criminals. Yet a significant body of research has shown that, on the whole, severe and persistent poverty leads to a host of children's problems including compromised health and well-being, lower school performance, and behavioral troubles associated with delinquency (Duncan & Brooks-Gunn, 1999). Moreover, growing up in neighborhoods with concentrated poverty increases the odds that a young person will gravitate toward gangs or crime, in part as a way to achieve self-efficacy in a context where they are typically less able to acquire this sense of power through more mainstream social institutions (Anderson, 2000).

We can likely agree that way too many children in Los Angeles County—more than 25 percent—are growing up poor (Willen et al., 2013). And unfortunately, the youth in our study who grew up with severe poverty seemed to have a harder time moving away from crime as young adults. It is truly unjust that a child like Mike, who had to steal groceries in order to eat dinner, would be criminalized at such a young age, rather than offered a hot meal or assistance. The act of stealing is the symptom of such a larger problem of entrenched poverty, hunger, and disparities in resources—in this case—in one of the wealthiest and most prosperous cities in the world.

Both historically and currently, social welfare policy in the United States has drawn a line between the "deserving" and the "undeserving" poor and assigned benefits accordingly (Gordon, 1994). The young people in this study largely came from families that policymakers and the public often cast as "undeserving": undocumented immigrants, racial and ethnic minorities, parents facing mental illness and drug addiction, single parents, and parents with criminal histories. Others had parents who simply could not make ends meet, even with public welfare support. There were key examples from our study that illustrated how strained finances directly contributed to delinquency. For example, Gabriel and Oscar both felt that their parents' long work hours resulted in less supervision at home, and accordingly, more time to get into trouble in the neighborhood. They also disclosed certain emotional drawbacks of their parents' work hours; both felt that in working so hard to supply for their family's needs, they lacked time to simply pay attention to their children's academic and social needs.

It is interesting to consider that the young adults in our study were born in the early 1990s; and as they were small children, their family's lives were influenced by dramatic changes in the structure of welfare benefits. In 1996, President Clinton authorized the most major overhaul of welfare benefits since the New Deal: replacing the federal Aid to Families with Dependent Children (AFDC) program to state block grants in the form of Temporary Assistance to Needy Families (TANF). Among other major changes, TANF imposed time limits on welfare benefits and allowed states to apply more discretion to TANF qualifications (Jannson, 2005). Of relevance to many of the families in this study, the law barred many immigrant families, both documented and undocumented, from receiving food stamps (Schwartz, 2001). As we listened to the young people whose parents were first-generation immigrants, we heard that as children they never felt that they had enough food or resources, despite their parents' hard work. Based on our data, we certainly cannot make any concrete conclusions about the relationship between the welfare reform generation and the path to the juvenile justice system. However, research has found adverse outcomes for children who experienced welfare reform (Gennetian, Duncan, Knox, Vargas, Clark-Kauffman, & London, 2004; Zaslow et al., 2002) and we believe that researchers should continue to examine the potential relationships between TANF, family poverty, and crime now that this generation has become adults.

The School-to-Prison Pipeline

A sizable number of the participants in this book began their journey to juvenile hall by way of the policies and practices of their local school system (Curtis, 2014). When these children acted out their home or other frustrations in school, the punishments they received often led them to stop going to school altogether. In turn, school disconnection translated to more time learning on the streets than in the classroom. The district then lost track of these transfers and eventually allowed these youth to fall into the black hole of alternative schools, like Peter, or to just drop out of school altogether, like Keira.

In the last several years, the school-to-prison pipeline has become a significant point of consideration in regard to preventing youth from entering the juvenile justice system. In 2013, the Los Angeles Unified

School District became the first district in the state of California to ban willful defiance as a reason for suspension. Willful defiance includes minor infractions such as coming to class unprepared or refusing to remove a hat (Los Angeles Unified School District, 2013). These willful defiance clauses and similar policies around the nation have disproportionately targeted students of color, particularly black males, with suspensions and expulsions that negatively impact their futures (Advancement Project 2010; Curtis, 2014). The state of California soon followed Los Angeles' lead, and in 2014, Governor Brown signed Assembly Bill 420, which eliminates willful defiance for expulsion and prevents administrators from using willful defiance to suspend students in kindergarten to third grade (Frey, 2014). This is a key piece of legislation that we anticipate will slow down or curb the school-to-prison pipeline in the future.

Based on the experiences of the young people in our study, we believe that the momentum toward policy change in the area of willful defiance is significant, yet not sufficient for altering the course of struggling public school students. Overhauling suspension and expulsion laws may help some students to remain in school, but they do not ensure a quality education or a learning environment that is safe or that fosters success. As long as school segregation and unequal funding formulas remain in place, students of color and poor students will continue to be marginalized and often forgotten within public school systems such as LAUSD. Many of the youth in our study were educationally disadvantaged due to a poor-quality education; while some LAUSD schools have high expectations and impressive graduation rates, the schools that these young people attended were, by their accounts, some of the most dismal with regard to academic achievement, resources, and school climate. Suspension and expulsion policies may represent an important step in creating an environment that is inclusive and supportive of all students, but on their own, won't change these equally important structural disparities.

A recently released report entitled *Black Minds Matter: Supporting the Educational Success of Black Children in California* (The Education Trust, 2015) lays out a series of concrete policy recommendations to bolster black students' academic success in California, including universal access to pre-kindergarten, desegregation through enhanced school choice, higher quality and rigorous education across schools, and improvements in school climate and discipline practices. We support these policy recommendations and believe that if properly implemented, they would help to prevent delinquency among all children, not only black students. One strategy highlighted in this study included extending classroom learning time to include academic, social, and skills-based activities to supplement what students learn during traditional school hours. This learning model has been shown to increase educational outcomes for black students in particular throughout California. Certainly for the young people that we interviewed, school improvements such as those outlined in this report may have helped to address some of the key behavioral, academic, and social difficulties they encountered in their early learning years.

Our study also illustrates how important it is to improve the educational climate for youth during the middle school years, the time period when a core group of our participants began disengaging from school and getting into more serious trouble with their peers. The report highlighted specific programs that have reduced delinquent behaviors by providing youth with opportunities for leadership and mentorship. We saw many examples when young men and women in our study exhibited leadership, ingenuity, and creativity, but they often lacked opportunities to channel their gifts into more positive activities. In other words, the same talents they used to survive on the streets could be useful in more pro-social settings. We believe that it is critical to invest in programs that can tap into and strengthen youths' assets, and expand their perspective on how they can use their skills to positively contribute to the world around them.

Crossover Youth and Child Welfare Systems

It is incredibly disturbing that so many of America's most vulnerable children, those raised in foster care, wind up in the throes of the juvenile justice system (Herz et al., 2012; Krinsky, 2010). Crossover youth also have the worst young adult outcomes across health, income, housing, and criminal justice domains compared to youth from either system on its own (Culhane et al., 2011). Given what is known about the serious problems that crossover youth face, it seems quite clear that our social institutions can no longer afford to fail our most vulnerable children in this way. The experiences of crossover youth in our study affirm what is known in the larger literature about being the most vulnerable to marginalization, particularly when they lost all sense of family support during adolescence. There may be no equivalent substitute for a healthy and thriving family that is free from maltreatment; however, we can certainly do better in preventing youth from crossing over from child welfare to juvenile justice. Based on these stories and the other research we have reviewed, we offer two major recommendations: improving foster care placements and examining the criminalization process.

Prevention for crossover youth must start with the child welfare system's responsibility to provide high-quality foster care and permanency planning for abused and neglected children. After considering and listening to the stories of the crossover youth, we are left with little doubt that many of their problems that occurred in adolescence and young adulthood could have been prevented by receiving higher quality foster care and sustained and supportive child welfare services. Several of our study participants expressed strong resentment toward DCFS for placing them in more abusive or unstable living situations. They saw themselves as the system's greatest throwaways. Prevention through child welfare systems means that these young people are not tossed from one abusive setting to another; that they are given a chance to thrive by improving child welfare systems, quality of placements, and permanency planning.

Poor-quality child welfare placements also clearly contribute to running away and to a pattern of additional instability and disadvantage. Resulting from this cycle of abuse and running away was a process of gradual criminalization that ended up further marginalizing and destabilizing foster youth. We must rethink social policies that criminalize youth for running away from foster care, which happened with nearly all of the young women in our study. Imagine if, rather than penalizing this behavior, child welfare workers were mandated to understand reasons why a young person would run away. What if running away was a signal for a young person's distress, rather than a trigger for a trip to juvenile hall?

All of these changes are possible and crossover youth policy is a tangible area for policy reform. Indeed, there are several initiatives currently underway that can benefit crossover youth, such as specialized courts, mandated multi-system collaborations between child welfare and probation, and specific practice models to implement when working with crossover youth in the courts (National Juvenile Justice Network, 2015). We consider these advances to be promising, provided that these newer modes of operating will be carefully evaluated, funded, and then replicated according to their successes. Our nation's most vulnerable children should not be unjustly criminalized or further disadvantaged for lack of a safe home to fall back on; in fact, this is a fragile point of intervention with major consequences for the child's future.

Thus, from the prevention standpoint, we have presented three potential angles to work from: family income support, school policies, and child welfare reform. While we recognize that none of these are simple tasks, we assert that making headway in just one of these areas can potentially disrupt the paths toward delinquency that emerged in our study. We find it imperative that we continue to seek solutions with a far-reaching prevention angle. For, once a child gets involved in the juvenile justice system, it is often quite difficult to break free.

INSIDE THE JUVENILE JUSTICE SYSTEM

There is a significant movement underway that is seeking to reform several key aspects of the juvenile justice system, with emerging support from both sides of the political aisle. As part of the backlash to decades of failed mass incarceration policies, advocates and policymakers have made great strides in several key juvenile justice arenas, including: (1) limiting the use of detention or formal probation for minor crimes (Mendel, 2011); (2) keeping youth out of the adult system by raising the age of criminal responsibility and scaling back mandatory transfer laws to criminal court (Campaign for Youth Justice, 2014); (3) limiting or abolishing the criteria for life without parole sentences for minors when tried in adult court (Calvin, Weir, Nahoray, & Breen, 2012); (4) making juvenile correctional institutions less punitive, safer, and reducing the use of solitary confinement (Mendel, 2015); and (5) more adequately addressing the needs of young women in the juvenile justice system (Center for the Study of Social Policy, 2015). In sum, the current era of juvenile justice reform is creating a safer and more just system in the service of children's rights and to promote greater social good.

For the young people in our study, their lives unfolded at a time when they did not benefit from these reforms. On the contrary, they endured detention and incarceration at some of the worst moments, when lawsuits charged abuses in the Los Angeles probation camps and when there were not enough beds to house all of the youth who the courts deemed in need of placement. A few of the study participants, like Shawn, were positioned to be prosecuted as adults for minor crimes due to very punitive policies initiated during the 1990s, when fear of crime and youth in particular reached its peak (Abrams, 2013). Moreover, nearly all of the young women and many of the young men had spent time in juvenile hall due to petty crimes, status offenses, or probation violations. To make matters worse, the facilities where these young people were sentenced often were not safe or humane, as abuses of power such as those that Peter described were commonplace.

There are numerous current policies on the table for improving juvenile justice systems and services, and we do not wish to reinvent the wheel on these recommendations (for an excellent summary of current juvenile justice reform in all 50 US states, see the website *Advances in Juvenile Justice Reform*, published by the National Network on Juvenile Justice). Rather, our findings lend themselves to support several key strategies. In particular, we see a pressing need for laws and policies that decriminalize minor infractions, probation violations, status offenses, and that seek to reduce the use of out-of-home placements for system-involved youth. For example, the state of Pennsylvania passed a law in 2011 requiring courts to justify any court-ordered out-of-home placement. By decriminalizing minor crimes and limiting the use of out-of-home placements, we believe that many of the young people in our study would have been spared from years and years of cycling through the juvenile justice maze. They may also have been better situated financially and emotionally to become adults.

If a young person requires an out-of-home placement, these institutions must be free from abuse and violent victimization by guards and youth. In addition to this very basic premise, we recommend practices that invite outside rehabilitation services, mentors, and community members to work with youth in supportive ways both within facilities and, once they are released, to the community. Many of the youth in our study were able to hang onto these relationships with program staff even when they exited the system, such as Irene, who found solace and support in her trusted mentor who she met while in CYA. They appreciated programs they saw as benefiting their overall development and sense of optimism—such as sports and writing. While there is a current pressure on public systems to fund only evidence-based juvenile justice interventions (Abrams, 2013), our findings lend support to the idea that programs cultivating positive youth development among incarcerated youth, such as the arts, fitness, and opportunities for expression (Lerner, Almerigi, Theokas, & Lerner, 2005) are just as relevant to producing positive outcomes as some of the more widely lauded evidence-based therapies.

It is also important to note that while progress is occurring on many fronts in regard to juvenile justice reform, racial disparities within the juvenile justice system are actually widening, rather than shrinking (Sickmund et al., 2013). African American youth in particular are not benefitting from these reforms in the same ways as their counterparts. Some have suggested that reforms are largely targeting those deemed most worthy of redemption—white youth, those who score lower on standardized risk assessments, and those who live in areas with more alternatives to incarceration (Hager, 2015). While we recognize the need for reform initiatives that will target all youth who become entangled with the juvenile justice system, we are skeptical of policies that do not explicitly target racial bias and disparities that permeate the system. If not directly addressed, we fear that youth of color may not gain from the potential benefits of these reforms.

POLICIES SUPPORTING DESISTANCE IN YOUNG ADULTHOOD

In recent years, we have witnessed an increase in policies, public funding, and services geared toward transition-age foster youth, such as extended benefits and care, housing, educational grants, and mental health services and supports. However, we haven't seen this same level of concern for and investment in youth who have been involved in the juvenile justice system. By and large and despite the significant challenges that lie before them, young people often exit the juvenile justice system to face adulthood on their own, without a concrete plan or tangible resources to help them adjust to life as adults. Additionally, as we discussed in chapter 2, many formerly incarcerated youth return to communities weighed down by their own set of challenges and without an abundance of resources to facilitate success.

The lack of a comprehensive blueprint for this group is especially concerning given that these are the young people who often have the worse set of adult outcomes with regard to unemployment, criminal activity, homelessness, and other indicators of well-being, even compared to other vulnerable emerging adult populations (Uggen & Wakefield, 2005). Earlier in this chapter we commented on the historic paradigm of the deserving versus underserving poor and associated implications for supporting families with young children. It is hard to disentangle this age-old social welfare construct from the discussion around policies for formerly incarcerated youth, given the demographics of youth who are disproportionately profiled, arrested, and incarcerated for their crimes. Would society feel more responsibility for these youth if they represented more of the deserving poor? How might that belief impact the types of policies and programs that are put in place to assist these youth? Below we draw attention to a few key barriers to desistance that emerged in our study that we believe require more systematic attention.

Employment

One point that scholars, practitioners, and youth generally agree upon in discussions around breaking the cycle of recidivism is the importance of employment (Seigle & Walsh, 2014). Our study findings were no different, in that participants who were able to secure a legal means of supporting themselves managed to stay away from criminal activity for longer periods of time. Moreover, looking deeper to underlying mechanisms, employment provided these young adults a sense of meaning and purpose associated with their transition to adult roles and responsibilities. In turn, success in achieving adult roles helped to support desistance. For many of our participants, the ability to view longevity in their work enabled them to envision futures that did not involve crime.

Yet even for some of the most successful of those who were making ends meet, like Shawn and Steven, longer term career paths were not always readily apparent or attainable without a college degree, and they didn't have time to work full time and go to school. Moreover, the majority of the participants did not find long-term or meaningful employment, and employment in and of itself was not sufficient to fully disrupt cycles of homelessness and recidivism. For example, when the men in Typologies Two and Three were employed, the positions were typically located in the food sector or retail industry. While these jobs certainly provided them with money that was critical to their survival, they did not inspire these young men to change their lives in significant ways. The women as a slightly younger group were a bit different in that they were trying to finish school and/or raise children, and they were not all seeking full-time work at the time that we met them. Nevertheless, they all aspired to career paths that involved a college degree, and it was unclear how they would be able to achieve this goal and simultaneously navigate the high cost of living in Los Angeles.

What then does this say about the types of employment pathways that are available for formerly incarcerated young people? The lack of a structured safety net for system-involved youth frequently results in their being tracked into jobs that are, simply put, a way to just barely make ends meet or to check a box on a condition of parole. In some ways, these lower-skilled jobs may not differ much from those held by young people in the same age range who do not have post-secondary degrees. A recent report from the Pew Research Center (2014) found that the wage disparities between college and non-college degree-holding millennials (ages 25–32) is wider than ever before, with high school graduates earning roughly $17,000 less per year than individuals who hold a college degree. Moreover, 42 percent reported having "just a job to get by" compared to only 14 percent of college graduates. However, formerly incarcerated youth are distinct in that they often have direct access to illegal means of making money. And the temptation to go this route may be particularly high for those like Mike, who viewed selling drugs as necessary for his survival. Another example of this conundrum is Chris, who professed a strong desire to avoid any further time behind bars, and to a lesser extent, criminal activity, yet he felt stuck because he hadn't been able to find stable work for more than two years and was contributing to the care of two children. He recognized that his unemployment represented a huge desistance barrier, and for that reason, he seemed open to any work that would provide a solid income. At the same time, his entrepreneurial spirit was evident in his numerous attempts to start a business.

In chapter 4, we argued that more privileged young adults don't necessarily have the same types of employment pressures as formerly incarcerated youth. Indeed, many are encouraged to use this phase of life to explore career paths that they are passionate about, which can include working a variety of internships, or not working at all, in order to develop the skills and pursue the education needed to support their goals. If you believe (as we do) that most formerly incarcerated youth are capable of changing their lives for the better, would it be reasonable to provide them with the same room for growth and development in emerging adulthood that more privileged youth tend to enjoy? While there is clearly a promising bipartisan movement to reduce mass incarceration, we need to be equally mindful of opening up opportunities for young adults on probation, community supervision, or diversion to transition into career opportunities that offer sustainable futures. There are a number of community-based programs in Los Angeles County that have demonstrated success in helping formerly incarcerated young adults carve out employment paths during and after confinement (Abrams, Daughtery, & Freisthler, 2011) and these are not unique just to Los Angeles. However, these programs are often at capacity and do not have the funding to meet the demand.

In our view, we must continue to chip away at multiple levels of barriers to employment for formerly incarcerated youth if we wish to provide economic safety nets and the opportunity for independence. In particular, we believe that the programs aiming to lift structural barriers to employment (such as ban the box campaigns), launch career paths (as opposed to temporary low-wage work), and provide ongoing support through mentoring or other direct services will be most apt to engage young people in a successful employment trajectory.

Finding Home

Finding home emerged as a key concept in this study, more visibly for the young women, but nevertheless important for the young men as well. Having a home provides the stable base from which to launch other aspects of their lives—jobs, education, and movement toward desistance. Yet several participants were insecurely housed or transient and only about one-quarter of the group were able to afford to rent their own room or apartment. Housing was clearly a problem for most and an ongoing source of stress, particularly in an expensive city such as Los Angeles, where economists have projected that one has to make $33 an hour to afford the average apartment (Green, Reina, & Hemp, 2014), and yet our employed participants were earning the minimum wage of then $8.25 per hour or slightly higher.

Finding a place to call home wasn't just logistical, but was also emotional and symbolic of their independence and idea of adulthood. So many of these young adults had not had a stable home since they were 12 years of age or even younger. Years of institutionalization had not prepared them, either emotionally or financially, to settle down, pay rent, and create a safe space for themselves. Our participants often found themselves bouncing from home to home, staying on couches, and at times, sleeping in their cars. Even when they were housed, they complained about neighborhood safety concerns, gangs, and police presence that disrupted the tentative sense of peace they were trying to establish.

There are federal laws and a host of local initiatives providing transitional housing (either supervised or less supervised) for youth who are aging out of foster are, and we suggest that similar policies need to be in place for youth who are aging out of the juvenile justice system. The Foster Care Independence Act (Chafee Act) enacted in 1999 made inroads into this arena with foster youth by increasing the provision of educational, vocational, and employment resources to promote independence during the transition-age years. Though some have critiqued this policy for being too narrowly focused and perhaps not recognizing that foster youth need lifelong connectedness and support, the Chafee Act was still significant in that it raised awareness of the significant needs that systems-involved young people have as they enter adulthood (Freundlich, 2010). Our study provides support to devote similar concerted attention to the housing needs of formerly incarcerated youth.

Police Profiling

It is difficult, if not impossible, to discuss policies and programs for formerly incarcerated young adults without addressing the structural problem of the disproportionate rates of police harassment, arrests, and unwarranted killings of young men of color. A recent *Washington Post* report found that black people, particularly those who are unarmed, have higher rates of being killed by the police compared to white people or any other ethnic minority group (Kindy, 2015). Popular media outlets with near constant depictions of heavy-handed police misconduct further paint the picture of the types of treatment youth of color are apt to receive when they come into contact with law enforcement. While a full detailing of the legalized harassment of youth of color is well defined in others' scholarship (cf. Goffman, 2014; Rios, 2011), these dynamics no doubt colored how our participants navigated their daily lives after they exited the system. Some felt that the sheer presence of the police in their neighborhoods represented a threat to desistance because it increased the likelihood that they would be stopped and harassed because of their past actions and/or current appearance. To be fair, we acknowledge that this line became blurred when the same youth who complained of this harassment also admitted to ongoing criminal activity. However, regardless of their level of criminal involvement, most of the participants perceived the police as a hindrance rather than a help to any efforts they were making to change their lives.

It is clear that any initiatives aimed at disrupting cycles of crime and incarceration among youth, and youth of color in particular, must be coupled with police reform. For even the most well-meaning prevention programs will have limited impact if these young people are living in a society where they have an increased likelihood of encounters with the police that can result in them being arrested, incarcerated, or at worst, dead. More broadly, policymakers, academics, and community members have crafted a range of possible solutions to initiate police reform, including the use of police body cameras, citizen review boards to monitor police shootings, and laws that require police to report data around deaths that occur while individuals are under police supervision (Chang & Sewell, 2014; Wilson, n.d.). These policies are intended not only to improve policing practices in communities of color, but also to combat the long-standing stereotype of youth of color as individuals with a greater proclivity toward crime and violence, and as more deserving of the most severe treatment and punishment.

Specific to Los Angeles, we believe that the current gang injunction policy ought to be studied for how it contributes to the profiling, harassment, and recidivism rates of young men of color. Injunctions negatively impacted many of the young men in our study, regardless of whether or not they were even consistently involved in crime or gang violence. A few of the young men also believed that in addition to per-petuating discrimination, injunctions contributed to unbreakable cycles of criminalization. As we illustrated in chapter 6, it is difficult to sustain the momentum toward change when you are constantly marked by your past. If gang injunctions are to remain an active crime suppression strat-egy, then we must at least question the current model that does not allow a person to be removed from such surveillance. It seems only fair that any gang injunction policy have a time limit or mechanisms for these policies to be lifted once a person has shown that she or he is a safe member of the community. It is also worth questioning to what extent injunctions serve to contribute to cycles of criminal recidivism among gang-involved youth, even in the absence of any new crimes.

In sum, there are several arenas of policy reform that can specifi-cally target young adults with incarceration histories. We have honed in on the areas of employment, housing, and policing, that we believe can directly address some of the obstacles that formerly incarcerated young adults are apt to face. This list is by no means exhaustive, as there are sev-eral other institutional arenas that can also be reshaped to better address the needs of this population. Nevertheless, working within our everyday desistance framework, we believe that providing opportunities to succeed along with strategies to decriminalize normal young adult behavior can help to facilitate desistance when young people are ready to take these critical steps.

Working with Formerly Incarcerated Young Adults

It is important to provide some practical implications for those working with formerly incarcerated youth, particularly probation and parole officers, who often have sustained one-on-one contact with young people once they enter into the juvenile or criminal justice systems. The supervisorial duties associated with these jobs can range from the devel-opment of aftercare plans to assist youth with community reentry (i.e., arranging job, housing, and social services), to the enforcement of court orders (i.e., conducting drug testing, searches, and re-arrests). Parole and probation officers act as gatekeepers in that the services they offer can provide youth with opportunities to avoid crime, yet they can also determine whether or not a young person reenters the system. These agents of the law thus play a critical role in shaping youths' opportunities for desistance. But what strategies are in place to improve their interactions with and oversight of the youth with whom they work?

A number of participants were able to recall encounters with officers of the law who influenced them in various directions. Shawn fortunately remembered the words of his probation officer, who told him to contact him if he ever needed a job, and then found steady work in his family's business. He admitted that he would have had a very difficult time in attaining independence without this consistent source of income. Gabriel, however, explained that his one and only arrest as an adult occurred simply because he missed an appointment with his probation officer. Despite the fact that he had left his gang, had a job, and had stayed out of trouble, he was detained nevertheless, and then quickly released in part due to the advocacy of the staff of community programs who wrote letters and appeared in court to speak up on his behalf. What types of options do probation and parole officers have to advocate for their clients who are actively working to better themselves? What would have happened to Gabriel if there had been no witnesses to provide testimony about his lifestyle changes? How might extended jail time have impinged upon his ability to find another job or place to live after he was released? And if he was unable to readily find these things, how might he have dealt with the weight of having a family to support with no legal source of income? For other participants, their probation services were abruptly cut when they turned 18, like Lupe and Desiree, leaving them scrambling for housing and income support as youth who had relied on that system for food and shelter.

Probation and parole services appear to be a mixed blessing, at times offering supportive words or relationships; and at other times, operating simply as an arm of the law with established rigidity and bureaucracy. As some of our participants experienced, these formal systems have limitations on the type of help they provide. From a law enforcement perspective, desistance is undoubtedly tied to legal mandates; following probation conditions, staying away from associates with criminal backgrounds, cutting gang ties, and most important, terminating criminal activities. Probation officers and other contracted service providers often emulate this model, and are required to measure success through official arrest rates or reconviction rates and standardized instruments, rather than subjective measures of change. Our study supports other scholars' contentions that these official measures do not always represent the best method for assessing recidivism or propensity for desistance (Miller, 2014; Salole, 2016). For example, Gabriel, Steven, and Oscar were among the most committed to the road to desistance, yet all three had been arrested or detained as adults. All of this is to say that the unknowns involved in everyday desistance and the abrupt changes that these young people experience can make it hard for formulaic programs to truly capture how a young person is doing at a given time or even predict how they may act in the future.

Despite these complexities, our findings illustrate how programs can target their resources to impact young people who may want to abstain from crime, but are struggling to sustain their motivation and/or enact major behavioral change. We would argue that the majority of young people in our study were at this exact juncture of struggle when we met them. It is likely that there were key moments to engage someone like Carlos, who exited juvenile camp not fully ready to leave his gang, but with a mind-set to work, go to school, and move toward desistance in his own way, mostly by altering his appearance and following the terms of his probation. We didn't know Carlos during this period of life, so it's difficult to pinpoint the exact set of factors that caused him to stray from these goals. However, after hearing his story, we were left wondering how a probation officer might have worked with Carlos to better support him in incremental changes he was willing to make at that time.

At the same time, the people who work with formerly incarcerated youth must take into account that not all of their clients are necessarily open to receiving support, particularly from agents of the state. Histories of public welfare services and confinement and simply being young people who were anxious to be in charge of their own lives for the first time left many of the participants in our study hesitant to access formal social services. Some also expressed being reluctant to enroll in programs targeted toward formerly incarcerated youth, either because of the associated stigma, or because it was difficult to focus on their goals while surrounded by other young people who were all at different phases of their own desistance journeys. Thus, while some of the young people had established relationships with probation officers, mentors, and community-based programs that helped to shift their life trajectories, others wanted the freedom to sort out their lives without constant oversight and monitoring. All of these insights further emphasize the point that there is no one universal program or strategy that can create a pathway toward desistance. Rather, we must continue to seek out moments of engagement that may trigger pathways toward desistance at various stages of the process, and in concert with the young person's most pressing needs, motivations, and circumstances.

CONCLUSION

In this concluding chapter, we have offered our ideas on strategies for improving the life chances of formerly incarcerated young adults from prevention through adulthood. We recognize the limitations of social safety nets in providing youth with everything needed to overcome barriers to criminal desistance. This includes the love and support of family and friends, the strength that comes from knowing that people believe in you in spite of your mistakes, and the internal motivation to change course. Nevertheless, we believe that as a society we can do more to care for young people who have been considerably disadvantaged by their involvement in the juvenile justice system.

We also find it critical that young people who have experienced incarceration have room to experience all that young adulthood entails. This range of experiences encompasses having the room to make mistakes and bad decisions alongside the opportunity to recover from and rebuild afterward. The value of second chances is partially reflected in certain policy initiatives directed for youth with criminal histories. For example, policies in California allow records to be sealed if they are from juvenile court, which can facilitate greater access to employment, a driver's license, or public housing. By and large, however, there are few ways to account for missteps once these young people become legal adults. While all young people should be held to the same standard in terms of following the law, it also seems clear that the zero-tolerance policies only serve to breed ongoing marginalization and life disruption rather than positive change.

As we listened to the narratives of our participants and watched their adult lives unfold, we were amazed at the ingenuity and resilience of these young men and women to navigate immense obstacles they faced. Their life paths were varied and changed considerably even during the time that we met them. Yet in the end, their stories taught us that all young people have the capacity to reach beyond the labels assigned to them. Thus we believe that with a blend of concerted policy changes from prevention through to adulthood, we can most certainly do more to help formerly incarcerated youth succeed in living their lives free from state control and with abundant opportunities to fulfill their aspirations.

Acknowledgments

There are many people who helped to make this project possible, and we are grateful for all of their support. We wish to begin by thanking Peter Mickulas, our fabulous editor at Rutgers University Press (RUP), who ushered us through this process from start to finish. Through the RUP editorial process we also received in-depth feedback and advice on our proposal and our completed book from Professor Mercer Sullivan of Rutgers University. These comments were very useful in strengthening our conclusions and theory. We also thank Michelle Inderbitzin for reading the manuscript and framing the book for the readers in the context of scholarship and practice.

Several students and scholars contributed to this project at many stages. First we wish to thank Dr. Christina Tam, who collected data with us and also made the maps included in the book. We so appreciate all of your hard work and support. In addition, many graduate students worked on aspects of the data collection, analysis, and proofreading: Elizabeth Shaper, Liz Ul, Sunnaa Mohammad, Charles Lea, and Matthew Mizel. Thank you all for your time, insight, and dedication.

We received a great deal of institutional support from UCLA Luskin School of Public Affairs, and particularly wish to acknowledge Department Chair Dr. Todd Franke for his enthusiasm for our work. We also received gracious assistance, office space, and recruitment opportunities from multiple community-based agencies and schools and we thank all of them for their help.

Last but certainly not least, we could not have completed the book without the support of our families. Thank you to Laura's husband Owen Fighter, sons Eli Fighter and Noah Fighter, and parents Richard and Jane Abrams for an endless supply of love and humor. Thank you to Diane's husband La Mont Terry, sons LJ, DJ, and KJ (all of whom were born during the project), and parents Donald and Charlotte Fields, who provided motivation, feedback, and necessary distractions. We hope that this book helps to contribute to a more just world for our sons and all of the young people of their generation.

APPENDIX

The Research Process

THE TWO OF US embarked upon this project in the fall of 2010, in part for Diane's doctoral dissertation, with Laura serving as her PhD advisor in the department of social welfare at UCLA. With a mutual interest in criminal justice, young people, and reentry, we had been working together on related projects for several years. The impetus to pursue this desistance study was a natural extension of our collaborative research in the local juvenile halls, camps, and community-based reentry programs. This appendix presents more detailed information about the process of synthesizing our many years of work together to complete this book.

As a team, we approached this study from different standpoints and perspectives that we discussed throughout the conceptualization, data collection, analysis, and writing phases. Diane had a very personal interest in reentry research based on relationships with people in her life who had been incarcerated, and also as a result of her work in the child welfare field where she witnessed how fluid the boundaries were between the foster care, juvenile, and adult criminal justice systems. The projects she had worked on with Laura provided an opportunity to continue exploring these topics from various angles. By the time her dissertation project emerged, she was excited to conduct more in-depth research with members of a population who they both felt were not receiving the attention they warranted.

Laura had limited personal experiences with incarceration and reentry, but had immersed herself in the juvenile justice field for many years prior. Her ethnographic book on juvenile corrections was then well underway (Abrams & Anderson-Nathe, 2013), so she wanted to delve into her next project on reentry. However, she was encountering some barriers in obtaining funding the study. After some starts, stops, and missteps, she was eager to get back into the field and talk to young people directly in partnership with Diane. This project was exciting and motivating for both of us.

Recruiting Participants

Recruitment for the study took place in several waves. In the initial wave, we had a list of young men to contact who had taken part in our telephone survey of formerly incarcerated young men (Abrams & Franke, 2013; Abrams, Terry, & Franke, 2011). At the end of that survey, we asked the participants to indicate their willingness to be contacted for a future study. As such, we already had the human subjects consent required to contact these participants directly. At that time, we looked through our prior survey sample of 75 young men and identified those who were still between the ages of 18 and 25. We then wrote letters and emails, asking them to contact us if they had an interest in taking part in a separate study.

At least 20 young men made contact with us at that juncture. However, securing a meeting place and time was not always an easy task. If the participant did not want to meet at his home, we tried community centers, libraries, or other spaces in proximity to where they lived, worked, or went to school. We ruled out coffee shops or restaurants due to the noise level and absence of privacy. Diane worked tirelessly to locate spaces in the community that were safe, private, and willing to lend us a meeting room. Typically we would arrive at a meeting space having never met the participant before. We were always anxious to know if he would show up, and if so, if he would have time to talk for an hour or more or be open to sharing his story with us. If all went well and we were able to meet and conduct the first interview, we would then contact the participant for a second meeting. While some missed appointments or arrived very late or with little time to spare, we were fortunate that for the most part, our strategies to locate meeting places were successful.

For Diane's dissertation work with 15 young men, she was present for all of the initial 30 interviews (two per participant). Laura attended about three-quarters of these interviews and otherwise Diane conducted them herself. We often took turns occupying the lead interviewer role with the other person taking notes, recording impressions and ideas, and then asking follow-up questions. We found a very natural synergy in our joint interviewing skills, which also improved over the course of our work together. On most occasions, we were able to debrief after the interviews, sharing our thoughts, points of concern to follow up on with the youth, and at times, our mixture of feelings which ranged from sorrow to hopefulness and inspiration.

Once Diane had collected her dissertation data (and gave birth to her first son in the course of it all), we decided that the project was worth continuing in order to craft a larger project, and eventually we hoped to turn all of our findings into a book. At this point, we decided to diversify the sample to include women and also men from other recruitment sites. So while Diane was completing her dissertation and tending to her infant son, Laura wrote a small faculty grant to acquire more funding for the project and hired Christina Tam, then a first-year PhD student in social welfare, to continue the project.

Christina and Laura then secured two additional recruitment sites: a reentry program and an alternative school serving probation youth. These organizations were willing to let us recruit and interview at their sites, which was extremely helpful for planning purposes. At that point we recruited eight young women and two additional young men through group presentations to potentially eligible participants. Christina and Laura conducted the remaining series of two interviews per participant, along with the occasional assistance of Elizabeth Shaper, then an MSW student at UCLA. Christina was new to qualitative interviewing but very interested in the subject matter and the research training. She proved to be an excellent researcher and connected very well with the participants, particularly with the young women.

Once Diane had completed her dissertation (Terry, 2012) and began working at a community-based organization, we regrouped to talk about next steps. We decided to try to follow a select group of young men and women for a longer period than our initially planned sequence of two interviews. Accordingly, we looked through the pool and purposively asked some of the young men and women for follow-up interviews based on their diverse stories, time availability, and what we assessed as their ability to contribute to the research process through insights and experiences. Cesar, Oscar, John, Mike, Irene, and Desiree all participated in four to five interviews over the course of two years, and four others (Carina, Evan, Lupe, and Tyrone) participated in three interviews. This part of the data collection definitely added significant perspective to the research, particularly in how rapidly the participants' lives changed in between each meeting. It also seemed to provide the participants with additional time to reflect on their desistance experiences, including the progress and setbacks they had experienced since we met them. Table A.1 lists the names of each participant, the number of interviews they completed, and the time span between the first and last interview.

CONDUCTING INTERVIEWS

This project relied on in-depth interviews as our main method of gathering stories and insights. Initially we planned a series of two interviews, the first being a comprehensive life history interview that often took a full two hours to complete. This life history covered topics such as family, schooling, delinquency, and other domains. The second interview included four parts: clarification of the life history information, focused questions pertaining to the transition to adulthood and desistance from crime, a social support exercise, and a neighborhood mapping exercise. The second interview usually lasted 60 to 90 minutes, but occasionally took longer. When we met with participants for the third meeting and beyond, we did not use a structured guide, but rather checked in with them about many aspects of their lives and discussed changes in their experiences with crime, social support, concerns, and plans for jobs, schooling, and housing, among other topics. The conversations by then were more familiar, and they flowed very comfortably.

For the most part, the young people who participated in the project were willing and eager to share their life experiences with us. With a few exceptions, the young women were initially more open to talking openly relative to the young men. However, by the second interview, the young men were also typically very open to sharing their insights. Several participants mentioned at the end of our interviews that they appreciated the chance to tell their stories and reflect on their overall life histories in ways they had not experienced in the past. We were always very appreciative of the young men and women for sharing their stories, and in return, we offered our thanks as well as gift cards for their time. However, we are aware that in this power configuration of researchers and participants, ultimately their openness benefitted our work perhaps more than the experience or compensation benefitted them.

TABLE A.1.

List of Interviews Completed

Name	Number of Interviews	Time Span from First to Last Interview
Anthony	2	1 month
Amber	2	4 months
Carina	3	6 months
Carlos	2	< 1 month
Cesar	4	24 months
Chris	2	< 1 month
Desiree	5	10 months
Eduardo	2	< 1 month
Evan	3	5 months
Gabriel	2	3 months
Greg	2	< 1 month
Irene	5	12 months
Jerry	2	2 months
John	4	18 months
Keira	2	< 1 month
Lupe	3	5 months
Maria	2	2 months
Mario	2	2 months
Mike	4	19 months
Oscar	4	24 months
Paul	2	< 1 month
Sara	2	2 months
Shawn	2	< 1 month
Steven	2	< 1 month
Tyrone	3	16 months

While the interview approach yielded very rich information, it also presented some key limitations. To begin, we could not necessarily ascertain the truthfulness of their stories and recollections. We did not "fact check" any information, and want to be clear that we do not contend that the events recounted in this book are indeed factual. Rather, they are told through the sieve of the participants' memories and retrospective view of their lives. The book should be interpreted with this caution in mind. We have reported and analyzed the information relayed to us from memory and experience, and changed relevant details only when the participants requested such changes, or when we felt that we needed to do so in order to protect their confidentiality. Altering small details is a common tool in qualitative research to protect confidentiality and potential reader identification of the subject (Kaiser, 2009). Another limitation of the method is that we did not have an abundance of opportunity to interact with the participants beyond the interview scenario. In this way, our purview on their lives was more limited than it would be in a project that included more observations of daily life.

To compensate for these limitations, we decided to frame their experiences within the context of Los Angeles County—what we know was happening around the timeframe of 2011–2013 with regard to juvenile justice, reentry, schooling, unemployment, crime, housing and policing. We felt compelled while writing this book not only to tell the participants' stories, but also to place them within a larger system of social relations that indeed shaped their life experiences, understandings, and perceptions. For example, consider Desiree's story of being reported to DCFS at the group home for pregnant and parenting foster teens. While we don't know if the events leading to that report were entirely congruent with her telling of that story, by providing relevant contextual information about DCFS, we tried to show why Desiree saw the agency as her enemy. This is similar for the men's accounts of their interactions with the police; with some historical understanding of the LAPD, one can see why these young men had a high level of suspicion and distrust of the police. So while we weren't there to witness the events ourselves, we hope that providing a context helps the reader to better comprehend the participants' understandings and lived experiences.

ANALYSIS

One of the greatest challenges of conducting qualitative research is the analysis phase. We had 70 transcribed interviews averaging about 40 pages each, along with written interview notes, memos, social support diagrams, and neighborhood maps. In short, there was an abundance of material to synthesize. We organized the material in several ways, including shared cloud-based folders for each participant along with actual notebooks full of the printed materials and raw data (transcripts, maps, email correspondence, etc.). Two former MSW students, Liz Ul and Sunnaa Mohammad, also compiled basic information about each participant and summarized each person's life history time line and significant events. They helped us a great deal in getting organized for our in-depth analysis process.

While Diane had completed a great deal of analysis on the desistance stories of the initial 15 young men, we had the added challenge of the ten new participants and the extended interviews. So while we retained many of the core concepts that Diane had discovered for her dissertation (Terry, 2012), we also had to refine, expand, and add to these ideas as we covered more ground for the book. This process resulted in a few changes and modifications to her initial analysis. To analyze the data, we used a combination of computer-assisted data coding and retrieval along with consistently returning to hard copies of the materials, stories, and narratives to confirm our working hypotheses and assumptions. We also used charts, tables, and other organizational mechanisms to record our codes, themes, and findings. Since almost half of the data had not been previously analyzed for the dissertation, the analysis work was a fairly arduous process.

We were very fortunate to bring the study findings back to three participants to confirm our hunches and to gather their interpretations. Member checking helps to ensure that the researcher is not inserting too much of her or his own bias into the interpretation of the stories (Lincoln & Guba, 1984). While we did not present the information to all 25 participants, the member checking process really increased our confidence about the material and commentary presented within the book.

WRITING THE BOOK

After completing our follow-up interviews in February 2013 and sitting with the data for about a year, we finally decided that it was time to put it all together into a book. We crafted a book prospectus that we submitted to Rutgers University Press. By fall 2014 and with a contract in hand, we started to dig back into the data and write.

At that point, Diane had two sons then under the age of three, was working as a postdoctoral scholar at Loyola Marymount University, and teaching part-time at UCLA. Laura was involved in several other projects and was also consumed with her responsibilities as a professor and doctoral program chair. We both also had significant time commitments in the evenings with our sons. So carving out time to write the book was not easy. We started to meet once a week at a café for three-hour blocks, which helped to keep our momentum going. Soon we eased into a routine of catching up on life and work, ordering our favorite breakfast burritos, drinking coffee, and writing. We usually worked on different sections or chapters but passed our work back and forth to each other for editing, commenting, and adding. While the writing could have been accomplished without the face-to-face meetings, they helped to ground us in the process and keep our work in sync.

These meetings also helped us with another important aspect of this process; to keep the work firmly planted in its relevant context. During our intensive writing period, the police killings of Michael Brown, Eric Garner, Ezell Ford, and other high-profile shootings throughout the country also unfolded. The #blacklivesmatter movement sprung into action. Public attention was turning to matters of race, justice, and law enforcement accountability. With Diane being black and Laura being white, we definitely had different emotions related to these events. While both of us are raising sons, we have a very different set of fears and worries about our sons' safety based on our racial locations. Our writing sessions thus also turned into times where we could discuss these events and our different emotional responses to them. These events also very much related to our book, as we sat and re-read stories from the young men (mostly) about the police, fear, and racism. At times we definitely felt a sense of hopelessness. Yet we were also very fortunate to have had access to these stories at a time when we felt that black and brown voices needed to be heard. We both aspire to use our academic privilege to put in writing that these experiences are important, and that these young people's lives indeed do matter a great deal; that they have many hopes and dreams for their futures that can and should be fulfilled.

We hope that we have done justice to these young people's experiences and their stories. We have many discussions about the balance between realism and pessimism that we presented in this book. Neither of us wanted the reader to walk away feeling defeated. Still, with ethical and scholarly integrity, we also have to tell the stories as they were recounted to us. By placing the stories into their context, we attempted to provide the readership with optimism that young people can change and succeed given a more robust set of opportunities. We also aimed to provide the reader a more nuanced and contextualized view of the process of criminal desistance. While we indeed discovered young people who represented various ends of the desistance typologies we created, what we mostly found was a group of young people who were trying to make it in life, and who had encountered both challenges and successes in trying to get there.

In sum, the experience of conducting this project together was rich, emotional, and ultimately extremely rewarding. We hope that this methodological appendix provides useful guidance, to researchers, doctoral students, and anyone interested in pursuing a scholarly career, about how to piece together individual life histories into a holistic story.

BIBLIOGRAPHY

Abram, K., Teplin, L., McClelland, G., & Dulcan, M. (2003). Co-morbid psychiatric disorders in youth in juvenile detention. *Archives of General Psychiatry, 60*(11), 1097–1108.

Abrams, L. S. (2007). From corrections to community: Youth offenders' perceptions of the challenges of transition. *Journal of Offender Rehabilitation, 44*(2/3), 31–53.

Abrams, L. S. (2013). Juvenile justice at a crossroads: Science, evidence, and twenty-first century reform. *Social Service Review, 87*(4), 725–752.

Abrams, L. S., & Anderson-Nathe, B. (2013). *Compassionate confinement: A year in the life of unit C.* New Brunswick, NJ: Rutgers University Press.

Abrams, L. S., Daughtery, J., & Freisthler, B. (2011). *The Los Angeles County young offender reentry blueprint.* Los Angeles, CA: Los Angeles Commission on Community and Senior Services. Retrieved from http://luskin.ucla.edu/sites/default/files/download-pdfs/bueprint—websiteversion2.8.11.pdf

Abrams, L. S., & Franke, T. (2013). Post-secondary education among formerly incarcerated transition age young men. *Journal of Offender Rehabilitation, 52*(4), 233–253.

Abrams, L. S., & Freisthler, B. (2010). A spatial analysis of risks and resources for reentry youth in Los Angeles County. *Journal of the Society for Social Work Research, 1*(1), 41–55.

Abrams, L. S., & Snyder, S. (2010). Youth offender reentry: Conceptual models for intervention and directions for future inquiry. *Children and Youth Services Review, 32*(12), 1787–1795.

Abrams, L. S., & Terry, D. (2014). "You can run but you can't hide": How formerly incarcerated young men navigate neighborhood risks. *Children and Youth Services Review, 47*(1), 61–69.

Abrams, L. S., Terry, D., & Franke, T. (2011). Community-based juvenile reentry services: The effects of service dosage on juvenile and adult recidivism. *Journal of Offender Rehabilitation, 50*, 492–510.

Advancement Project. (2010, March). *Test, punish, and push out: How zero tolerance policies and high stakes testing funnel youth into the school-to-prison pipeline.* Washington, DC: Author. Retrieved from http://www.advancementproject.org/resources/entry/test-punish-and-push-out-how-zero-tolerance-and-high-stakes-testing-funnel

Advancement Project. (2011). *A call to action: Los Angeles' quest to achieve community safety.* Washington, DC: Author. Retrieved from http://www.advancementprojectca.org/sites/default/files/imce/AP%20Call%20to%20Action_LAQuest%20To%20Achieve%20Community%20Safety%20-%20EXEC%20SUMM.pdf

Anderson, E. (2000). *Code of the street: Decency, violence, and the moral life of the inner city.* New York: W. W. Norton & Company.

Arnett, J. J. (2000). Emerging adulthood: A theory of development from the late teens through the twenties. *American Psychologist, 55*(5), 469–480.

Bandura, A. (1989). Human agency in social cognitive theory. *American Psychologist,*
    44, 1175–1184.
Benda, B. B. (2005). Gender differences in life-course theory of recidivism: A sur-
    vival analysis. *International Journal of Offender Therapy and Comparative Criminology,*
    49(3), 325–342.
Bernstein, N. (2014). *Burning down the house: The end of juvenile prison.* New York:
    The New Press.
Bersani, B. E., & Doherty, E. E. (2013). When the ties that bind unwind: Examin-
    ing the enduring and situational processes of change behind the marriage ef-
    fect. *Criminology, 51*(2), 399–433.
Bloom, B., Owen, B., Deschenes, E. P., & Rosenbaum, J. (2002). Moving toward
    justice for female offenders in the new millennium: Modeling gender-specific
    policies and programs. *Journal of Contemporary Criminal Justice, 18,* 37–56.
Blue Ribbon Commission on Child Protection. (2014, April). *Final report of the*
    Los Angeles County blue ribbon commission on child protection. Los Angeles, CA:
    Author. Retrieved from http://ceo.lacounty.gov/pdf/brc/BRCCP_Final_Re-
    port_April_18_2014.pdf
Bullis, M., & Yovanoff, P. (2006). Idle hands: Community employment experiences
    of formerly incarcerated youth. *Journal of Emotional and Behavioral Disorders,*
    14(71), 71–85.
California Department of Education. (2013a). *Standardized testing and reporting*
    (STAR). Sacramento, CA: Author. Retrieved from: http://star.cde.ca.gov/
California Department of Education. (2013b). *Cohort outcome data: California longitu-*
    dinal pupil achievement data system (CALPADS) cohort outcome data reported by race/
    ethnicity, program participating, and gender. Sacramento, CA: Author. Retrieved from
    http://www.cde.ca.gov/ds/sd/sd/filescohort.asp
California Department of Education. (2013c). *Dropouts by grade, 2012–2013.*
    Sacramento, CA: Author. Retrieved from http://dq.cde.ca.gov/dataquest/Drop-
    outReporting/DrpByGrade.aspx?cDistrictName=LOS%20ANGELES%20UNI
    FIED&CDSCode=19647330000000&Level=District&TheReport=GradeOnly
    &ProgramName=All&cYear=2012–13&cAggSum=DTotGrade&cGender=B
California Department of Corrections and Rehabilitation. (n.d.). "History of the
    DJJ." Sacramento, CA: Division of Juvenile Justice. Retrieved from http://www.
    cdcr.ca.gov/Juvenile_Justice/DJJ_History/Index.html
Calvin, E., Weir, A., Nahoray, D., & Breen, A. (2012, March). *When I die—they'll*
    send me home: Youth sentenced to life in prison without parole in California: An update.
    Los Angeles, CA: Human Rights Watch. Retrieved from https://www.hrw.org/
    report/2012/03/01/when-i-dietheyll-send-me-home/youth-sentenced-life-
    prison-without-parole
Campaign for Youth Justice. (2014). *State trends: Updates from the 2013–2014 Legisla-*
    tive session. Washington, DC: Campaign for Youth Justice. Retrieved from http://
    www.campaignforyouthjustice.org/images/nationalreports/state_trends-_up-
    dates_from_the_2013–2014_legislative_session.pdf
Carlyle, E. J. (2012). Inner city kids have higher rates of PTSD than combat
    veterans—California's Children. Retrieved from http://californiaschildren.
    typepad.com/californiaschildren/2012/05/may-8–2012-youth-living-in-inner-
    cities-show-a-higher-prevalence-ofpost-traumatic-stress-syndrome-ptsd-than-
    us-soldiers.html#.Um0kmRbalUQ
Cauffman, E. (2008). Understanding the female offender. *The Future of Children,*
    18(2), 119–142.
Center for the Study of Social Policy. (2015). *Dismantling the pipeline: Addressing the*

needs of young women and girls of color involved in intervening public systems. Washington, DC: Author. Retrieved from http://www.cssp.org/pages/body/WGOC-policy-oct2015-spreads.pdf

Chang, C., & Sewell, A. (2014). L.A. County sheriff's department to get civilian oversight. *L.A. Times.* Retrieved from http://www.latimes.com/local/california/la-me-sheriff-oversight-20141210-story.html#page=1

Chemerinsky, E. (2000). The rampart scandal and the criminal justice system in Los Angeles County. *Guild Practitioner, 57,* 121.

Christopher, W. (Ed.). (1991). *Report of the independent commission on the Los Angeles Police Department.* Darby, PA: Diane Publishing.

Chung, H. L., Little, M., & Steinberg, L. (2005). The transition to adulthood for adolescents in the juvenile justice system: A developmental perspective. In D. W. Osgood, E. M. Foster, C. Flanagan, & G. R. Ruth (Eds.), *On your own a net: The transition to adulthood for vulnerable populations* (pp. 68–91). Chicago: University of Chicago Press.

Correll, J., & Keesee, T. (2009). Racial bias in the decision to shoot? *The Police Chief,* 54–58.

Culhane, D., Byrne, T., Metraux, S., Moreno, M., Toros, H., & Stevens, M. (2011). *Young adult outcomes of youth exiting dependent or delinquent care in Los Angeles County.* Agoura Hills, CA: Conrad N. Hilton Foundation. Retrieved from http://www.hiltonfoundation.org/images/stories/PriorityAreas/FosterYouth/Downloads/Hilton_Foundation_Report_Final.pdf

Curtis, A. (2014). Tracing the school-to-prison pipeline from zero-tolerance policies to juvenile justice dispositions. *Georgetown Law Review, 102,* 1251–1277.

Davis, M. (2006). *City of quartz: Excavating the future in Los Angeles.* New York: Verso Books.

Duke, N. N., Pettingell, S. L., McMorris, B. J., & Borowsky, I. W. (2010). Adolescent violence perpetration: Associations with multiple types of adverse childhood experiences. *Pediatrics, 125*(4), e778–786.

Duncan, G. J., & Brooks-Gunn, J. (Eds.). (1999). *The consequences of growing up poor.* New York: Russell Sage Foundation.

EdSource. (2016). *Welcome to the local control funding formula guide.* Retrieved from http://edsource.org/wp-content/uploads/2016/02/lcff-guide-print-version.pdf

Fabelo, T., Thompson, M. D., Plotkin, M., Carmichael, D., Marchbanks III, M. P., & Booth, E. A. (2011). Breaking schools' rules: A statewide study of how school discipline relates to students' success and juvenile justice involvement. New York: Council of State Governments Justice Center.

Fader, J. (2013). *Falling back: Incarceration and transitions to adulthood among urban youth.* New Brunswick, NJ: Rutgers University Press.

Federal Interagency Forum on Child and Family Statistics. (2014). *America's young adults: Special issue 2014.* Washington, DC: US Government Printing Office. Retrieved from http://www.childstats.gov/pdf/ac2014/YA_14.pdf

Fisher, E. (2011, July 21). *Los Angeles millionaire growth second in nation.* Retrieved from http://www.huffingtonpost.com/2011/07/21/la-ranks-2-for-millionair_n_906197.html

Foster, E. M., & Gifford, E. J. (2005). The transition to adulthood for youth leaving public systems: Challenges to policies and research. In R. A. Setterson, F. Furstenberg, & R. C. Rumbaut (Eds.), *On the frontier of adulthood: theory, research, and public policy* (pp. 501–533). Chicago: University of Chicago Press.

Freundlich, M. (2010, April). *Chafee plus ten: a vision for the next decade.* St. Louis, MO: The Jim Casey Youth Opportunities Initiative. Retrieved from http://www.jimcaseyyouth.org/sites/default/files/documents/Chafee%20 FINAL_3.3B.pdf

Frey, S. (2014). *New law limits student discipline measure.* Oakland, CA: EdSource. Retrieved from http://edsource.org/2014/new-law-limits-student-discipline-measure/67836

Fridell, L. A. (2008). Racially biased policing: The law enforcement response to the implicit black-crime association. In M. E. Lynch, E. B. Patterson, and K. K. Childs, (Eds.), *Racial divide: Race, ethnicity and criminal justice* (pp. 39–59). Monsey, NY: Criminal Justice Press.

Furstenberg, F. (2010). On a new schedule: Transitions to adulthood and family change. *The Future of Children, 20*(1), 67–87.

Furstenberg, F., Rumbaut, R. G., & Settersten, R. A. (2005). On the frontier of adulthood: An introduction. In R. A. Settersten, F. Furstenberg, & R. G. Rumbaut (Eds.), *On the frontier of adulthood: Theory, research, and public policy* (pp. 3–28). Chicago: University of Chicago Press.

Gennetian, L. A., Duncan, G., Knox, V., Vargas, W., Clark-Kauffman, E., & London, A. S. (2004). How welfare policies affect adolescents' school outcomes: A synthesis of evidence from experimental studies. *Journal of Research on Adolescence, 14*, 399–423.

Giordano, P. C., Cernkovich, S. A., & Rudolph, J. L. (2002). Gender, crime, and desistance: Toward a theory of cognitive transformation. *American Journal of Sociology, 107*(4), 990–1064.

Glueck, S., & Glueck, E. (1950). *Unraveling juvenile delinquency.* New York: Commonwealth Fund.

Goffman, A. (2014). *On the run: Fugitive life in the inner-city.* Chicago: University of Chicago Press.

Gordon, L. (1994). *Pitied but not entitled: Single mothers and the history of welfare, 1890–1935.* New York: The Free Press.

Green, R. K., Reina, V., & Hemp, S. (2014). *2014 Casden multifamily forecast.* Los Angeles, CA: Kemp Center at the University of Southern California. Retrieved from http://lusk.usc.edu/sites/default/files/2014-USC-Casden-Multifamily-Forecast.pdf

Grunwald, H. E., Lockwood, B., Harris, P .W., & Mennis, J. (2010). Influences of neighborhood context, individual history and parenting behavior on recidivism among juvenile offenders. *Journal of Youth and Adolescence, 39*(9), 1067–1079.

Hager, E. (2015, November 18). *Our prisons in black and white: The race gap for adults is shrinking. Why is it widening for juveniles?* New York: The Marshall Project. Retrieved from https://www.themarshallproject.org/2015/11/18/our-prisons-in-black-and-white#.nhW0q00Hx

Harris, M. S., & Hackett, W. (2008). Decision points in child welfare: An action research model to address disproportionality. *Children and Youth Services Review, 30*(2), 199–215.

Heitzeg, N. A. (2009). Education or incarceration: Zero tolerance policies and the school to prison pipeline. *Forum on Public Policy, 2*, 1–21.

Henig, R. S., & Henig, S. (2012). *Twentysomething: Why do young adults seem stuck?* New York: Hudson Street Press.

Herz, D., Lee, P., Lutz, L, Stewart, M., Tuell, J., & Wiig, J. (2012). *Addressing the needs of multi-system youth: Strengthening the connections between child welfare and juvenile justice systems.* Washington, DC: Center for Juvenile Justice Reform. Retrieved from http://cjjr.georgetown.edu/wp-content/uploads/2015/03/MultiSystemYouth_March2012.pdf

Herz, D., & Ryan, J. P. (2008, September). *Exploring the characteristics and outcomes of 241.1 youth crossing over from dependency to delinquency in Los Angeles County.* Sacramento, CA: Center for Families, Children, and the Courts. Retrieved from http://www.courts.ca.gov/documents/AB129-ExploringReseachUpdate.pdf

Jansson, B. S. (2005). *The reluctant welfare state: American social welfare policies—past, present, and future.* New York: Wadsworth Publishing Company.

Jay, M. (2012). *The defining decade: Why your twenties matter, and how to make the most of them now.* New York: Hatchett Book Group.

Kaiser, K. (2009). Protecting respondent confidentiality in qualitative research. *Qualitative Health Research, 19*(11), 1632–1641.

Kazemian, L. (2007). Desistance from crime: Theoretical, empirical, methodological, and policy considerations. *Journal of Contemporary Criminal Justice, 23*(1), 5–27.

Kindy, K. (2015). Fatal police shootings in 2015 approaching 400 nationwide. *Washington Post.* Retrieved from https://www.washingtonpost.com/national/fatal-police-shootings-in-2015-approaching-400-nationwide/2015/05/30/d322256a-058e-11e5-a428-c984eb077d4e_story.html

Krinsky, A. M. (2010). Disrupting the pathway from foster care to the justice system—a former prosecutor's perspectives on reform. *Family Court Review, 48*(2), 322–337.

Kubrin, C. E., & Stewart, E. A. (2006). Predicting who reoffends: The neglected role of neighborhood context in recidivism studies. *Criminology, 44*(1), 165–197.

Laub, J. H., & Boonstoppel, S. L. (2012). Understanding desistance from juvenile offending: Challenges and opportunities. In D. M. Bishop & B. Feld (Eds.), *The Oxford handbook of juvenile crime and juvenile justice* (pp. 373–394). New York: Oxford University Press.

Laub, J. H., & Sampson, R. J. (2003). *Shared beginnings, divergent lives: Delinquent boys to age 70.* Cambridge, MA: Harvard University Press.

LeBel, T. P., Burnett, R., Maruna, S., & Bushway, S. (2008). The chicken and egg of subjective and social factors in desistance from crime. *European Journal of Criminology, 5*(2), 131–159.

Lerner, R. M., Almerigi, J. B., Theokas, C., & Lerner, J. V. (2005). Positive youth development. *Journal of Early Adolescence, 25*(1), 10–16.

Leverentz, A. M. (2006). The love of a good man? Romantic relationships as a source of support or hindrance for female ex-offenders. *Journal of Research in Crime and Delinquency, 43*(4), 459–488.

Lincoln, Y. S., & Guba, E. G. (1985). *Naturalistic Inquiry.* Newbury Park, CA: Sage Publications.

Los Angeles Almanac. (2014). *Gang populations: Los Angeles county and city, countywide.* Los Angeles, CA: Author. Retrieved from http://www.laalmanac.com/crime/cr03v.htm.

Los Angeles Police Department. (2014). *Gangs.* Los Angeles, CA: Los Angeles Police Foundation and the LAPD. Retrieved from http://www.lapdonline.org/get_informed/content_basic_view/1396

Los Angeles Unified School District. (2013). *L.A. unified adopts new policy on student behavior.* Los Angeles, CA: Author. Retrieved from http://home.lausd.net/apps/news/article/311093

Losen, D., Martinez, T., & Gillespie, J. (2012). *Suspended education in California.* Los Angeles, CA: The UCLA Civil Rights Project. Retrieved from http://civilrightsproject.ucla.edu/resources/projects/center-for-civil-rights-remedies/school-to-prison-folder/summary-reports/suspended-education-in-california/SuspendedEd-final3.pdf

Lynn-Whaley, J., & Russi, A. (2011). *Improving juvenile justice policy in California: A closer look at transfer laws impact on young men and boys of color.* Berkeley, CA: The Chief Justice Earl Warren Institute on Law and Social Policy. Retrieved from https://www.law.berkeley.edu/files/BMOC_Brief_Juvenile_Justice_CA_final. pdf

Maroney, T. (2011). Adolescent brain science and juvenile justice. In M. Freeman (Ed.), *Law and neuroscience: Current issues 2010.* New York: Oxford University Press.

Maruna, S. (2001). *Making good: How ex-convicts reform and rebuild their lives.* Washington, DC: American Psychological Association.

Massoglia, M., & Uggen, C. (2010). Settling down and aging out: toward an interactionist theory of desistance and the transition to adulthood. *American Journal of Sociology, 116*(2), 543–582.

Matsunaga, M. (2008). *Concentrated poverty neighborhoods in Los Angeles.* Los Angeles, CA: Los Angeles Chamber of Commerce. Retrieved from http://www.lachamber.com/clientuploads/LUCH_committee/052610_ConcentratedPoverty.pdf

Matsunaga, M. (2011, September). *Unemployment and under-employment: Los Angeles County, California and the United States.* Retrieved from https://economicrt.org/resource/unemployment-and-under-employment-rates-for-the-united-states-california-and-los-angeles-county-new/

Mears, D. P., & Travis, J. (2004). Youth development and reentry. *Youth Violence and Juvenile Justice, 2,* 3–20.

Mendel, R. A. (2011). *No place for kids: The case for reducing juvenile incarceration.* Baltimore, MD: The Annie E. Casey Foundation. Retrieved from http://www.aecf. org/OurWork/JuvenileJustice/~/media/Pubs/Topics/Juvenile%20Justice/Detention%20Reform/NoPlaceForKids/JJ_NoPlaceForKidsEmbargoed.pdf

Mendel, R. A. (2015). *Maltreatment of youth in U.S. juvenile correctional facilities: An update.* Baltimore, MD: Annie E. Casey Foundation. Retrieved from http://cfc.ncmhjj.com/wp-content/uploads/2015/07/aecf-maltreatmentyouthuscorrections-2015.pdf

Mennis, J., & Harris, P. (2011). Contagion and repeat offending among urban juvenile delinquents. *Journal of Adolescence, 34*(5), 951–963.

Miller, R. (2014). Devolving the carceral state: Race, prisoner reentry and the micro-politics of urban poverty management. *Punishment and Society, 16*(3), 305–335.

Moffitt, T. E. (1993). Life course persistent and adolescent limited antisocial behavior: A developmental taxonomy. *Psychological Review, 100*(4), 674–701.

Monahan, K. C., Steinberg, L., Cauffman, E., & Mulvey, E. P. (2009). Trajectories of antisocial behavior and psychosocial maturity from adolescence to young adulthood. *Developmental Psychology, 45*(6), 1654.

Monteith, M. L. (2010). *Transnational gangs: The MS-13 gang and others.* New York: Nova Science.

Mulvey, E., Steinberg, L., Fagan, J., Cauffman, E., Piquero, A., Chassin, L., Knight, R., Schubert, C., Hecker, T., & Losoya, S. (2004). Theory and research on desistance from antisocial activity among serious adolescent offenders. *Youth Violence and Juvenile Justice, 2,* 213–236.

National Juvenile Justice Network (2015). *Advances in juvenile justice reform: Adjudication and sentencing.* Washington, DC: Author. Retrieved from http://www.njjn. org/our-work/juvenile-justice-reform-advances-adjudication-and-sentencing

Needell, B., Webster, D., Armijo, M., Lee, S., Dawson, W., Magruder, J., Exel, M., Cuccaro-Alamin, S., Putnam-Hornstein, E., Sandoval, A., Yee, H., Mason, F.,

Benton, C., Lou, C., Peng, C., King, B., & Lawson, J. (2014). *California child welfare indicators project (CCWIP) reports.* Berkeley, CA: California Child Welfare Indicators Project, University of California at Berkeley. Retrieved from http://cssr.berkeley.edu/ucb_childwelfare

Newell, M., & Leap, J. (2013, November). *Reforming the nation's largest juvenile justice system.* Los Angeles, CA: Children's Defense Fund. Retrieved from http://www.cdfca.org/library/publications/2013/reforming-the-nations.pdf

Orfield, G., Siegel-Hawley, G., & Kucsera, J. (2011). Divided we fail: Segregated and unequal schools in the Southland. Retrieved from http://civilrightsproject.ucla.edu/research/metro-and-regional-inequalities/lasanti-project-los-angeles-san-diego-tijuana/divided-we-fail-segregated-and-unequal-schools-in-the-southfield

Osgood, D. W., Foster, M., & Courtney, M. (2010). Vulnerable populations and the transition to adulthood. *The Future of Children, 20*(1), 209–229. Retrieved from http://www.princeton.edu/futureofchildren/publications/docs/20_01_10.pdf

Perruti, A., Schindler, M., & Zeidenberg, J. (2014). *Sticker shock: Calculating the full price of youth incarceration.* Washington, DC: Justice Policy Institute. Retrieved from http://www.justicepolicy.org/uploads/justicepolicy/documents/sticker_shock_final_v2.pdf

Pew Charitable Trusts. (2015). *Re-examining juvenile incarceration: High cost, poor outcomes spark shift to alternatives.* Washington, DC: Author. Retrieved from http://www.pewtrusts.org/en/research-and-analysis/issue-briefs/2015/04/reexamining-juvenile-incarceration

Pew Research Center. (2014). *The rising cost of not going to college.* Washington, DC: Author. Retrieved from http://www.pewsocialtrends.org/2014/02/11/the-rising-cost-of-not-going-to-college/

Piquero, A. R., Schubert, C. A., & Brame, R. (2014). Comparing official and self-report records of offending across gender and race/ethnicity in a longitudinal study of serious youthful offenders. *Journal of Research in Crime and Delinquency, 51*(4), 526–556.

Public Policy Institute of California. (2014). Realignment, incarceration, and crime trends in California. Public Policy Institute of California. Retrieved from http://www.ppic.org/main/publication_quick.asp?i=1151

Rios, V. (2011). *Punished: Policing the lives of black and Latino boys.* New York: New York University Press.

Ross, R. (2012). *Juvenile-in-justice.* New York: The Image of Justice. Retrieved from http://www.juvenile-in-justice.com/

Salole, A. (2016). Penal assemblages: Governing youth in the penal voluntary sector. In L. S. Abrams, E. Hughes, M. Inderbitzin, & R. Meek (Eds.), *The voluntary sector in prisons: Encouraging institutional and personal change.* Washington, DC: Palgrave.

Salvatore, C., & Taniguchi, T. A. (2012). Do social bonds matter for emerging adults? *Deviant Behavior, 33*(9), 738–756.

Sampson, R. J., & Laub, J. (1993). *Crime in the making.* Cambridge, MA: Harvard University Press.

Sampson, R. J., Raudenbush, S. W., & Earls, F. (1997). Neighborhoods and violent crime: A multilevel study of collective efficacy. *Science, 277,* 918–924.

Schwartz, S. (2001). Immigrant access to food stamps: Overcoming barriers to participation. *Clearinghouse Review, 35,* 260–275.

Seigle, E., & Walsh, N. (2014). *Core principles for reducing recidivism and improving other outcomes for youth in the juvenile justice system.* Washington, DC: The National Reentry Research Center. Retrieved from https://csgjusticecenter.org/wp-content/uploads/2014/07/Core-Principles-for-Reducing-Recidivism-and-Improving-Other-Outcomes-for-Youth-in-the-Juvenile-Justice-System.pdf

Sickmund, M., Sladky, A., & Kang, W. (2015). *Easy access to juvenile court statistics: 1985–2013.* Washington, DC: Office of Juvenile Justice and Delinquency Prevention. Retrieved from http://www.ojjdp.gov/ojstatbb/ezajcs/

Sickmund, M., Sladky, T. J., Kang, W., & Puzzanchera, C. (2013). *Easy access to the census of juveniles in residential placement.* Washington DC: Office of Juvenile Justice and Delinquency Prevention. Retrieved from http://www.ojjdp.gov/ojstatbb/ezacjrp/

Smalley, S. (2009, February 6). How do you leave a gang? *Newsweek.* Retrieved from http://www.newsweek.com/how-do-you-leave-gang-82499

The Advancement Project. (2006). A Call to Action. Advancement Project. Retrieved from http://advancementprojectca.org/wp/wp-content/uploads/2015/09/imce/p3_report.pdf

The Council of State Governments Justice Center. (2015). "Locked out: improving educational and vocational outcomes for incarcerated youth." New York: The Council of State Governments Justice Center. Retrieved from https://csgjusticecenter.org/wp-content/uploads/2015/11/LOCKED_OUT_Improving_Educational_and_Vocational_Outcomes_for_Incarcerated_Youth.pdf

The Education Trust. (2015). *Black minds matter: Supporting the educational success of black children in California.* Oakland, CA: The Education Trust–West. Retrieved from http://west.edtrust.org/wp-content/uploads/sites/3/2015/10/Ed-Trust-West-Black-Minds-Matter-FINAL-PDF.pdf

Terry, D. J. (2012). *Social supports and criminal desistance in the transition to adulthood.* A doctoral dissertation completed at UCLA.

Thornberry, T. P., Huizinga, D., & Loeber, R. (2004). The causes and correlates studies: Findings and policy implications. *Juvenile Justice, 9*(1), 3–19.

Trulson, C. R., Marquart, J. W., Mullings, J. L., & Caeti, T. (2005). In between adolescence and adulthood: Recidivism outcomes of a cohort of state delinquents. *Youth Violence and Juvenile Justice, 3*(4), 355–387.

Trupin, E. W., Stewart, D. G., Beach, B., & Boesky, L. (2002). Effectiveness of a dialectical behavior therapy program for incarcerated female juvenile offenders. *Child and Adolescent Mental Health, 7*(3), 121–127.

Uggen, C., & Kruttschnitt, C. (1998). Crime in the breaking: Gender differences in desistance. *Law and Society Review, 32,* 339–366.

Uggen, C., & Wakefield, S. (2005). Young adults reentering the community from the criminal justice system: The challenge. In D. W. Osgood, E. M. Foster, C. Flanagan, & G. Ruth (Eds.), *On your own without a net: The transition to adulthood for vulnerable populations* (pp. 114–144). Chicago: University of Chicago Press.

US Bureau of Labor Statistics. (2013). *Employment projections: Employment 2012 and projected 2022, by typical entry-level and training assignment.* Washington, DC: US Department of Labor. Retrieved from http://www.bls.gov/emp/ep_table_education_summary.htm

US Census Bureau. (2012). *State and county quickfacts: Los Angeles county, California.* Washington, DC: US Department of Commerce. Retrieved from http://quickfacts.census.gov/qfd/states/06/06037.html

US Census Bureau. (March, 2014). *American fact finder.* Washington, DC: US Department of Commerce. Retrieved from http://factfinder.census.gov/faces/nav/jsf/pages/community_facts.xhtml

US Department of Education. (2011). *Status dropout rates of 16- through 24-year-olds in the civilian, non-institutionalized population, by race/ethnicity: Selected years, 1980–*

2009. In US Department of Education, National Center for Education Statistics (Ed.), *The condition of education 2011* (NCES 2011–033), indicator 20. Washington, DC. Retrieved from http://nces.ed.gov/fastfacts/display.asp?id=16

Vigil, J. D. (1988). *Barrio: The rise of Latino street gangs.* Austin, TX: University of Texas Press.

Vigil, J. D. (2008). Community dynamics and the rise of street gangs. In M. Suarez-Orozco & M. Paez (Eds.), *Latinos: Remaking America* (pp. 97–109). Berkeley: University of California Press.

Watson, L., & Edelman, P. (2012). *Improving the juvenile justice system for girls: Lessons from the states.* Washington, DC: Georgetown Center on Poverty, Inequality, and Public Policy. Retrieved from http://www.law.georgetown.edu/academics/centers-institutes/poverty-inequality/upload/JDS_V1R4_Web_Singles.pdf

Willen, C., Mattingly, M., Levin, M. Danielson, C., & Bohn S. (2013). *A portrait of poverty within California counties and demographic groups.* Palo Alto, CA: The Stanford Center on Poverty and Inequality. Retrieved from http://web.stanford.edu/group/scspi/poverty/cpm/CPMBrief_CPI.pdf

Wilson, R. (n.d.). Police accountability measures flood state legislatures after Ferguson, Staten Island. *Washington Post.* Retrieved from https://www.washingtonpost.com/blogs/govbeat/wp/2015/02/04/police-accountability-measures-flood-state-legislatures-after-ferguson-staten-island/

Zaslow, M. J., Moore, K. A., Brooks, J. L., Morris, P. A., Tout, K., Redd, Z. A., & Emig, C. A. (2002). Experimental studies of welfare reform and children. *The Future of Children, 12*(1), 79–95.

Index

Page numbers followed by a *t* indicate a table.

About the Authors

Laura S. Abrams, PhD, MSW, is a professor of social welfare at the Meyer and Renee Luskin School of Public Affairs at UCLA. She is the author of *Compassionate Confinement: A Year in the Life of Unit C* (2013) and the lead editor of *The Voluntary Sector in Prisons: Encouraging Institutional and Personal Change* (2016).

Diane J. Terry, PhD, MSW, is a senior research associate at the Psychology Applied Research Center at Loyola Marymount University. She is the author of several publications concerning the needs and experiences of formerly incarcerated youth.

CPSIA information can be obtained
at www.ICGtesting.com
Printed in the USA
LVOW10s0910100517

533935LV00004B/4/P